OpenOffice.org Writer

OpenOffice.org Writer

The Free Alternative to Microsoft Word

Jean Hollis Weber

O'REILLY®
COMMUNITY PRESS

Beijing · Cambridge · Farnham · Köln · Paris · Sebastopol · Taipei · Tokyo

OpenOffice.org Writer: The Free Alternative to Microsoft Word
by Jean Hollis Weber

Published by O'Reilly Media, Inc., 1005 Gravenstein Highway North, Sebastopol, CA 95472.

O'Reilly books may be purchased for educational, business, or sales promotional use. Online editions are also available for most titles (*safari.oreilly.com*). For more information, contact our corporate/institutional sales department: 800-998-9938 or *corporate@oreilly.com*.

Editor: David Brickner

Production Editor: Matt Hutchinson

Cover Designer: Edie Freedman

Printing History:

July 2004:	First Edition.

RepKover™
This book uses RepKover™, a durable and flexible lay-flat binding.

ISBN: 0-596-00826-0

[M]

*To Eric Lindsay, for putting up with me
during the research and writing of this book,
assisting with technical problems, and providing
food and drink at appropriate intervals.*

Table of Contents

Preface

What Is OpenOffice.org Writer?

OpenOffice.org Writer is the word-processing component of the open source project through which Sun Microsystems has released the technology for the popular StarOffice Productivity Suite. Other OpenOffice.org capabilities include spreadsheets (Calc), presentations (Impress), drawings (Draw), and file conversion facilities including those for Microsoft Office formats. OpenOffice.org runs on Linux, Solaris, and Windows. For more information, visit *http://www.openoffice.org/*.

Who Is This Book For?

This book is for intermediate and advanced users of OpenOffice.org Writer. You may not have used this program before, but you have used another word processor (such as Microsoft Word or Corel WordPerfect) and are familiar with the basics of word processing.

Typical users include academic writers, technical writers, and other business and professional writers—anyone who produces books, research papers, proposals, or other documents requiring the use of more than the basic features. For example, you need to use styles instead of direct formatting of headings and other paragraphs, and you need to include chapter information in the footers of pages, or you want to use master documents to control a book containing many chapters, perhaps written by different people.

I have not attempted to cover all the features and functions of Writer—that would take a book several times the size of this one. Some topics are covered only briefly, leaving you to work out the details for yourself. A few major topics are not covered at all; these include macros, forms, and exchanging data with other OpenOffice.org applications.

Prerequisites—What Do You Need to Do Before You Use This Book?

This book assumes that:

- You know how to use your computer's operating system, including finding, opening, saving, moving, copying, and deleting files; setting up printers; etc.
- You have successfully installed OpenOffice.org on your computer and can view, edit, and print files.
- You can perform basic word processing in Writer, including copying, pasting, and direct formatting of text.
- You are familiar with basic computing, word processing, and desktop publishing terms for applications using a graphical user interface (GUI).

Other Sources of Information

- Official OpenOffice.org website and its associated mailing lists:
  http://www.openoffice.org/
- List of user resources including websites and books:
  http://www.mackmoon.com/OOoHelpOutline.html

Conventions Used in This Book

The following typographical conventions are used in this book:

Plain text
Indicates menu titles, menu options, menu buttons, and keyboard accelerators (such as Alt and Ctrl).

Italic
Indicates new terms, URLs, email addresses, filenames, file extensions, pathnames, and directories.

`Constant width`
Indicates commands, options, variables, attributes, functions, types, classes, properties, parameters, values, objects, XML tags, HTML tags, macros, the contents of files, or the output from commands.

`Constant width bold`
Shows commands or other text that should be typed literally by the user.

`Constant width italic`
Shows text that should be replaced with user-supplied values.

Tips, notes, and bugs are presented as follows.

| **Tip** | This is a tip. It is set off by lines above and below. |

Technical Notes

This book was written entirely in OpenOffice.org Writer 1.1.1 running on Windows ME. It was printed to a PostScript file using the Acrobat Distiller printer driver, then converted to PDF (Portable Document Format) using Adobe Acrobat Distiller 5.05.

Acknowledgments

I am indebted to numerous people who have contributed to my knowledge of how to use OpenOffice.org Writer: the members of several discussion lists on the OpenOffice.org site, and the people who read and commented on a draft of an earlier (self-published) version of this book, titled *Taming OpenOffice.org Writer*.

These people reviewed the earlier version for usability and technical problems and tested the instructions: Craig Hadden, Nancy Herbert, Shane Herring, Rebbecca Martin, Ed Matthews, and Deborah Salvarda, plus some others who looked at only part of the book.

David Brickner and Matt Hutchinson of O'Reilly assisted greatly with the conversion of my earlier book into the O'Reilly style, catching several errors in the process.

Any errors remaining in this book are entirely my responsibility.

1

Setting Up Writer to Work Your Way

If you use OpenOffice.org Writer a lot, you'll want to take the time to set up the interface to suit your work and your personal preferences. But even if you use Writer only occasionally, you can make a few quick changes to make your work much easier.

The Options dialog controls many settings in the OpenOffice.org set of applications. Some settings apply to all the applications; other settings apply to only one.

This chapter covers some options of particular interest to writers and editors, and some that are a bit obscure or hard to find when you first start using the program. It does not cover all the options in detail.

In addition to setting options, you can change other Writer features to suit your preferences and working habits. For more information on all options and other customizable features, check the Contents of the online help for General Information for OpenOffice.org Writer > Configuring and Modifying OpenOffice.org.

Choosing Options That Affect All the OpenOffice.org Applications

This section covers some of the settings that apply to all the applications. For information on settings not discussed here, see the online help.

1. Click Tools > Options.
2. Click the + sign to the left of OpenOffice.org in the left-hand section. A list of subsections drops down.

General Options

1. In the Options dialog, click OpenOffice.org > General.
2. On the Options – OpenOffice.org – General dialog (Figure 1-1), the options are:

    Year (two digits)
    Specify how two-digit years are interpreted. For example, if the two-digit year is set to 1930, and you enter a date of 1/1/30 or later into your document, the date is interpreted as 1/1/1930 or later. An "earlier" date is interpreted as being in the following century; that is, 1/1/20 is interpreted as 1/1/2020.

    Help Agent
    To turn off the Help Agent (OpenOffice.org's equivalent to Microsoft's Office Assistant), deselect Activate. If the Help Agent is active, you can specify how long it remains open before it is automatically closed. To restore the default Help Agent behavior, click Reset.

    OpenOffice.org Help formatting
    To display Help in high contrast for accessibility, choose one of the high-contrast style sheets from the list.

    Open/Save dialogs
    To use the standard Open and Save dialogs for your operating system, deselect the Use OpenOffice.org dialogs checkbox.

    Document status
    Choose whether printing a document counts as changing the document. If this option is selected, then the next time you close the document after printing, the print date is recorded in the document properties as a change and you'll be prompted to save the document again, even if you didn't make any other changes.

    Back button (same behavior on all options dialogs)
    Resets options to the values that were in place when you opened OpenOffice.org.

3. Continue to the next topic, or click OK to save your changes and close the dialog.

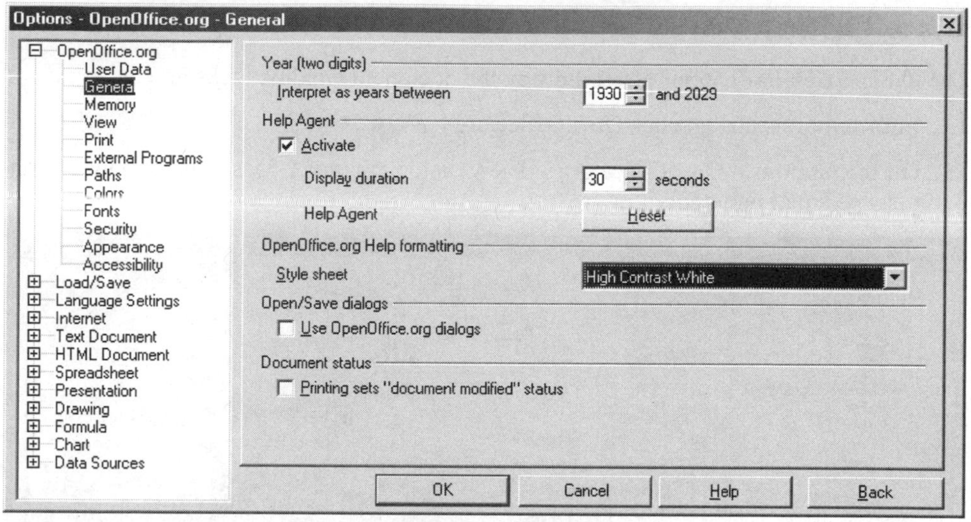

Figure 1-1. Setting general options for the OpenOffice.org applications

Memory Options

1. In the Options dialog, click OpenOffice.org > Memory.

2. On the Options – OpenOffice.org – Memory dialog (Figure 1-2):

    *   Consider the trade-offs of convenience against speed or insufficient memory. For example, more undo steps require more memory.

    *   To load the Quickstarter (an icon on the desktop or in the system tray) when you start your computer, select the checkbox near the bottom of the dialog.

3. Continue to the next topic, or click OK to save your changes and close the dialog.

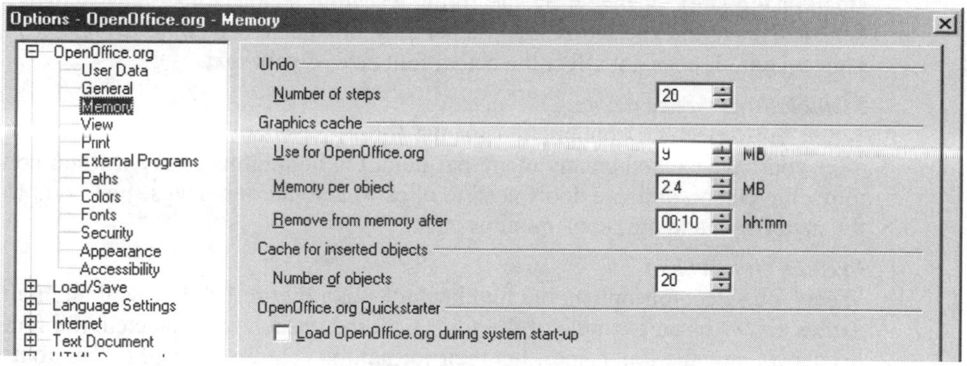

Figure 1-2. Choosing Memory options for the OpenOffice.org applications

View Options

The choices of View options affect the way the document window looks and behaves.

1. In the Options dialog, click OpenOffice.org > View.

2. On the Options – OpenOffice.org – View dialog (Figure 1-3), set the options to suit your personal preferences.

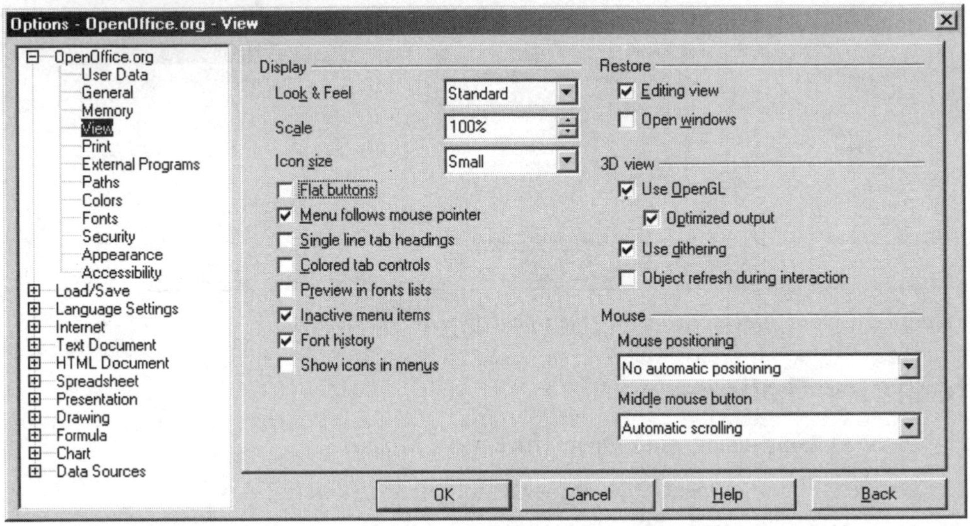

Figure 1-3. Choosing View options for the OpenOffice.org applications

Some options are:

Scale

If the text in the help files and on the menus of the OOo user interface is too small or too large, change it by specifying a scaling factor. Sometimes a change here can have unexpected results, depending on the screen fonts available on your system. It does not affect the actual font size of your text.

Menu follows mouse pointer

When you select this option, the menus follow standard Windows behavior: after you have clicked on any menu bar item, the highlighting moves when you move the cursor, and you don't need to click to activate submenus (just point to the menu item and the submenu pops out).

Preview in fonts lists

When you select this option, the font list looks like Figure 1-4, left, with the font names shown as an example of the font; with the checkbox deselected, the font list shows only the font names, not their formatting (Figure 1-4, right). The fonts you will see listed are those that are installed on your system.

Inactive menu items

Select this option if you want inactive menu items to be visible but grayed out. Deselect it to prevent inactive menu items from appearing on the menu.

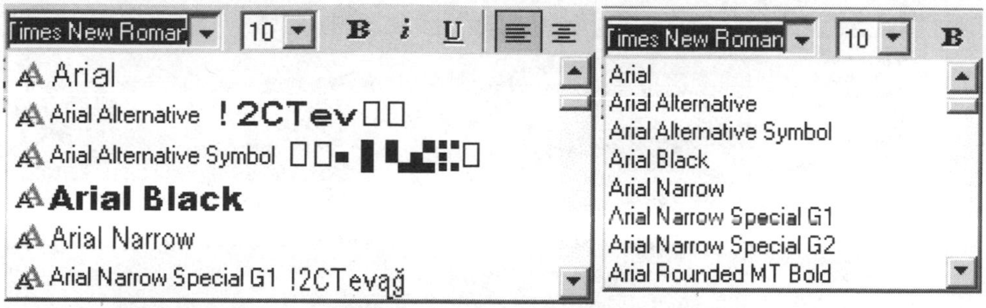

Figure 1-4. (Left) Font list showing preview; (Right) Font list without preview

Font history

When you select this option, the last five fonts you have assigned to the current document are displayed at the top of the font list.

Restore – Editing view

Select this option if you want to open documents at the place the cursor was located when you previously closed the document. Deselect this option to always open documents at the first page.

Restore – Open windows

Select this option if you want all documents and windows that are open when you close OpenOffice.org to be restored when you restart it.

3D view

These options are for use with Draw and Impress. For more information, see the online help or other documentation on these applications.

Mouse

Use these options to choose how the mouse is positioned in newly opened dialogs and to select the function of the middle mouse button.

3.　Continue to the next topic, or click OK to save your changes and close the dialog.

Print Options

Set the print options to suit your default printer and your most common printing method. You can change these settings at any time, either through this dialog or during the printing process (by clicking the Options button on the Print dialog).

1.　In the Options dialog, click OpenOffice.org > Print.

2.　On the Options – OpenOffice.org – Print dialog (Figure 1-5), look at the Printer warnings section near the bottom. Here you can choose whether to be warned if the paper size or orientation specified in your document does not match the paper size or orientation available for your printer. Having these warnings turned on can be quite helpful, particularly if you work with documents produced by people in other countries where the standard paper size is different from yours.

3.　Continue to the next topic, or click OK to save your changes and close the dialog.

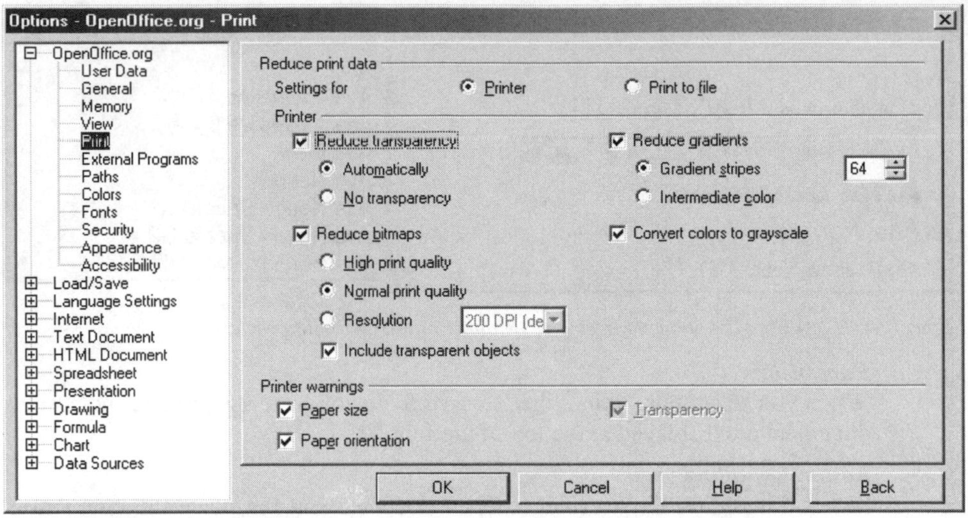

Figure 1-5. Choosing general printing options to apply to all OpenOffice.org applications

> **Tip**   If your printouts are coming out incorrectly placed on the page or chopped
> off at the top, bottom, or sides, or the printer is refusing to print, the most
> likely cause is page size incompatibility.

Paths

You can change the location of files associated with, or used by, OpenOffice.org to suit
your working situation. In a Windows system, for example, you might want to store
documents by default somewhere other than My Documents.

1.   In the Options dialog, click OpenOffice.org > Paths.

2.   To make changes, select an item in the list shown in Figure 1-6 and click Edit. On
     the Select Paths dialog (not shown), add or delete folders as required, and then click
     OK to return to the Options dialog. Note that many items have at least two paths
     listed: one to a shared folder (which might be on a network) and one to a user-
     specific folder (normally on the user's personal computer).

3.   Continue to the next topic, or click OK on the Options dialog to save your changes
     and close the dialog.

> **Tip**   You can use the entries in the Options – OpenOffice.org – Paths dialog to
> compile a list of files, such as those containing AutoText, that you need to
> back up or copy to another computer.

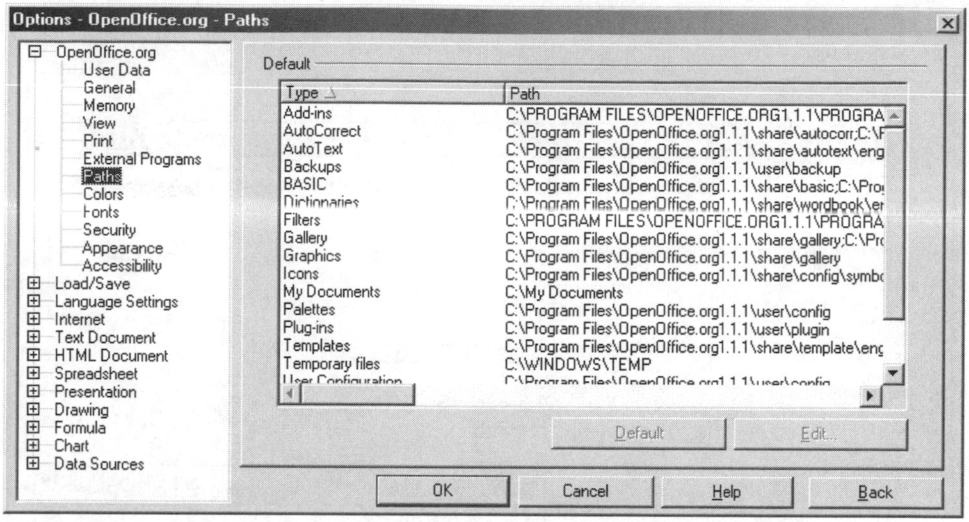

Figure 1-6.Viewing the paths of files used by OpenOffice.org

Font Options

You can define replacements for any fonts that might appear in your documents. If you receive from someone else a document containing fonts that you don't have on your system. OpenOffice.org will substitute fonts for those it doesn't find, but you might prefer to specify a different font from the one the program chooses.

1. In the Options dialog, click OpenOffice.org > Fonts.

2. On the Options – OpenOffice.org – Fonts dialog (Figure 1-7):

    *   Select the Apply Replacement Table checkbox.

    *   Select or type the name of the font to be replaced in the Font box. (If you don't have this font on your system, it won't appear in the drop-down list in this box, so you need to type it in.)

    *   In the Replace with box, select a suitable font from the drop-down list of fonts installed on your computer.

3. The checkmark to the right of the Replace with box turns green. Click on this checkmark. A row of information now appears in the larger box below the input boxes. Select the checkboxes under Always and Screen.

4. In the bottom section of the dialog, you can change the typeface and size of the font used to display source code such as HTML and Basic (in macros).

5. Continue to the next topic, or click OK to save your changes and close the dialog.

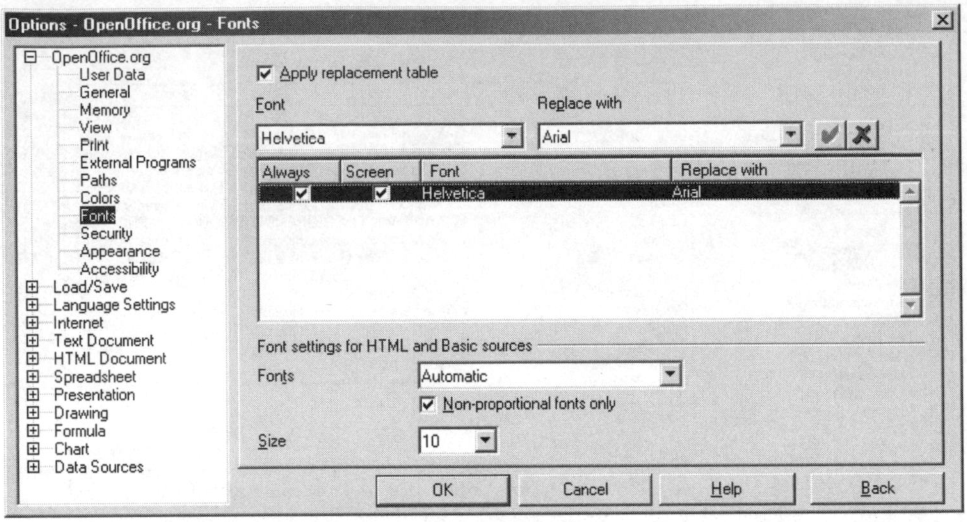

Figure 1-7. Defining a font to be substituted for another font

Appearance Options

Writing, editing, and page layout are often easier to do when you can see as much as possible of what's going on in your document. For example, you need to know if any tables or graphics are too wide and intrude into the margins of the page.

On the Options – OpenOffice.org – Appearance dialog (Figure 1-8), you can specify which items are visible and the colors used to display various items.

1. In the Options dialog, click OpenOffice.org > Appearance.

2. To show or hide items such as text boundaries, select or deselect the checkboxes next to the names of the items.

    To change the default colors for items, click the down-arrow in the Color Setting column by the name of the item and select a color from the pop-up box.

3. To save your color changes as a color scheme, type a name in the Scheme box and click Save.

4. Continue to the next topic, or click OK to save your changes and close the dialog.

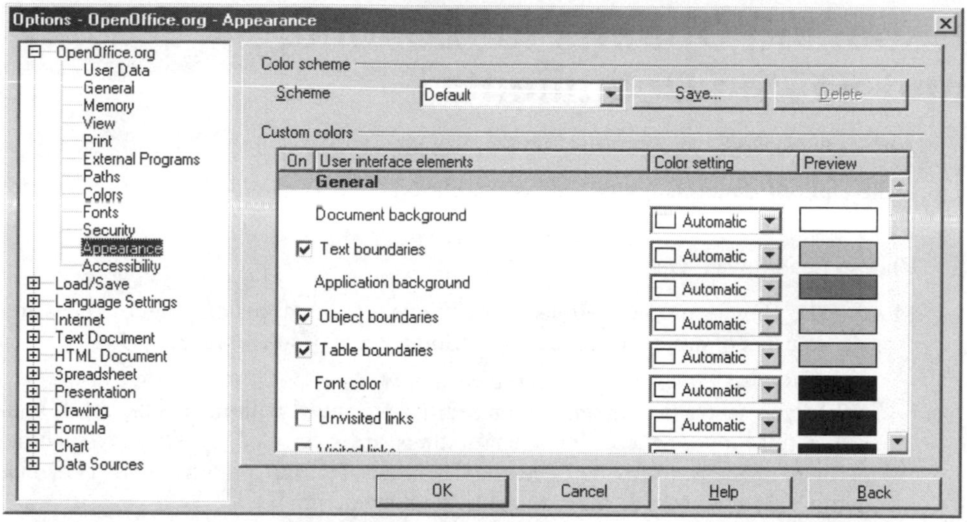

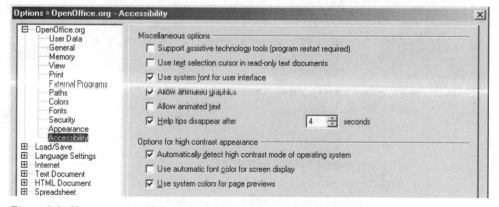

Figure 1-8. Showing or hiding text, object, and table boundaries

Accessibility Options

Accessibility options include whether to allow animated graphics or text, how long help tips remain showing, some options for high contrast display, and a way to change the font for the user interface of the OpenOffice.org program (see Figure 1-9).

1. In the Options dialog, click OpenOffice.org > Accessibility.

2. Select or deselect the options as required.

3. Continue to the next topic, or click OK to save your changes and close the dialog.

Figure 1-9. Choosing accessibility options

Choosing Options for Loading and Saving Documents

You can set the Load/Save options to suit the way you work.

1.   If the Options dialog is not already open, click Tools > Options. Click the + sign to the left of Load/Save.

2.   Choose Load/Save > General.

Most of the choices on the Options – Load/Save – General dialog (Figure 1-10) are familiar to users of other word processors. Some items of interest are:

Load user-specific settings with the document
When you save a document, certain settings are saved with the document. If you select this option, these document settings are overruled by the user-specific settings of the person who opens it. If you deselect this option, users' personal settings do not overrule the settings in the document.

For example, your choice on the Options – Text Document – General dialog (Figure 1-13) of how to update links (Always, on Request, Never) is a user-specific setting that is affected by this option. Some settings (printer name, data source linked to the document) are always loaded with a document, whether or not this checkbox is selected.

Edit document properties before saving
When you select this option, then the first time you save a new document (or whenever you use Save As), the Document Properties dialog pops up to prompt you to enter relevant information.

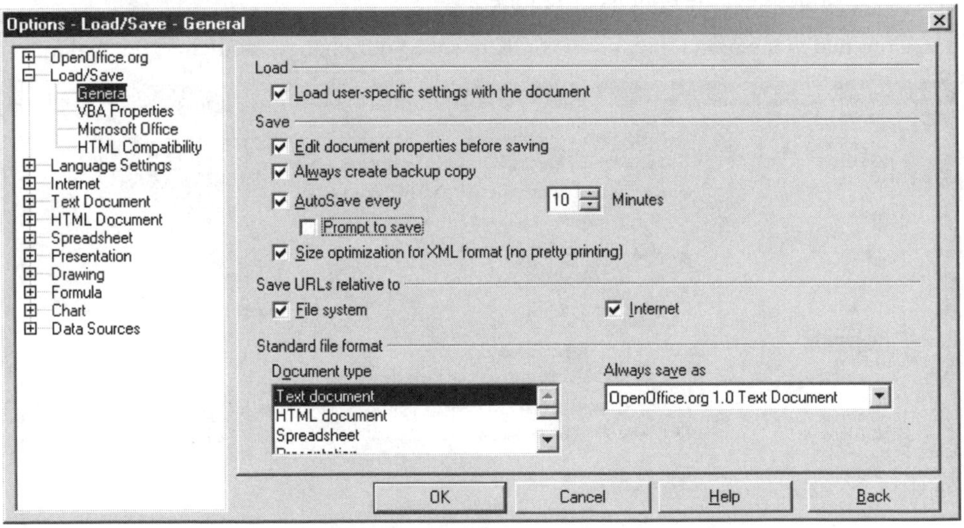

Figure 1-10. Choosing Load and Save options

AutoSave
Note that AutoSave in OpenOffice.org overwrites the original file.

Size optimization for XML format (no pretty printing)
OpenOffice.org documents are XML files. When you select this option, OOo writes the XML data without indents and line breaks; the resulting file size is smaller, and documents are saved and opened more quickly. If you want to read the XML files in a text editor in a structured form, deselect this option.

3. If you routinely share documents with users of Microsoft Word, you might want to change the Always save as attribute for text documents in the Standard file format section to one of the Word document types.

4. Choose Load/Save > VBA Properties.

5. On the Options – Load/Save – VBA Properties dialog (Figure 1-11), you can choose whether to keep any macros in MSOffice documents opened in OpenOffice.org.

   - If you choose Save original Basic code, the macros will not work in OOo but are retained if you save the file into Microsoft Office format.

   - If you choose Load Basic code to edit, the changed code is saved in an OOo document but is not retained if you save into an MSOffice format.

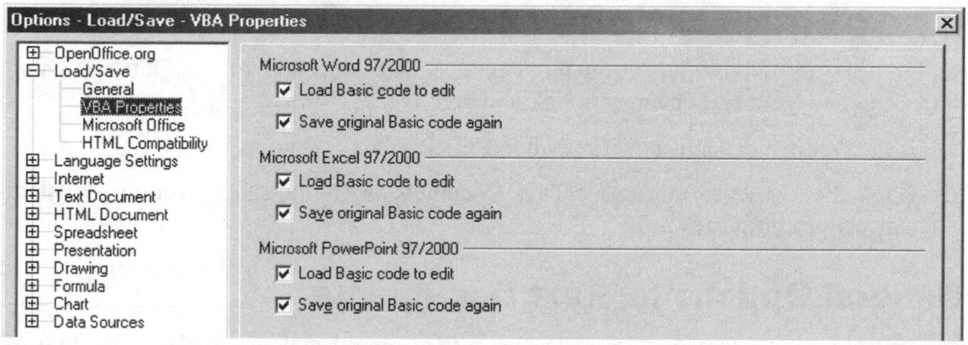

Figure 1-11. Choosing Load/Save VBA Properties

6. Choose Load/Save > Microsoft Office.

7. On the Options – Load/Save – Microsoft Office dialog (Figure 1-12), you can choose what to do when importing and exporting Microsoft Office OLE objects (linked or embedded objects or documents such as spreadsheets or equations).

   Select the [L] checkboxes to convert Microsoft OLE objects into the corresponding OpenOffice.org OLE objects when a Microsoft document is loaded into OOo.

   Select the [S] checkboxes to convert OpenOffice.org OLE objects into the correspnding Microsoft OLE objects when a document is saved in a Microsoft format.

8. Continue to the next topic, or click OK to save your changes and close the dialog.

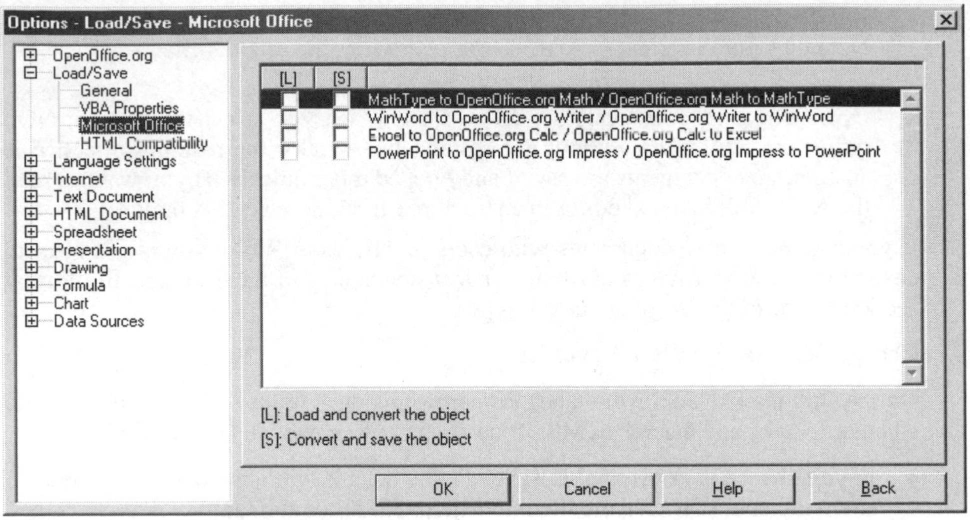

Figure 1-12. Choosing Load/Save Microsoft Office options

Choosing Options for Text Documents

Settings chosen on the dialogs in the Text Document section of the Options dialog determine how your text documents look and behave.

1. If the Options dialog is not already open, click Tools > Options.

2. Click the + sign to the left of Text Document in the left-hand section. A list of subsections drops down.

General Options for Text Documents

The choices on the Options – Text Document – General dialog affect the updating of links and fields, the units used for rulers and other measurements, whether captions are automatically added to selected objects such as tables or figures, paragraph spacing, and tab stop behavior.

1. Choose Text Document > General on the Options dialog (Figure 1-13).

2. Some considerations to keep in mind when selecting options on this dialog:

    Update links when loading
    Depending on your work patterns, you may not want links to be updated when you load a document. For example, if your file links to other files on a network, you won't want those links to update when you are not connected to the network.

    Update fields and charts automatically
    You may not want fields or charts to update automatically when you are working because that slows down performance.

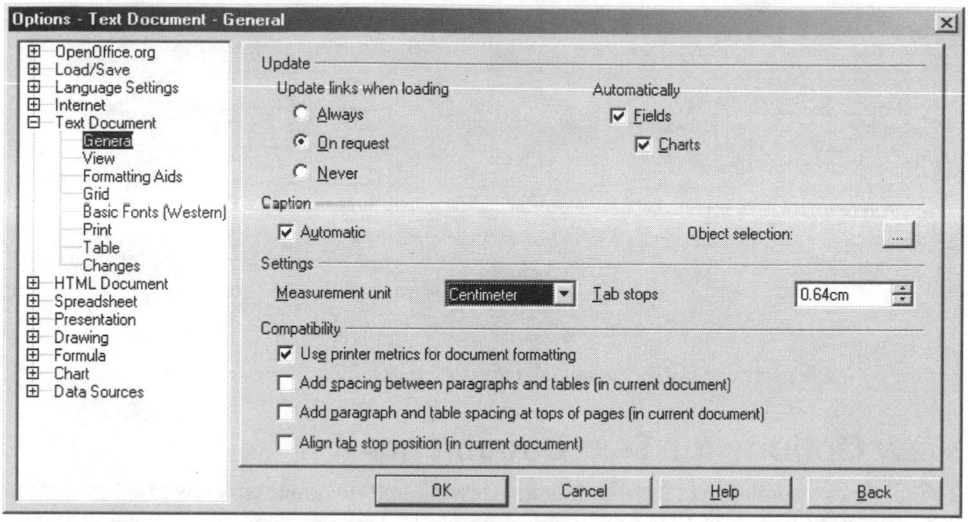

Figure 1-13. Choosing general options for text documents

Compatibility

Do you want your Writer documents to be compatible with Microsoft Word? If so, you may want to select some or all of these settings. Unlike some other options, the compatibility settings are valid only for the current document and thus must be defined separately for each document.

Settings – Tab stops

The Tab stop setting is also used for the indent distance applied by the Increase Indent and Decrease Indent icons on the Object Bar.

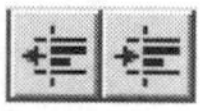

Captions

Do you want OOo to automatically insert captions for tables, graphics, frames, and OLE objects that have been inserted in a text document? You may not always want captions for every table, for example, if you use tables for layout as well as for tables of data. You can always add captions to individual tables, graphics, or other objects.

If you do want automatic captions on one or more object types:

a) Select Caption – Automatic, then click the Object Selection button.

b) On the Caption dialog (Figure 1-14), choose which objects will be automatically captioned, and specify the characteristics of the captions. If the term you want for the caption label is not in the drop-down Category list, type the required term in the box; you are not limited to the supplied categories. In the example shown, I have added the category "Figure" to the list.

c) Click OK to return to the Options dialog.

d) See "Adding Captions to Graphics" on page 183 for more about captions.

3. After you have made your selections, continue to the next topic, or click OK on the Options dialog to save your changes and close the dialog.

Figure 1-14. Choosing settings for automatic captions on graphics

View Options for Text Documents

Two dialogs of options set the defaults for viewing text documents: View and Formatting Aids (described on page 14).

1. Choose Text Document – View on the Options dialog (Figure 1-15).

2. If the items on this dialog are not self-explanatory, you can easily test their effect in a blank document.

    This is a good dialog to check if, for example, you can't see graphics on the screen, or you see field codes instead of the text or numbers you are expecting.

3. After you have made your selections, continue to the next topic, or click OK to save your changes and close the dialog.

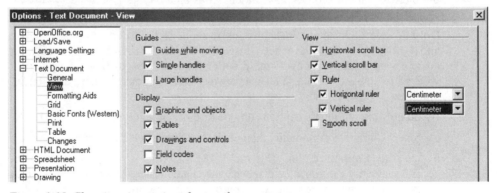

Figure 1-15. Choosing view options for text documents

Formatting Aids Options for Text Documents

The display of symbols such as paragraph ends and tabs help you when writing, editing, and doing page layout. For example, when you need to know if any blank paragraphs or tabs are included, or if any tables or graphics are too wide and intrude into the margins of the page.

1. On the Options – Text Document – Formatting Aids dialog (Figure 1-16), select the required checkboxes.

2. After you have made your selections, continue to the next topic, or click OK to save your changes and close the dialog.

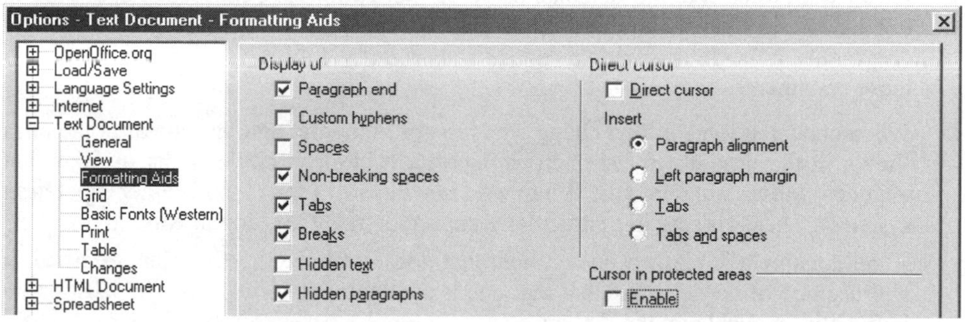

Figure 1-16. Choosing formatting aid options for text documents

---

Tip *Direct cursor* enables you to enter text at any position within the type area in your text document. This feature is incompatible with rigorous use of styles and can lead to many formatting oddities, so it should be avoided by professional writers.

Grid Options for Text Documents

Specifying "snap to grid" can be very helpful when you are trying to align several objects such as graphics or tables. If the grid intervals (subdivisions) are too large, you may find that you don't have enough control in placing the objects.

1. On the Options – Text Document – Grid dialog (Figure 1-17), you can choose whether to enable this feature, and what grid intervals to use.

2. After you have made your selections, continue to the next topic, or click OK to save your changes and close the dialog.

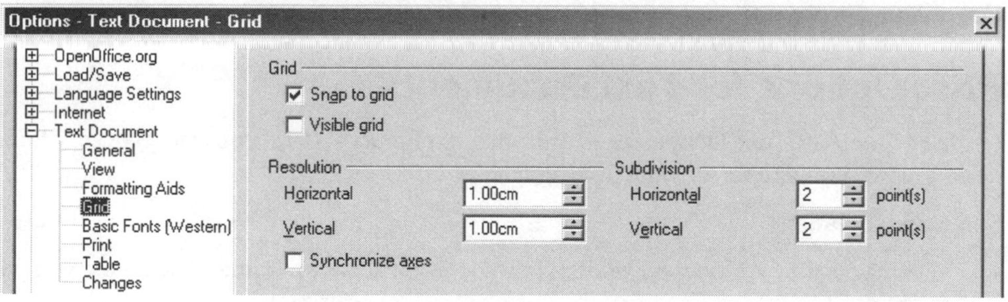

Figure 1-17. Choosing grid options for text documents

Default Fonts for Text Documents

The default fonts specified on the Basic Fonts dialog apply to both text documents and HTML (Web) documents.

1. If you want to change the defaults, do so on the Options – Text Document – Basic Fonts dialog (Figure 1-18). You can, of course, choose other fonts for use in specific documents, either by applying direct formatting or by defining and applying styles in those documents.

2. When choosing fonts in this dialog, you are not limited to single fonts or to the ones shown in the drop-down list. You can specify a "font family"—a set of fonts that includes those suitable for Windows, Macintosh, Linux, and other operating systerms. These choices are particularly important in HTML documents.

    If the document is viewed on a system that does not have the first font specified, it will use one of the other fonts if that one is available. Otherwise, it will substitute a font that is available on the system.

    Type the list of fonts, separated by commas, in the boxes. If you want these defaults to apply to the current document only, select that checkbox. The Default button at the bottom of the dialog (not shown) resets the values on this dialog to the defaults installed with OpenOffice.org.

3. After you have made your selections, continue to the next topic, or click OK to save your changes and close the dialog.

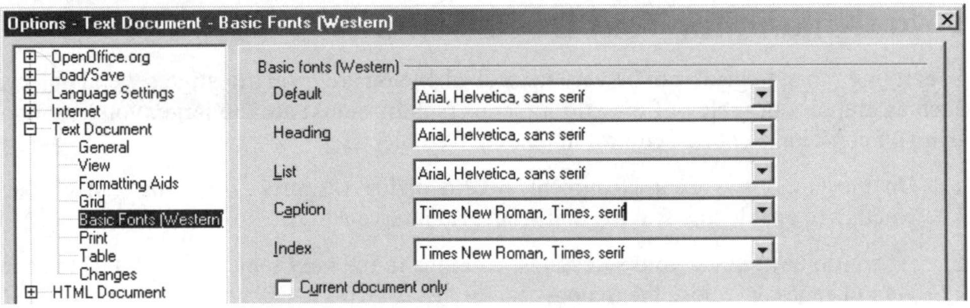

Figure 1-18. Choosing default fonts for text documents

Print Options for Text Documents

On the Options – Text Document – Print dialog (Figure 1-19), you can choose which items are printed with the document by default.

Some considerations:

*   When you are working on drafts, and you want to save printer ink or toner, you might want to deselect some of the items in the Contents section.

*   The Print black selection causes color text (but not graphics) to print as black on a color printer; on a black-and-white printer, this option causes color text to print as solid black instead of shades of gray (dithered). Contrast with Convert colors to

grayscale on the Options – OpenOffice.org – Print dialog (Figure 1-5), which prints all graphics as grayscale on color printers. (On black-and-white printers, color in graphics normally prints as grayscale.)

- If you're printing double-sided on a non-duplexing printer, you might choose to print only left or right pages, then turn the stack over and print the other pages.

- Depending on how your printer ejects pages (face up or face down), you might need to print the pages in reverse order so they stack in the correct order as they are printed.

- For more about Notes, see "Insert Notes and Questions" on page 39.

After you have made your selections, continue to the next topic, or click OK to save your changes and close the dialog.

Tip   You can override any of these defaults when printing a document. Click File > Print, then click the Options button on the Print dialog to display the dialog in Figure 1-19.

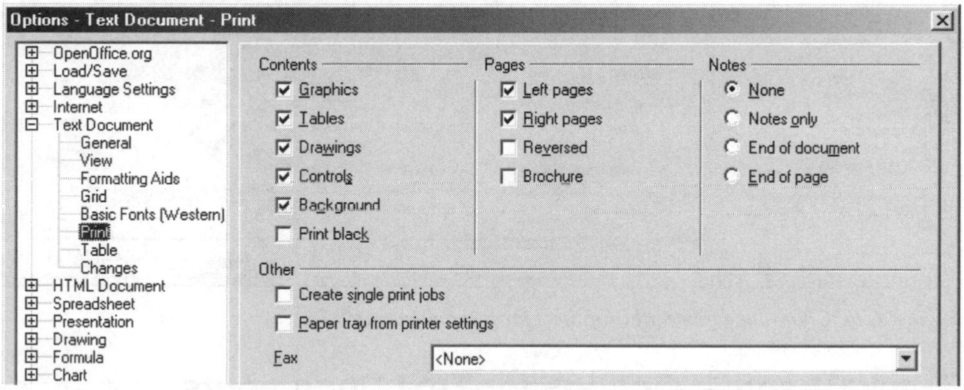

Figure 1-19. Choosing print options for text documents

Default Table Options for Text Documents

On the Options – Text Document – Table dialog (Figure 1-20), you can specify the default table behavior.

Some considerations:

- If most of your tables will require borders or headings, select those checkboxes; most of my tables are used for page layout, so I don't use either borders or headings.

- Number recognition can be very useful if most of your tables contain numerical data; Writer will recognize dates or currency, for example, and format the numbers appropriately. However, in many cases you want the numbers to remain as ordinary text, so this feature can be quite irritating. I generally deselect it.

- The Keyboard handling section specifies the distances cells will move when you use keyboard shortcuts to move them, and the size of rows and columns inserted using keyboard shortcuts. See "Control Spacing Within Table Cells" on page 62 for more about using keyboard shortcuts with tables.

- The choices in the Behavior of rows/columns section determine the effects that changes to rows or columns have on adjacent rows or columns and the entire table. You may need to test these selections to fully understand the effects.

After you have made your selections, continue to the next topic, or click OK to save your changes and close the dialog.

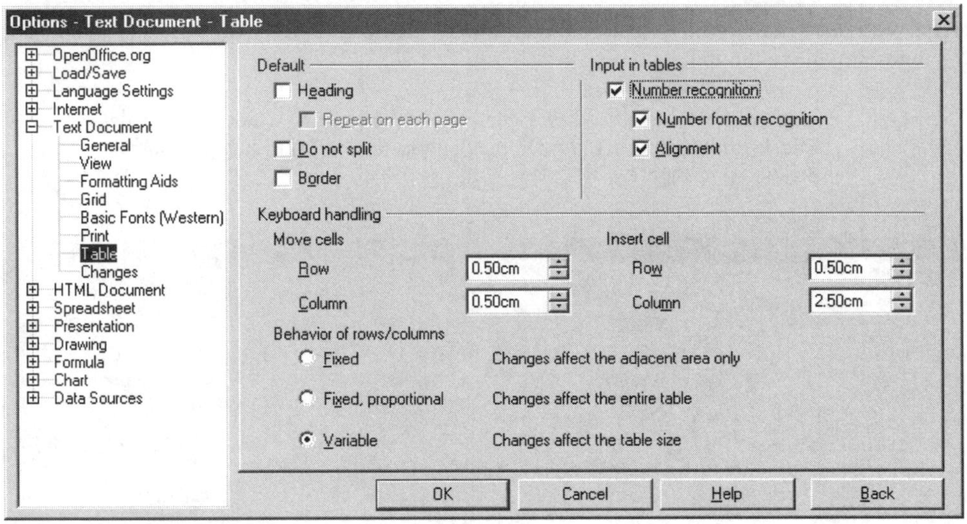

Figure 1-20. Choosing default table options for text documents

Track Changes Options for Text Documents

If you plan to use the change-tracking feature of Writer, use the Options – Text Document – Changes dialog (Figure 1-21) to choose the way inserted and deleted material is marked, whether and how attribute changes are marked, and whether and how change bars are marked in the margins. (The use of the change-tracking feature is covered in "Marking and Tracking Changes" on page 37.)

When you are done making all your changes, click OK to save them and close the dialog.

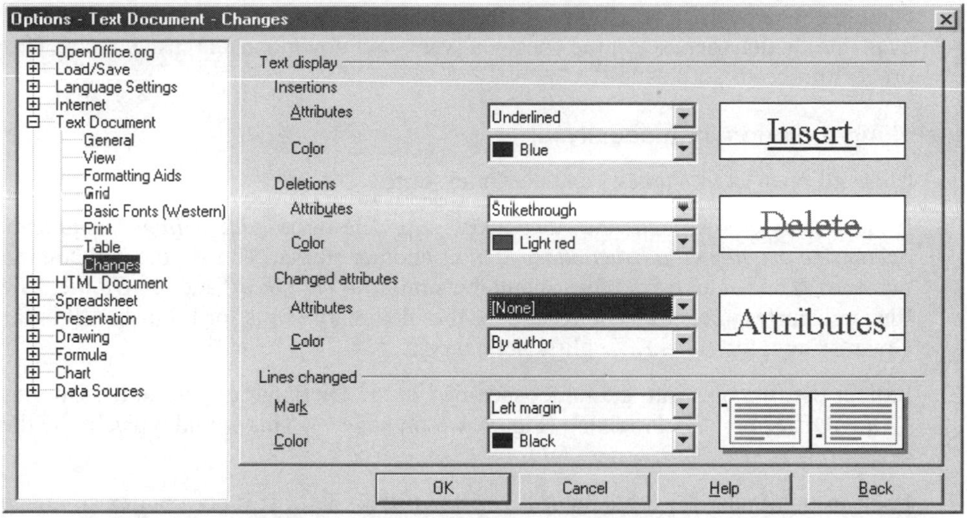

Figure 1-21. Choosing options for tracking changes in text documents

Preparing to Check Spelling

You may need to do several things to set the spelling options to what you want:

- Install the required dictionaries.
- Choose the dictionaries and spelling options.
- Change the default language for documents.
- Set the version of English to be checked.
- Create and use a custom dictionary.
- Create and use an exception dictionary.

Install the Required Dictionaries

OpenOffice.org 1.1.1 automatically installs several dictionaries with the program. To add other dictionaries, you can use the AutoPilot (not available in versions of OOo before 1.1.1) or install them manually.

Using the AutoPilot

1. Be sure you have write permission on the folder *<OOo>/share/dict/ooo* and on the file *<OOo>/share/dict/ooo/dictionary.lst*.

2. Be sure you are connected to the Internet, unless you have already downloaded a language pack or have one on a CD.

3. Click File > AutoPilot > Install new dictionaries. OOo opens a file (*DicOOo.sxw*) containing instructions in several languages and macro buttons to start the download and installation process. (The available dictionaries are for many more languages than those used in the instructions.)

4. Click the macro button and follow the instructions in the wizard to download a list of available dictionaries, select the ones you want, and download and install them. This process proceeds automatically.

Installing a dictionary manually

1. Close all open OOo windows and the Quickstarter.

2. If necessary, download the dictionary zip file from *http://lingucomponent. openoffice.org/download_dictionary.html* or another source. The zip file will contain two files. The names of the files should be similar to *en_GB.aff* and *en_GB.dic*. The filename corresponds to the language for the dictionary (*en* is for English; *GB* is for Great Britain, for the U.K. English dictionary).

3. Extract the two files into the folder specified in the Dictionaries path in the Options – OpenOffice.org – Paths dialog (Figure 1-6 on page 7). This would typically be the `<OOo>/share/dict/ooo` *folder*.

4. Look in this folder for a file named `dictionary.lst`. If it does not exist, create it.

5. Open this file in a text editor such as Notepad. Add this line to the file:

    `DICT en GB en_GB` (Change the filename to match the dictionary filename.)

6. Save the file as plain text.

Choose the Dictionaries and Spelling Options

After installing the dictionaries (either automatically or manually), you need to register them with Writer:

1. Start Writer (if it's not already running) and click Tools > Options.

2. Expand Language Settings and choose Writing Aids (Figure 1-22).

3. Make sure OpenOffice MySpell SpellChecker under Available language modules is selected, then click the Edit button at the top right of the dialog.

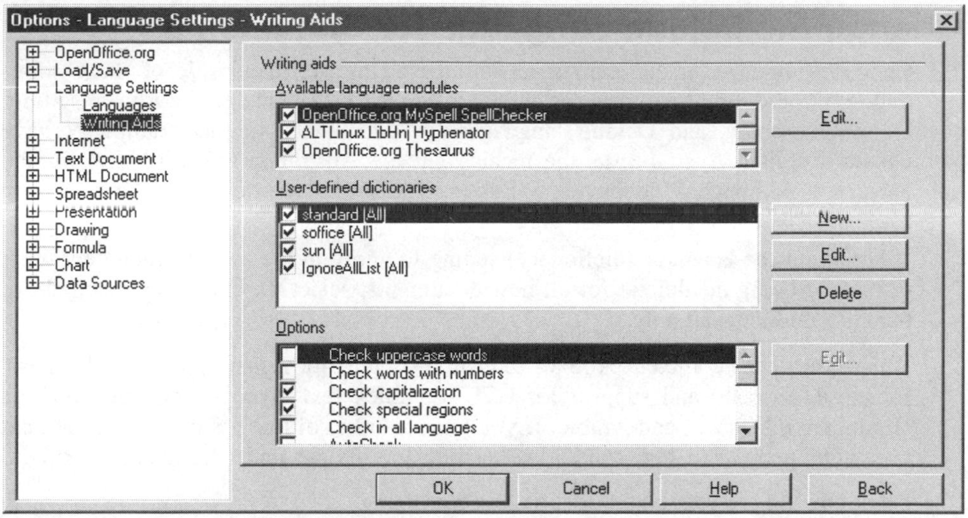

Figure 1-22. Choosing languages, dictionaries, and options for checking spelling

4. In the Edit Modules dialog (Figure 1-23), select the language from the list at the top, then select OpenOffice MySpell SpellChecker under Spelling. Click Close.

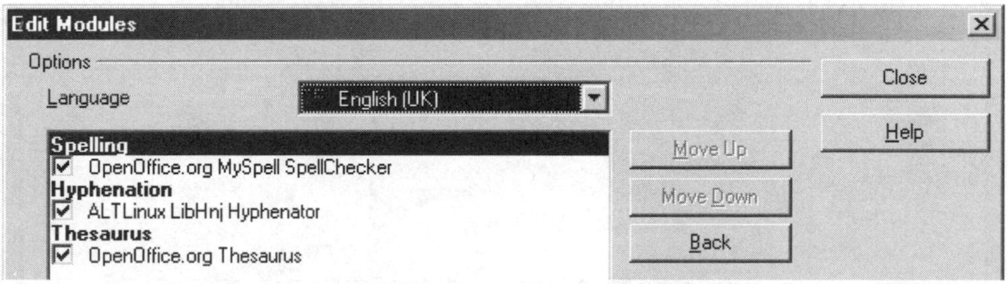

Figure 1-23. Registering a new dictionary

5. Back on the Writing Aids dialog, choose the settings that are useful for you. Some considerations:

    •   I select Do not mark errors (because these marks annoy and distract me) and deselect AutoCheck. (To find these items, scroll down in the Options list.)

    •   Because I use a custom dictionary that includes words in all uppercase and words with numbers (for example, AS/400), I select Check uppercase words and Check words with numbers.

    •   I select Check special regions to include headers, footers, frames, and tables when checking spelling.

    •   Here you can also check which user-defined (custom) dictionaries are active by default, and add or remove dictionaries, by clicking the New or Delete buttons. See "Create and Use a Custom Dictionary" on page 22.

Change the Default Language for Documents

1. Choose Languages under Language Settings on the left-hand side of the Options dialog. On the right-hand side (as shown in Figure 1-24), change the Locale setting, Default currency, and Default languages for documents. In the example, I have chosen English (Australia) as the locale, and the Australian dollar (AUD) for the currency. Although I do have an English (Australia) dictionary, I have chosen English (UK) as the default language.

    If you want the language (dictionary) setting to apply to the current document only, instead of being the default for all new documents, select the checkbox labelled For the current document only.

    If necessary, select the checkboxes to enable support for Asian languages (Chinese, Japanese, Korean) and support for CTL (complex text layout) languages such as Hindi, Thai, Hebrew, and Arabic. If you choose either of these checkboxes, the next time you open this dialog, you will see some extra dialogs under Language Settings.

2. Click OK to save your changes and close the dialog.

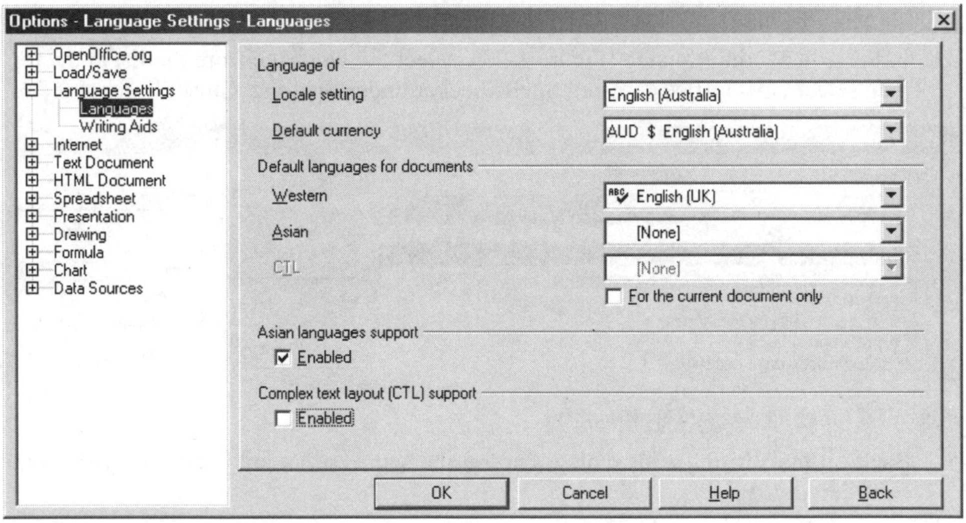

Figure 1-24. Choosing language options

Create and Use a Custom Dictionary

Many writing projects include large numbers of terms that are not in the supplied dictionaries. Technical terms and product names are the most common. To make sure they are spelled correctly, you can do one of these things:

*   The first time the spelling checker encounters the term in a document, click the Ignore All button. It will then skip all other instances of the word and add the word to the IgnoreAllList dictionary.

- If the word appears in several documents, you may wish to add it to a custom (user-defined) dictionary. Writer comes with several custom dictionaries that you can edit as needed. You can also create as many other custom dictionaries as you need. You may want separate custom dictionaries for different clients or for different projects.

Selecting one or more custom dictionaries to use with a document

On the Options – Language Settings – Writing Aids dialog (Figure 1-22), select or deselect the checkboxes for the various dictionaries in the User-defined dictionaries section. You may need to look at the contents of those dictionaries to determine which are useful. Click OK.

Editing an existing custom dictionary

1. In the Options – Language Settings – Writing Aids dialog (Figure 1-22), select the dictionary and click the Edit button to the right of the list of user-defined dictionaries. You must be authorized before you can edit a shared dictionary.

2. On the Edit Custom Dictionary dialog (Figure 1-25), type in the Word field the first word you want to put in the dictionary. Click New. Repeat for as many words as you want to add. Click Close to finish.

Edit Custom Dictionary		✕
Book	standard [All] ▼	
Language	[All] ▼	
Word		
Airlie		New
email		Delete
online		
	Help	Close

Figure 1-25. Adding words to a custom (user-defined) dictionary

Creating a new custom dictionary

1. In the Options – Language Settings – Writing Aids dialog (Figure 1-22), click New.

2. In the New Dictionary dialog (Figure 1-26), type a useful name for the dictionary and choose the language this dictionary applies to, or leave as [All]. Do *not* select the Exception checkbox. Click OK.

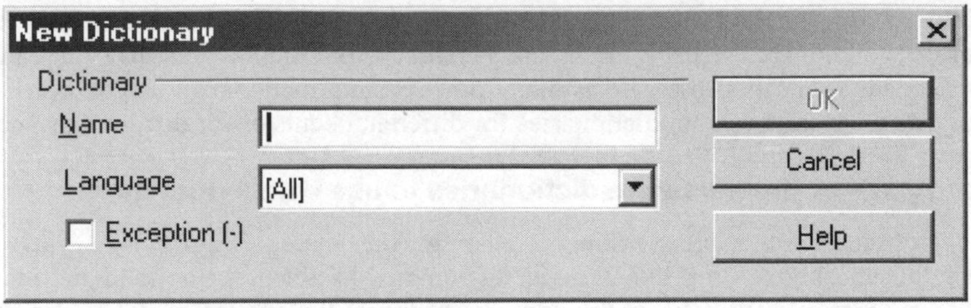

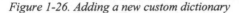

Figure 1-26. Adding a new custom dictionary

3. Back on the Writing Aids dialog, select the new dictionary (to put a mark in the checkbox and activate the dictionary) and click the Edit button to the right of the list of user-defined dictionaries.

4. On the Edit Custom Dictionary dialog (Figure 1-25), type in the Word field the first word you want to put in the dictionary. Click New. Repeat for as many words as you want to add. Click Close to finish.

You can return to this dialog at any time to add or delete entries. If you want to disable the dictionary, return to the Writing Aids dialog and deselect the checkbox next to its name.

Create and Use an Exception Dictionary

You can use an exception dictionary to find correctly spelled words that are not the right ones for the situation or are not your preferred spelling.

After you add words to the exception dictionary, the spelling checker will question them the next time you check spelling. You can then decide whether the word is the correct one or change it if necessary.

To create an exception dictionary:

1. In the Options – Language Settings – Writing Aids dialog (Figure 1-22), click New.

2. In the New Dictionary dialog (Figure 1-27), type a useful name (for example, Exclude), choose the language this dictionary applies to (or leave as [All]), and select the Exception (-) checkbox. Click OK.

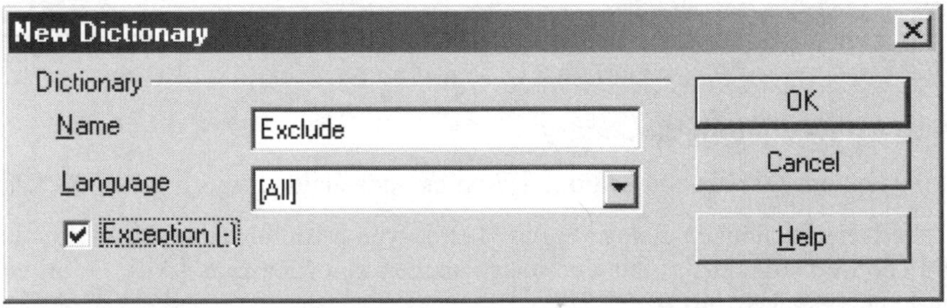

Figure 1-27. Adding an exception dictionary

3. Back on the Writing Aids dialog, select the dictionary named Exclude (to put a mark in the checkbox and activate the dictionary) and click the Edit button to the right of the list of user-defined dictionaries.

4. The Edit Custom Dictionary dialog (Figure 1-28) now has an extra field: Replace By. Type in the Word field the first word you want to put in the exception dictionary. You can type a suggested replacement in the Replace By field or leave it blank, as I have done in the example. Click New to add the word to the list. Repeat for as many words as you want to add. Click Close to finish.

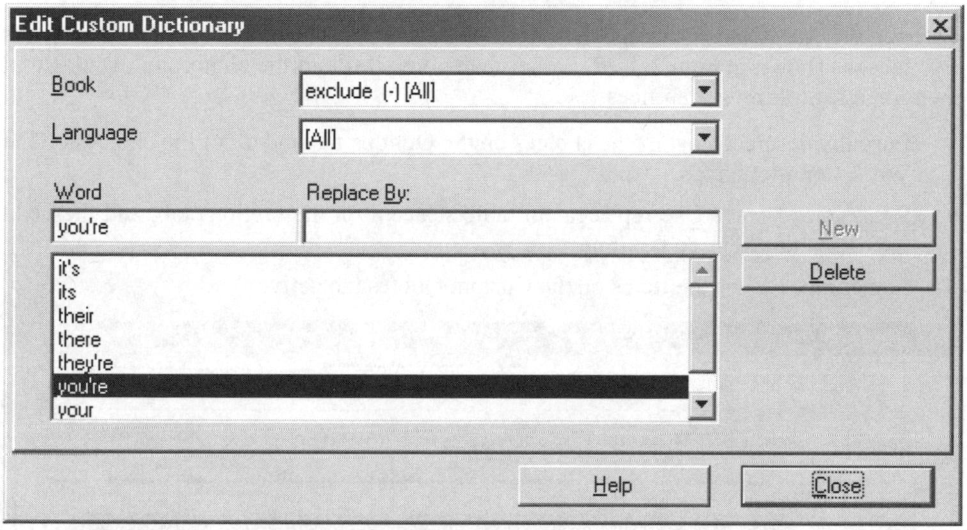

Figure 1-28. Adding words to an exception dictionary

You can return to this dialog at any time to add or delete entries or change the suggested replacement words. If you want to disable the dictionary, return to the Writing Aids dialog and deselect the checkbox next to its name.

Correcting Your User Information

Because Writer's revision features mark your changes and comments with the name or initials stored in User Information, you'll want to ensure that your name and initials appear there. To do this, open the Options – OpenOffice.org – User Data dialog. If anything on this dialog is incorrect, delete it and type the correct information. Click OK after making any changes.

Controlling Writer's AutoCorrect Functions

You may find that some or all of the items in any word processing program's AutoCorrect function are very annoying because what you type will often change when you don't want it to. Many people find some of the AutoCorrect functions quite helpful; if you do, then select the relevant checkboxes. But if you find unexplained changes appearing in your text, this is a good place to look to find the cause.

To open the AutoCorrect dialog, click Tools > AutoCorrect/AutoFormat. This dialog has five tabs, as shown in Figure 1-29. Rather than going through the choices in detail, I will mention a few of my preferences.

- I usually deselect most of the choices on the Options tab and all of the choices on the Word Completion tab.

- Sometimes I leave Use replacement table selected on the Options tab, and then edit the list on the Replace tab if necessary.

- Sometimes I leave the items on the Custom Quotes tab active.

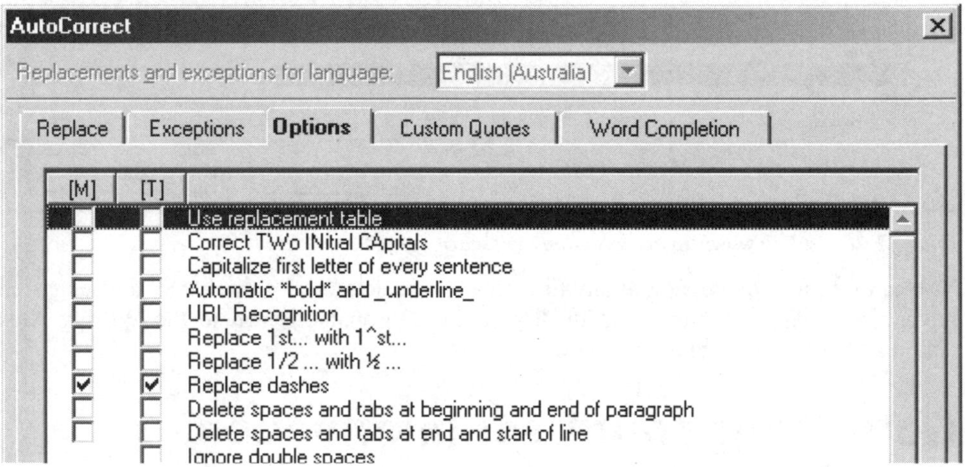

Figure 1-29. The AutoCorrect dialog, showing the five tabs and some of the choices on the Options tab

Writing, Editing, and Reviewing Documents

Writer provides many ways to write, edit, review, and comment on documents. This chapter covers some of those techniques, plus some other tips.

Parts of the Main Window

Figure 2-1 shows the terms that OpenOffice.org uses for parts of the main window.

Fly-Out Toolbars

OpenOffice.org also has fly-out toolbars on many of the toolbar and object bar icons. Icons with these toolbars have a tiny arrow in their upper right-hand corner; this arrow may be pointing down or to the right. If you click and hold one of these icons, a fly-out toolbar will appear. (Writer calls this *long-clicking*.) Move the mouse pointer over the icons on the fly-out toolbar and release it on the required icon. You can also detach any of these small toolbars and make them floating or dock them in a convenient place.

Main toolbar   Menu bar   Function bar   Object bar

Figure 2-1. Parts of the main Writer window

Keyboard Shortcuts, Extended Tips, and Right-Click Menus

If you use Writer a lot, you'll want to learn some of the many keyboard shortcuts. Look in the online help on the Contents page under Help about OpenOffice.org Writer > Shortcut Keys for Text Documents and General Shortcut Keys in OpenOffice.org.

If you're not sure what the toolbar icons are, click Help > Tips to show brief tooltips when you hover the mouse pointer over an icon or control in the main window. For more information about the options in a dialog, click Help > Extended Tips to pop up more information about a field, checkbox, or other control.

You'll find many useful functions on the right-click pop-up (context) menus, which often provide faster and easier access to the same functions that are available through the menu bar. It's well worth your time to check the right-click menu when you want to do something.

Special-Purpose Object Bars

OpenOffice.org provides several special-purpose object bars that you can display in certain situations. For example, when you click on the Numbering On/Off icon or the Bullets On/Off icon to turn on bullets or list numbering, a left-pointing arrow appears at the right-hand end of the Formatting object bar. If you click this arrow, the Formatting icons are replaced by the Numbering and Bullets object bar (see Figure 4-20 on page 89).

Similarly, when you insert a table and the cursor is within the table, the Table object bar can be turned on and off (see Figure 3-25 on page 67).

Selecting a graphic displays the Graphics object bar (see Figure 8-12 on page 176). Other inserted objects have their own object bars.

The Navigator

The Navigator is a very useful tool that helps you move quickly to specific parts of your document and also provides information about the content of the document.

To activate the Navigator (Figure 2-2), click Edit > Navigator, press F5, or click the Navigator icon ✦ on the function bar.

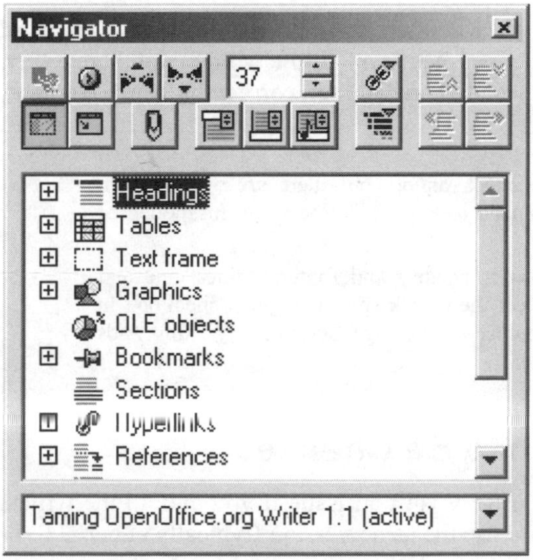

Figure 2-2. The Navigator for a Writer document

In Writer, the Navigator includes lists of the graphics and tables in your document. Click the + sign by any list to display the contents of the list. You can double-click an entry in the Navigator and jump immediately to that place in your document.

If you have structured a document by using heading styles, you can change the sequence and hierarchical levels of chapters and subchapters using the Navigator. Select an item and click one of the Promote or Demote icons.

Click the Navigation icon at the top of the Navigator to open a toolbar that you can turn into a floating toolbar. Use the small icons on this toolbar to jump quickly to different parts of your document. The online help describes the Navigator's functions in more detail.

The Navigator is a bit different in master documents, as described in "Creating and Using Master Documents" on page 149.

Checking Spelling

Although software won't find correctly spelled words that are used incorrectly, the spelling checker can be useful for making initial corrections. When used in combination with an exception dictionary, you can even find words that are wrongly used; see "Create and use an Exception Dictionary" on page 24 for details.

"Preparing to Check Spelling" on page 19 described how to choose languages and set up dictionaries in Writer.

The basics of checking spelling are the same as in other word processors, although some of the details differ. This section describes some of these differences and some features you might find useful.

You can choose to check the spelling only in selected text or in the full document.

Writer searches first through the selected user-defined (custom) dictionaries. If the word is not found there, it searches through the main dictionary. If the word is not there either, the Spellcheck dialog (Figure 2-3) is displayed. You can then correct the word, ignore it, or add it to a dictionary.

Tips   If you want to open the Spellcheck dialog, but there are no unknown words in your document, you need to enter a deliberately misspelled or unknown word.

If you want the spelling of text in headers and footers, tables, and text frames to be checked, then select the Check special regions checkbox in the Options section of the Options – Language Settings – Writing Aids dialog (Figure 1-22 on page 21).

Set the Version of English to Be Checked

The "version of English to be checked" usually isn't an issue if you and all the writers you work with have your systems set up to use the same version (typically either U.S. or U.K. English). "Change the Default Language for Documents" on page 22 shows how to do this.

If you work with some documents requiring U.S. English spelling and other documents requiring U.K. English spelling, you may need to change some documents to not use the default language.

To change the language for the current document:

1. Click Tools > Options.

2. On the Options – Language Settings – Languages dialog (Figure 1-24 on page 22), choose the required language and select the Only for the current document checkbox.

Add Words to a Custom Dictionary
While Checking Spelling

"Create and Use a Custom Dictionary" on page 22 describes how to add words directly to a custom dictionary. You can also add words while checking spelling.

1. Click Tools > Spellcheck > Check (or press F7) to open the Spellcheck dialog (Figure 2-3).

2. When a word is shown as incorrect or unknown, but it is spelled the way you want, you can either ignore the word or add it to a dictionary. To add it to a dictionary, first select the dictionary from the list near the bottom of the dialog; then click Add.

    On this dialog you can also change the language of the highlighted word, and you can call up the thesaurus or directly reach the Writing Aids dialog (by clicking Options). The Writing Aids dialog reached in this way (shown in Figure 2-4) is slightly different from the one shown in Figure 1-22 on page 21, as it contains only the list of user-defined dictionaries and the list of options for hyphenation and spellchecking.

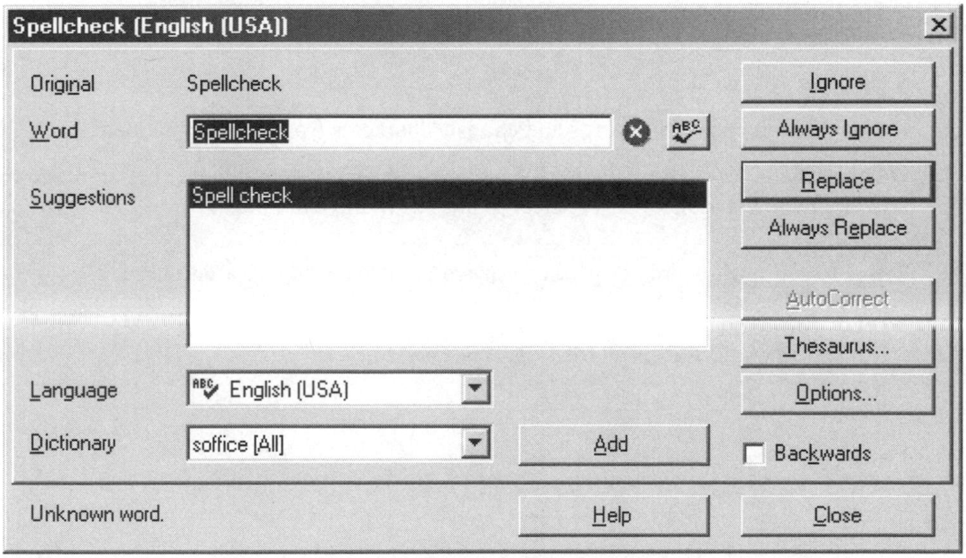

Figure 2-3. Ignoring a word or adding it to a custom dictionary

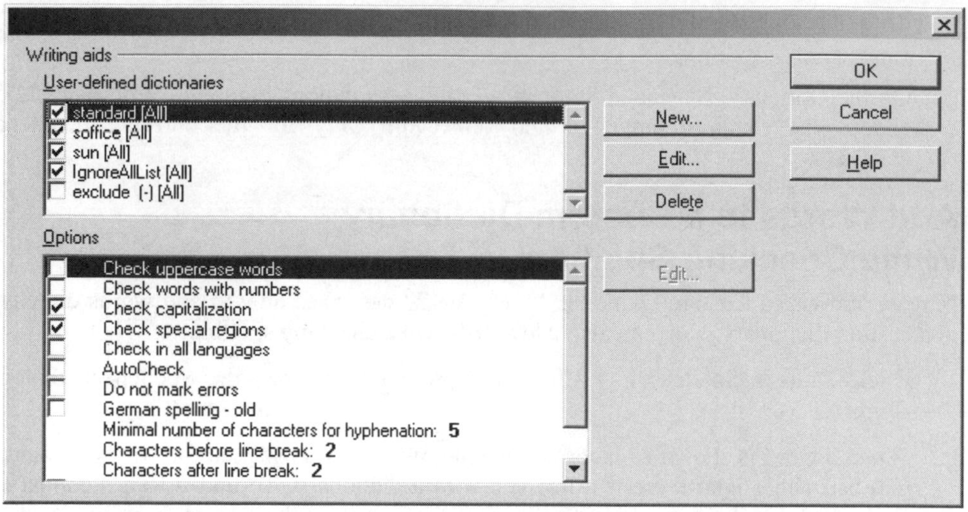

Figure 2-4. Changing information about writing aids during spellchecking

Ignore Some Text While Checking Spelling

To mark full paragraphs of text (such as code samples) to be ignored while checking spelling, create a paragraph style that specifies the language as [None]. See "Working with Styles" on page 79 for information on creating styles.

To exclude individual words or phrases from the spellcheck:

1. Select the words.

2. Right-click on one of the words and choose Character from the pop-up menu.

3. On the Character dialog (Figure 2-5), choose the Font tab and set the language to any language you don't use, or select [None] as in the example.

Tip   For single words or phrases that are used frequently in a document, a better solution is to add them to a custom dictionary. That way, they're checked but not flagged as errors unless you mistyped them. See "Create and Use an Exception Dictionary" on page 24.

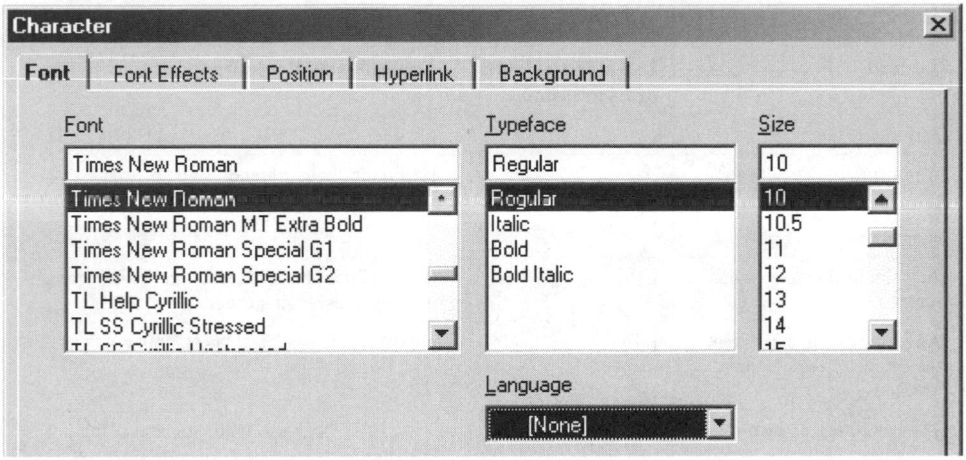

Figure 2-5. Setting a word's language to [None]

Finding and Replacing Text and Formatting

To open the Find & Replace dialog, click Edit > Find & Replace or press the shortcut keys Ctrl+F. This section assumes you know the basics of finding and replacing words or phrases, so it covers some advanced ways to use this function to make editing your work faster and easier.

Using the various buttons on the dialog, you can:

- Use wildcards and regular expressions to fine-tune a search
- Find and replace specific formatting
- Find and replace paragraph styles
- Plan a multiple-pass find and replace

Use Wildcards and Regular Expressions to Fine-Tune a Search

A *wildcard* is a keyboard character that can be used to represent one or many characters when you are searching for something. A *regular expression* combines wildcards with other characters that instruct OOo how to treat the wildcards (see Table 2-1).

Table 2-1. Examples of search wildcards

To find	Use this wildcard or expression	Examples and comments
Any single character	.	b.d finds "bad," "bud," "bid," and "bed."
Any string of characters	.*	b.*d finds "bad," "brand," and "board."
One of the specified characters	[ ]	b[iu]n finds "bin," and "bun."
Any single character in this range	[-]	[r-t]eed finds "reed," "seed," and "teed"; ranges must be in ascending order.
Any single character except the characters inside the brackets	[^]	p[^a]st finds "post" and "pest," but not "past."
The beginning of a word	\<	\<log finds "logbook" and "logistics," but not "catalog."
The end of a word	\>	log\> finds "catalog," but not "logistics."
A paragraph marker	$	Does not work as a replacement character. Use \n instead.
A line break	\n	Finds a line break that was inserted with Shift+Enter. When used as a replacement character, it inserts a paragraph marker.

Here are a few more things to be aware of:

- Many more regular expressions and their uses are described in the online help.
- To search for a character that is defined as a wildcard, type a backslash (\) before the character. For example, to find a phrase that includes a question mark (such as "how?"), you would search for "how\?".
- This feature did not work in Version 1.0.x of OpenOffice.org.

To use wildcards and regular expressions when searching and replacing:

1. On the Find & Replace dialog (Figure 2-6), select the Regular expressions checkbox.

2. Type your search text, including the wildcards, into the Search for and Replace with boxes.

3. Click Find, Replace, or Replace All (not recommended). If you're replacing text, it's a good idea to click Replace instead of Replace All; that way, you can confirm each replacement to make sure it's correct. Otherwise, you're likely to end up with some hilarious (and highly embarrassing) bloopers.

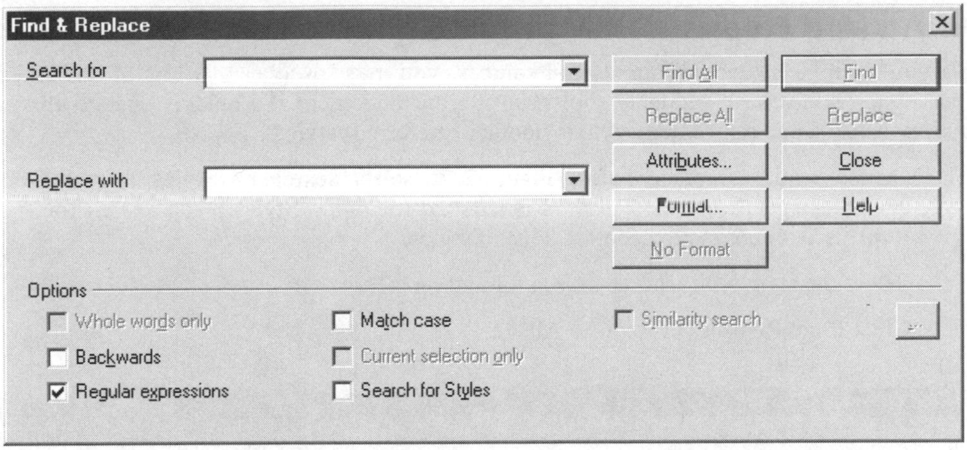

Figure 2-6. Using regular expressions (wildcards) in the Find & Replace dialog

Find and Replace Specific Formatting

A very powerful and handy use of Find & Replace takes advantage of the format option. For example, you might want to replace underlined words with italics. I'm sure you can find many other uses.

On the Find & Replace dialog:

1. To search for text with specific formatting, enter the text in the Search for box. To search for specific formatting only, delete any text in the Search for box.

2. Click Format, and then choose from the list the formats you want to search for. The names of selected formats appear under the Search for box.

3. To replace text, enter the replacement text in the Replace with box.

    To keep the same text but change the formatting, enter the same text in the Replace with box.

    To change formatting only, delete any text in the Replace with box. Click Format and choose the formats you want.

    To remove specific character formatting, click Format, select Font, then select the opposite format (for example, No Bold). The No Format button on the dialog clears all previously selected formats.

4. Click Find, Replace, or Replace All.

5. Unless you plan to search for other text using those same attributes, click No Format to remove the attributes. If you forget to do this, you may wonder why your next search fails to find words you know are in the document.

Find and Replace Paragraph Styles

If you combine material from several sources, you may discover that lots of unwanted paragraph styles have suddenly shown up in your document. To quickly change all the paragraphs of one (unwanted) style to another (preferred) style:

1. On the Find & Replace dialog (Figure 2-7), select Search for Styles. (If you have attributes specified, this checkbox is labelled Including Styles.) The Search for and Replace with boxes now contain a list of styles.

2. Select the styles you want to search for and replace.

3. Click Find, Replace, or Replace All.

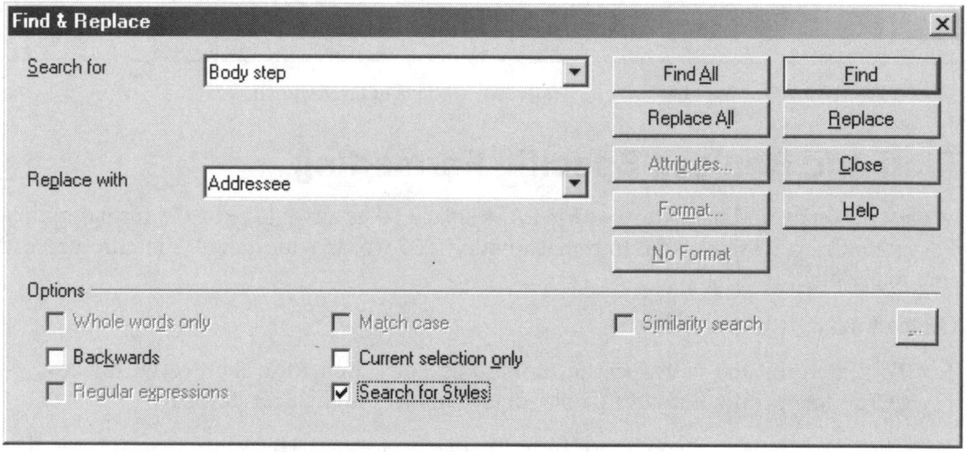

Figure 2-7. Searching for styles using the Find & Replace dialog

Plan a Multiple-Pass Find and Replace

Find and replace is a powerful feature, but it can be dangerous if you don't do a bit of planning first. You must consider the consequences of each step, so you do them in the correct order.

Example: replacing the formatting in part of a string of characters

Suppose you need to replace a string of characters in which one is a subscript or superscript (for example, H2O with H_2O) in a document where these occur frequently. Here are the steps you would take:

1. Replace all occurrences of H2O by (subscript) H2O using the Format option (Figure 2-8). Now you have $_{H2O}$.

2. Replace all occurrences of (subscript) H with normal H, again using the Format option (Figure 2-9). Now you have H_{2O}.

3. Replace all occurrences of (subscript) O with normal O. Now you have H_2O.

Figure 2-8. The first step of a multiple-pass find and replace

Figure 2-9. The second step of a multiple-pass find and replace

| Tip | You can do this particular substitution in other ways. For example, if you are typing in the text (instead of editing existing text), you can create one H_2O and make an AutoText entry to use in other situations where you need it. See "Using AutoText to Insert Often-Used Fields Quickly" on page 99. |

Marking and Tracking Changes

You can use several methods to keep track of changes made to a document. Which method you use, and whether you need to keep a record of changes, depends on your company's or client's policy.

- You can make your changes to a copy of the document (stored in a different folder, or under a different name, or both), then use Writer to compare the two files and show the changes you made. Click Edit > Compare Document. This technique is particularly useful if you are the only person working on the document, as it avoids the increase in file size and complexity caused by the other methods.

- You can save versions that are stored as part of the original file, but this method can cause problems with documents of any size or complexity, especially if you save a lot of versions. Avoid this method if you can.

- You can use Writer's change marks (often called "redlines" or "revision marks") to show where you have added or deleted material, or changed formatting. Later, you or another person can review and accept or reject each change.

Tip   Not all changes are recorded. For example, changing a tab stop from align left to align right, and changes in formulas (equations) or linked graphics are not recorded.

Prepare a Document for Editing or Review

Although you (or your editor or reviewers) can use Writer's revision feature to mark up a document that has not been prepared for review, you may want to do the preparation step first, so the editor or reviewer can't forget to turn on the revision marks. After you have protected the document, you must enter the correct password in order to turn off the function or accept or reject changes. *Passwords must contain at least five characters.*

1. Open the document. To check whether it contains multiple versions, click File > Versions. If multiple versions are listed, save the current version as a separate document with a different name, and use this new document as the review copy.

2. With the review copy open, click Edit > Changes > Protect Records. This opens the Enter Password dialog. Type a password (twice) and click OK.

Edit (Review) the Document

See "Track Changes Options for Text Documents" on page 18 for instructions on setting up how your changes will be displayed.

1. To begin tracking (recording) changes, click Edit > Changes > Record.

   To show or hide the display of changes, click Edit > Changes > Show.

Tip   Hover the mouse pointer over a marked change; you will see a Help Tip showing the type of change, the author, date, and time of day for the change. If you don't see this information, click Help > Tips. If the Extended Tips are also enabled, you will also see any comments recorded for this change.

2. To enter a comment on a marked change, place the cursor in the area of the change and then click Edit > Changes > Comment. (See Figure 2-10.) In addition to being displayed as an extended tip, the comment is also displayed in the list in the Accept or Reject Changes dialog.

   You can move from one marked change to the next by using the arrow buttons. If no comment has been recorded for a change, the Text field is blank.

3. To stop recording changes, click Edit > Changes > Record again.

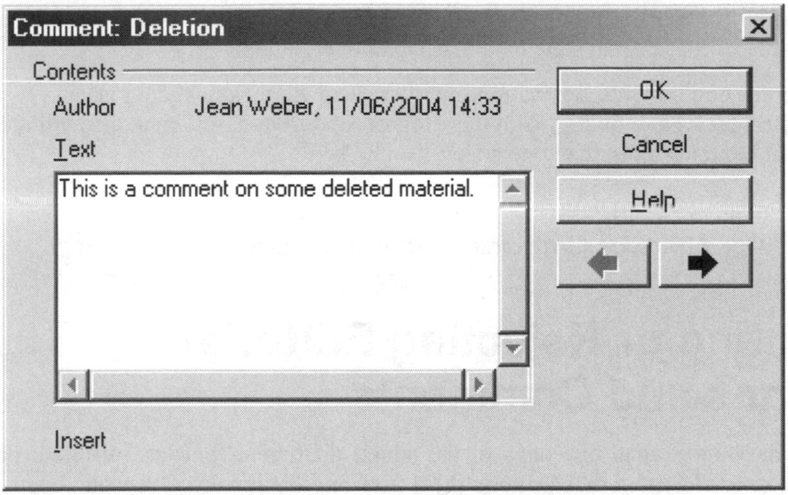

Figure 2-10. Inserting a comment on a deletion during change recording

Insert Notes and Questions

To insert a note or question that is not associated with a recorded change:

1. Position the cursor at the text you want to comment on, then click Insert > Note.

2. On the Insert Note dialog (Figure 2-11), type your note. Click Author to easily insert your name and the date and time.

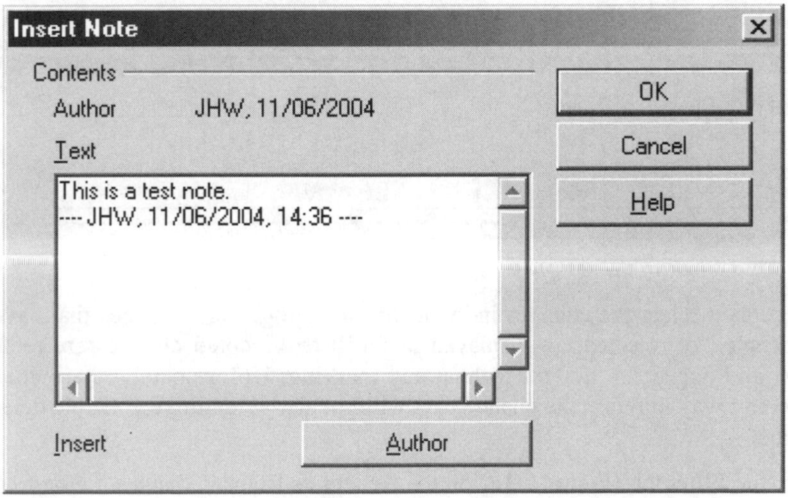

Figure 2-11. Inserting a note

To view a note, move the mouse pointer over the note marker (displayed as a small yellow square). Writer displays the note in a Tip above the text.

To edit a note, double-click on the note marker. The Edit Note dialog opens. It looks much like the Insert Note dialog, with the addition of forward and back arrow buttons if the document contains more than one note.

Tip	You can change the color of the note marker using the Options – OpenOffice.org – Appearance dialog (see Figure 1-8 on page 9).

Accepting or Rejecting Editorial Changes and Comments

1. If you have more than one copy of the edited document (because different people worked on different copies), merge them into one document. Open one copy, then click Edit > Changes > Merge Document and select another copy of the document to be merged with the first. Repeat until all copies are merged. All recorded changes will now be included in the open copy. Save this file under another name.

2. Now click Edit > Changes > Accept or Reject. The Accept or Reject Changes dialog (Figure 2-12) appears.

Figure 2-12. The List tab of the Accept or Reject Changes dialog

You can accept or reject the changes individually or all together. Changes that have not yet been accepted or rejected are displayed in the list. Accepted changes are removed from the list and appear in the text without any marking. Unfortunately, there does not appear to be any way to retain the change bars without also retaining the visible deletions and insertions.

You can use the Filter tab (Figure 2-13) on the Accept or Reject Changes dialog to show only the changes of certain people, or only the changes of the last day, or various other restrictions.

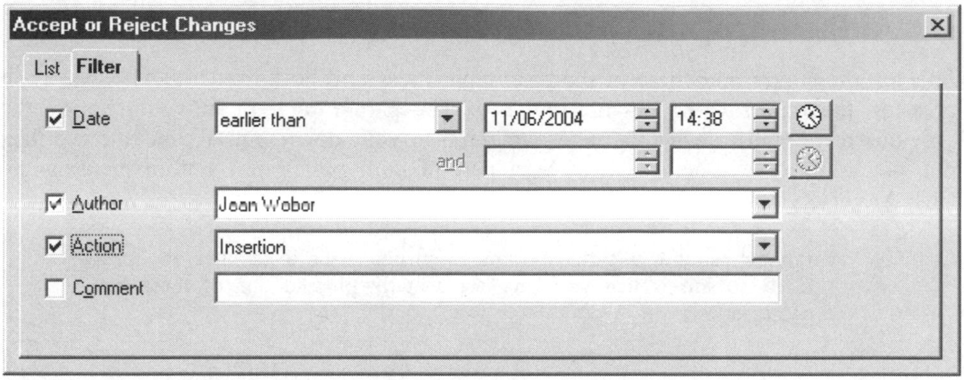

Figure 2-13. The Filter tab of the Accept or Reject Changes dialog

Changing Document Properties

Many people copy one document (often written by someone else, or for a different project) when they create another, or they create a template from an existing document, but they don't change the document properties. Unchanged properties can end up being quite embarrassing for someone, particularly if the properties include confidential information. To change document properties:

1. Click File > Properties.

2. On the Properties dialog, look at all the fields on the Description, User Defined, and Internet tabs, and change anything that needs amendment. Click OK.

See page 95 for more information about the User Defined tab. This book does not cover the Internet tab, which is used for HTML (Web) documents.

Useful Techniques

Here are some tricks you might find useful when writing and editing documents.

Undo Edits

You can click Edit > Undo, press Ctrl+Z on the keyboard, or click the Undo icon  to undo a series of edits or other actions, one at a time, working backward from the last action.

You can also long-click the Undo icon to see a list of the most recent actions you can undo. Scroll through the list until you find the action you want to undo, then click on it. Be careful, though: when you undo an action selected this way, you also undo all actions above it in the list. That result might not be what you want.

If Protect Records (see page 38) has been turned on, you cannot undo edits.

Move Paragraphs Quickly

Position the cursor anywhere in the paragraph. Press and hold the Ctrl+Alt keys while pressing the up-arrow or down-arrow key. The paragraph will move to before the previous paragraph or after the next paragraph in your document. To move more than one paragraph at a time, select at least part of both paragraphs before pressing the Ctrl+Alt+arrow keys.

Tip	If your paragraphs suddenly jump from one place to another, the most likely reason is that you have accidentally pressed one of these key combinations.

Paste Unformatted Text

When you copy text (from within OpenOffice.org or from another application) and paste it into a Writer document, the default is for the pasted text to retain some or all of its original formatting, including typeface and type size, attributes such as bold or italics, paragraph indentation, and so on, instead of taking on the attributes of the paragraph into which the text is pasted.

Sometimes this is what you want. However, if you do not want the pasted text to retain its attributes, click Edit > Paste Special and choose Unformatted text, or long-click on the Paste icon and choose Unformatted text from the drop-down menu. (See Figure 2-14. The choices on this menu vary a bit depending on the type of material.)

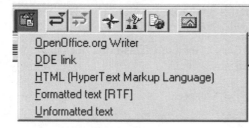

Figure 2-14. The Paste Special menu reached by long-clicking on the Paste icon

Select Items That Are Not Next to Each Other

Using the mouse to select nonconsecutive items

1. Select the first piece of text.

2. Hold down the Ctrl key and use the mouse to select the next piece of text.

3. Repeat as often as needed.

4. Now do what you want with the selected text (copy it, delete it, change the style, whatever).

Using the keyboard to select nonconsecutive items

1. Select the first piece of text.

2. Press Shift+F8.

3. Use the arrow keys to move to the start of the next piece of text to be selected. Hold down the Shift key and select the next piece of text.

4. Repeat as often as needed.

5. Now do what you want with the selected text (copy it, delete it, change the style, whatever).

6. Press Esc to cancel this mode.

Count the Number of Words

The File > Properties > Statistics tab gives the number of words for the entire document. Writer does not provide a way to count the words in a selection, but someone has written a macro to do this. You can find it here: *http://www.darwinwars.com/lunatic/bugs/oo_macros.html.*

This book does not cover the use of macros.

Number the First Page of a Document Something Other Than 1

Follow these instructions to start the page numbering in a document at a number greater than 1. (These instructions are for a page number in a footer, but you could use a header instead.)

| Tips | Do not set a starting page number that is an even number or you will end up with a blank page before the first page when you print the file or save it as a PDF. |
| | Do not use the offset value provided for the page field, as it does not work the way it should. The method described here, although a bit cumbersome, does work. |

1. Set the page style for the first page of your document. (See "Setting Up Page Styles for a Typical Document" on page 46 for more information.)

2. Click Insert > Footer > [page style] to activate the footer.

3. The cursor is now in the footer. To insert the page number, click Insert > Fields > Page Number. The page number will be 1.

4. Click in the first paragraph in the text area, or type a paragraph of text.

5. Click Format > Paragraph (or right-click and choose Paragraph from the pop-up menu) to display the Paragraph dialog (Figure 2-15).

6. Click the Text Flow tab. In the Breaks section, select Enable, With Page Style, and the page style you're using for the first page of the document.

7. The Page number field is now active. Type the page number you want to start with. Click OK to close the Paragraph dialog.

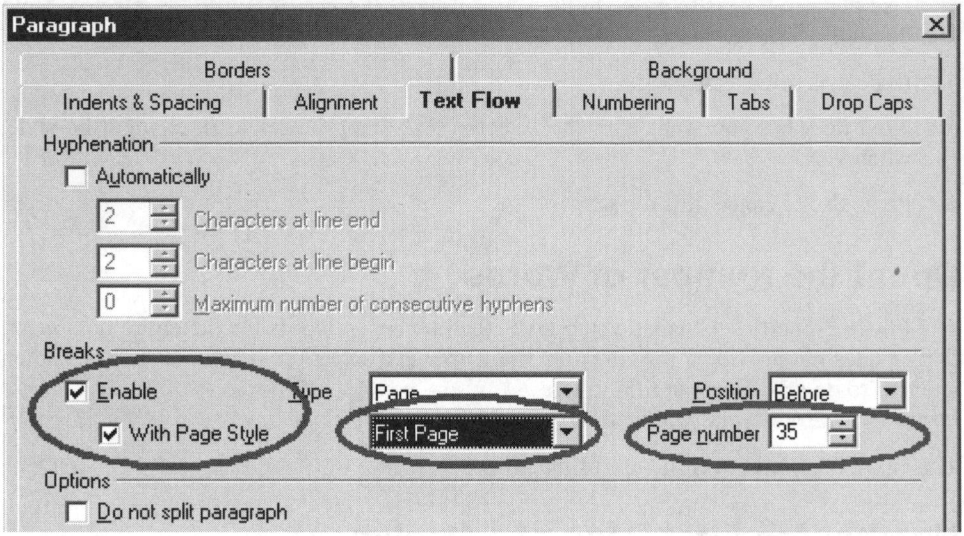

Figure 2-15. Changing the starting page number

3

Controlling Page Layout

Writer provides several ways for you to control page layouts by using:

- Page styles
- Tables
- Columns
- Frames

This chapter describes these methods and some associated techniques:

- Headers and footers
- Portrait headers on landscape pages
- Tabs
- Table control

Tip   When doing page layout, show text limits, table limits, and section limits
(in the Guides section of the Options – Text Document – View dialog) in
addition to the paragraph ends, tabs, breaks, and other items in the Display
section of the Options – Text Document – Formatting Aids dialog.

Setting Up Page Styles for a Typical Document

In Writer, *page styles* define the basic layout of all pages. Writer comes with several page styles, which you can use or modify, and you can define custom page styles. You can have one or many page styles in a single document.

Let's assume you want the first page of your document to always start on a right-hand page, and that the layout of the first page is different from the layout of the other pages in the chapter. The first page is followed by a left page, which is followed by a right page, and the pages continue to alternate left and right throughout the chapter. The left and right pages are mirror images of each other. (This book is designed that way.)

Define a First Page Style

For the first page, let's assume you want a large top margin (so the document title starts part way down the page), a wider binding margin on the left-hand side, and a footer (with a line above it to separate it visually from the main body of the page), but no header. Here's how to set up the First Page style:

1. Click Format > Styles > Catalog.

2. In the Style Catalog dialog (Figure 3-1), choose Page Styles and First Page, and then click Modify.

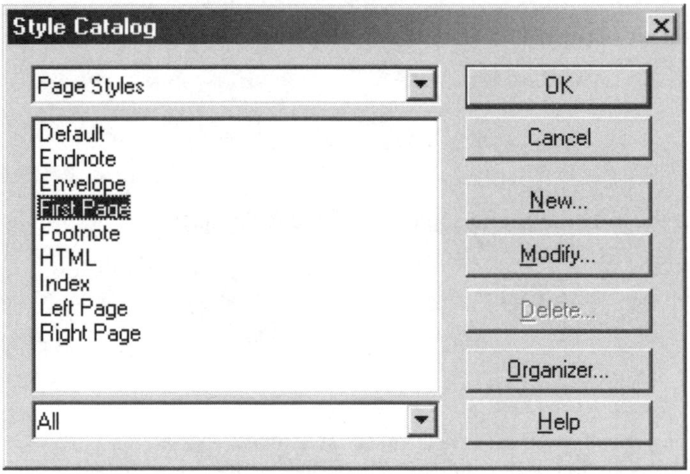

Figure 3-1. Choosing the First Page style from the Style Catalog

3. In the Page Style: First Page dialog, choose the Organizer tab (Figure 3-2). The page style name is already set to First Page, but the Next Style could be anything (probably First Page). Set the Next Style to Left Page because you want the first page to always be followed by a left page.

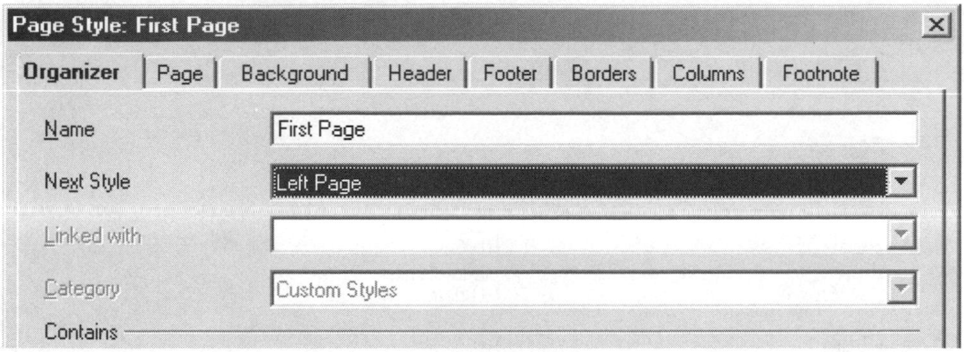

Figure 3-2. Setting the style for the next page on the Organizer tab

4. Choose the Page tab (Figure 3-3). Set your paper format (paper size) and margins, and choose Only right for Page Layout in the Layout Settings section because you want the first page to always be a right page. Some things to keep in mind:

    • Writer does not have a "gutter" setting, so you need to define the left margin to include the extra space.

    • Any headers and footers you define will go *inside* the page margins you set here.

    • On this tab you can also specify the format for any page numbers (1, 2, 3; i, ii, iii; or others). The page numbers won't appear until you insert a page number field; see "Editing Headers and Footers" on page 59.

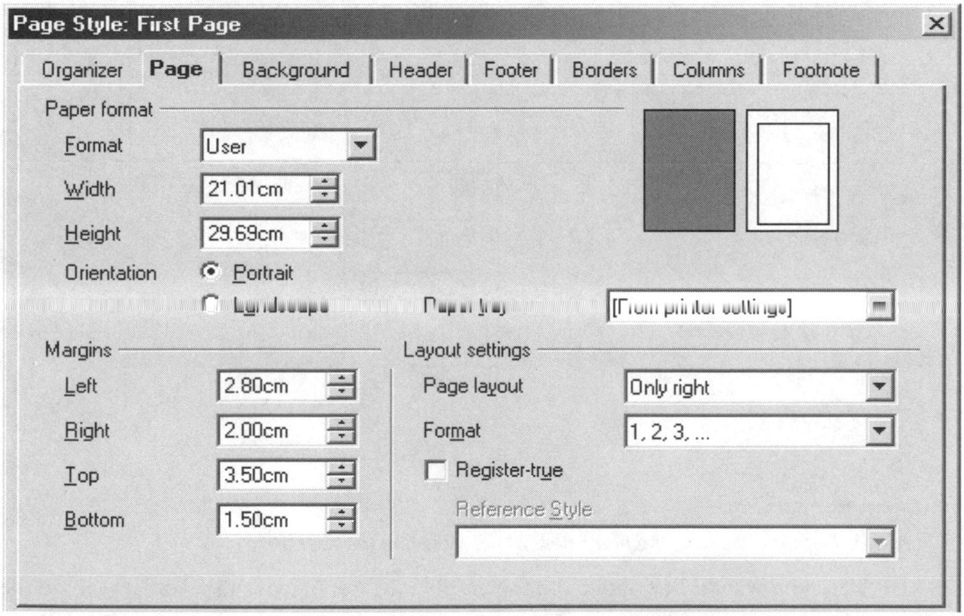

Figure 3-3. Defining the page format, margins, and page layout on the Page tab

5. Choose the Header tab (Figure 3-4). Deselect the Header on checkbox.

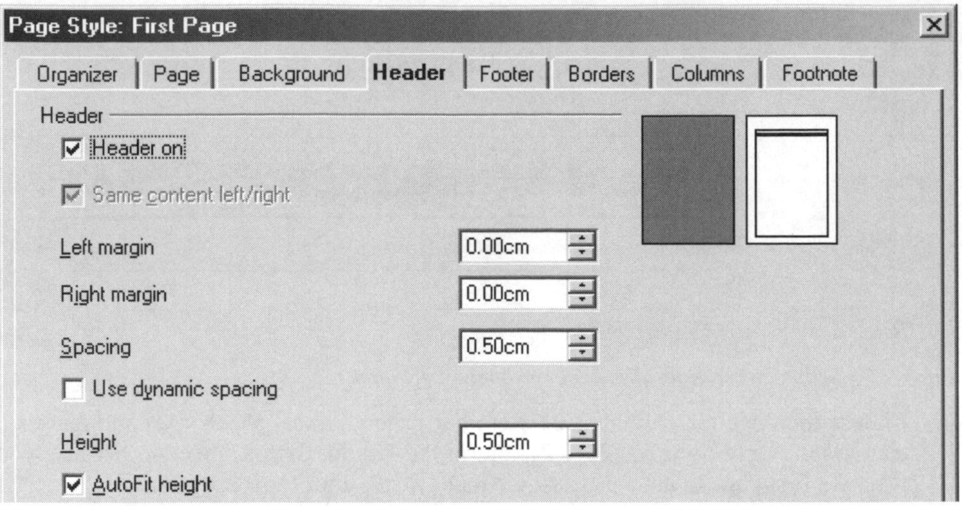

Figure 3-4. Turning off the header on the first page

6. Choose the Footer tab (Figure 3-5). Select the Footer on checkbox. You can use the Spacing field to change the space between the bottom of the footer to the top of the main body text on the page. You'll probably also want to select the AutoFit height checkbox, so the header adjusts to the size of the text and graphics in it.

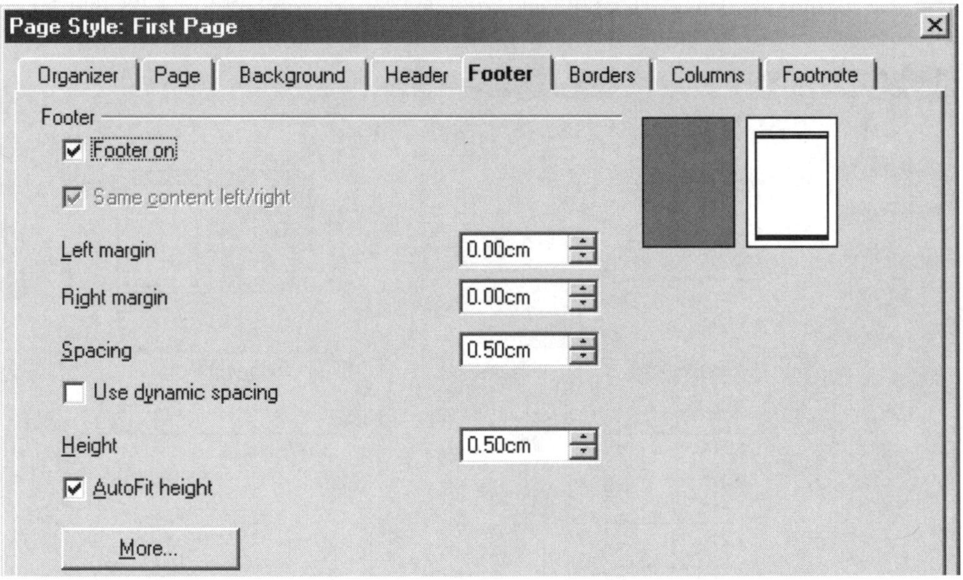

Figure 3-5. Defining the size and placement of the footer on the first page

7. Because you want a line above the footer, click More. Choose the Borders tab on the Border/Background dialog (Figure 3-6). Click in the Line arrangement box to activate only the line above, then choose the line weight and spacing from the footer text. Click OK to return to the Footer tab.

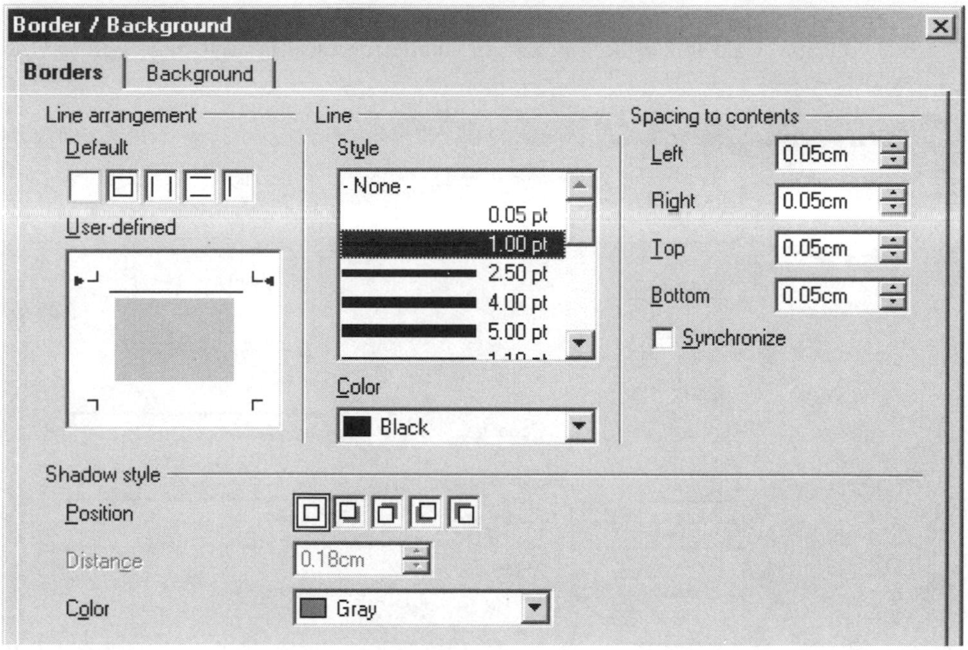

Figure 3-6. Defining the border above the first page footer

8. Click OK to finish defining the First Page style.

Define a Left Page Style

The steps in defining a Left Page style are similar to those for a First Page style, but the settings will be different.

Let's assume you want the left-hand pages of your document to have a wider binding margin on the right-hand side, a header (with a line below it to separate it visually from the main body of the page), and a footer (with a line above it). Here's how to set up the Left Page style:

1. If the Style Catalog is not open, click Format > Styles > Catalog to open it.

2. In the Style Catalog dialog (Figure 3-1), choose Page Styles and Left Page, and then click Modify.

3. In the Page Style: Left Page dialog, choose the Organizer tab. It will look similar to Figure 3-2, but the page style name is already set to Left Page and the Next Style could be anything (probably Left Page). Set the Next Style to Right Page because you want to alternate left and right page styles in this document.

4. Choose the Page tab (Figure 3-7). Set the paper format (paper size) and margins, and choose Mirrored in the Page Layout section. You'll probably want the Inner margin to match the Left margin on the first page, the Outer margin to match the Right

margin on the first page, and the Bottom margin to match the one on the first page, but you may want to set the top margin smaller because the left page will have a header.

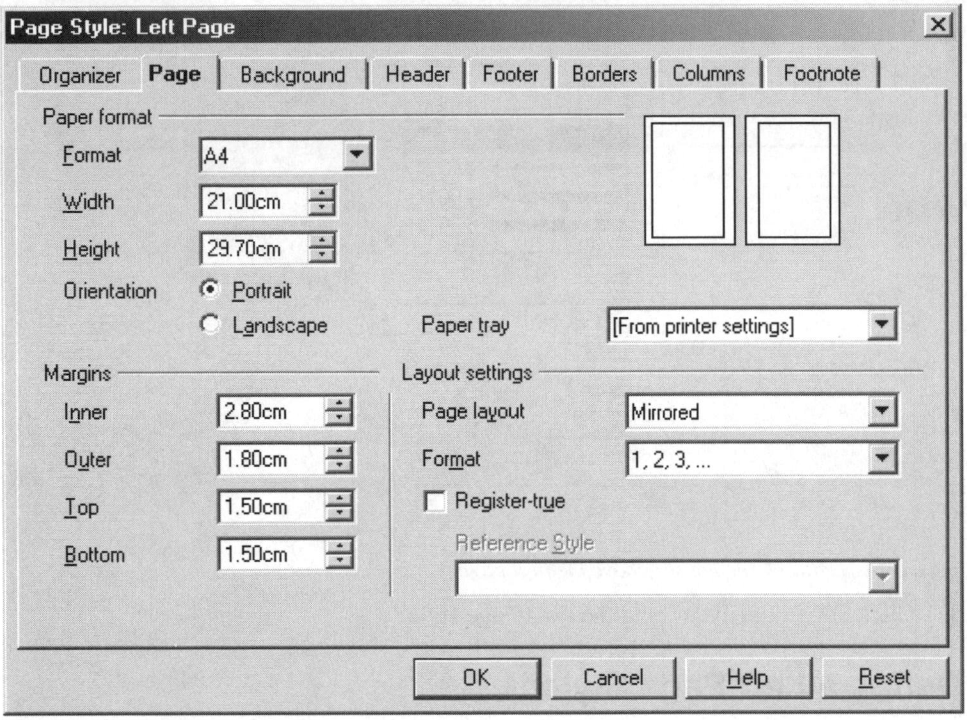

Figure 3-7. Defining the page format, margins, and page layout for the Left Page style

5. Choose the Header tab. Select the Header on checkbox, and make any other changes you wish. Click More. On the Border/Background dialog, choose the Borders tab and specify the details of the line under your header. Click OK.

6. Choose the Footer tab. Select the Footer on checkbox, and make any other changes you wish. Click More. On the Border/Background dialog, choose the Borders tab and specify the details of the line under your footer. Click OK.

7. Click OK on the Page Style dialog to finish defining the Left Page style.

Define a Right Page Style

The steps in defining a Right Page style are similar to those for a Left Page style, with only a few different settings.

Let's assume you want the right-hand pages of your document to "mirror" the left-hand pages; that is, right-hand pages will have a wider binding margin on the left-hand side, a header (with a line below it), and a footer (with a line above it). Here's how to set up the Right Page style:

1. If the Style Catalog is not open, click Format > Styles > Catalog to open it.

2. In the Style Catalog dialog, choose Page Styles and Right Page, and then click Modify.

3. In the Page Style: Right Page dialog, choose the Organizer tab. The page style name is already set to Right Page. Set the Next Style to Left Page because you want to alternate right and left page styles in this document.

4. Choose the Page tab. Set the paper format (paper size) and margins, and choose Mirrored in the Page Layout section, to automatically set the Inner margin to match the Outer margin on the left page, the Outer margin to match the Inner margin on the left page, and the Top and Bottom margins to match the ones on the left page.

5. Set up the headers and footers as you did for the left page.

6. Click OK on the Page Style dialog to finish defining the Right Page style.

Define Other Page Styles

For a book or other large document, you may need to define other page styles. You can add new page styles when you need them; you don't have to define them all at once. For example, you may need:

Title page
Different layout, no header or footer, no page numbers; next style Copyright page.

Copyright page
Different layout, no header or footer, no page numbers; next style Front matter first page.

Front matter (Preface and Table of Contents) first page
Similar to first page of main text, but with Roman page numbers (i, ii, iii); next style Front matter left page.

Front matter left and right pages
Similar to right and left pages of main text, but with Roman page numbers (i, ii, iii); next style Front matter right or left page.

Landscape page, or possibly Left Landscape and Right Landscape
Margins adjusted to match appearance of portrait pages, no specific next page style.

Tip   If you define a header or footer on a landscape page, they will be aligned with the long side of the page (the top and bottom), as you would expect. However, if your landscape pages are going to be inserted between portrait pages, you might want the headers and footers to be on the short sides of the landscape pages, so the final printed product has its headers and footers in the same orientation on all pages. See page 59 for instructions on how to put portrait header and footers on landscape pages.

Using Tables for Page Layout

Now that you have set up your basic page styles, you can look at the finer details of page layout. In many cases, you can control page layout by using paragraph styles alone. Most of this book is done that way. The main advantage to using paragraph styles alone is that you can add or delete text and graphics, and everything flows from one page to the next automatically—you don't need to control each page individually. (See "Working with Styles" on page 79 for more about paragraph styles.)

In some cases, however, you might need to use other methods to place text or graphics where you want them. One of those methods is to use tables.

Writer's tables can serve several purposes:

* To present tables of data, similar to those you might see in a spreadsheet (sometimes these tables are imported from Microsoft Excel or another program), and to perform some calculations

* To line up material that might otherwise be lined up using tabs and hanging indents

* To create page layouts by positioning various page elements in columns, or to line up graphics or sideheads in the margin with specific paragraphs

A full discussion of tables, their use, and how to control them is beyond the scope of this book. This section describes how to achieve some common layouts by using tables.

Create Sideheads Using Tables

Sideheads and marginal notes are commonly used in documents from resumes to computer user guides. The main body of the text is offset to leave white space (usually on the left-hand side) in which the sideheads or notes are placed. The first paragraph is aligned beside the sidehead, as in Figure 3-8.

Example of a sidehead	In some cases you may want to put only one or two paragraphs in the table itself and the rest of the text and graphics in ordinary paragraphs (formatted to line up with the paragraphs in the table), so that text and graphics will flow more easily from one page to another when you add or delete material.
	In other cases you might put each paragraph in a separate row of the table, and allow the table to break between pages.

Figure 3-8. Example of a sidehead

To create a table for use with a sidehead:

1. Place the cursor where you want the table to appear and click Insert > Table.

2. In the Insert Table dialog (Figure 3-9), define a two-column table with no border and no header. Click OK to create the table.

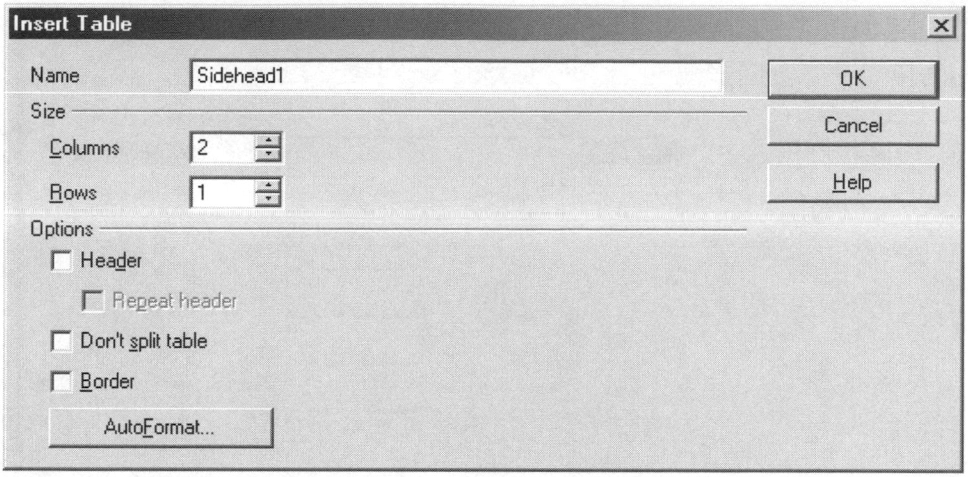

Figure 3-9. Defining a two-column borderless table with no header

3. With the cursor in the table, click Format > Table (or right-click and choose Table from the pop-up menu). On the Columns tab (Figure 3-10), make the columns the required width.

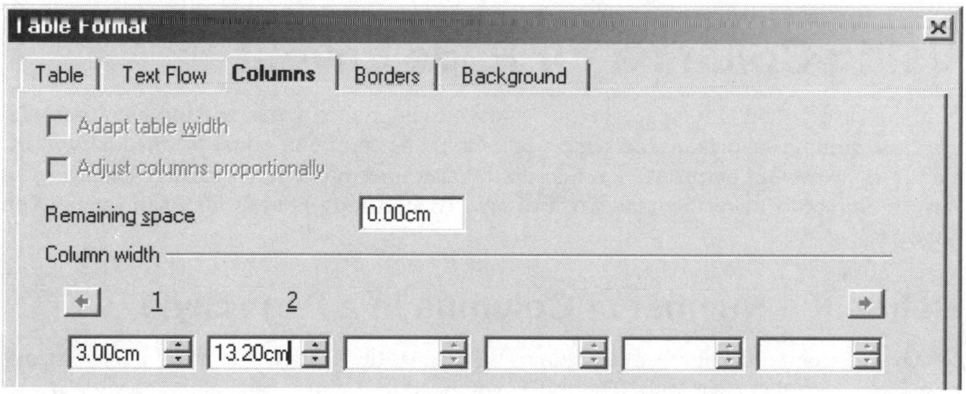

Figure 3-10. Defining a two-column table to line up with text offset at 3 cm

4. On the Table tab (Figure 3-11), in the Spacing section, make the Above and Below values the same as the Top and Bottom spacing you have defined for ordinary paragraphs of text. Click OK to save your settings.

You may also want to turn off number recognition, so that Writer won't try to format numbers if you want them to be plain text. To do this:

1. Position the cursor in the table and click Format > Number Format (or right-click and then click Number Format on the pop-up menu).

2. On the Number Format dialog, make sure the Category is set to Text. Click OK.

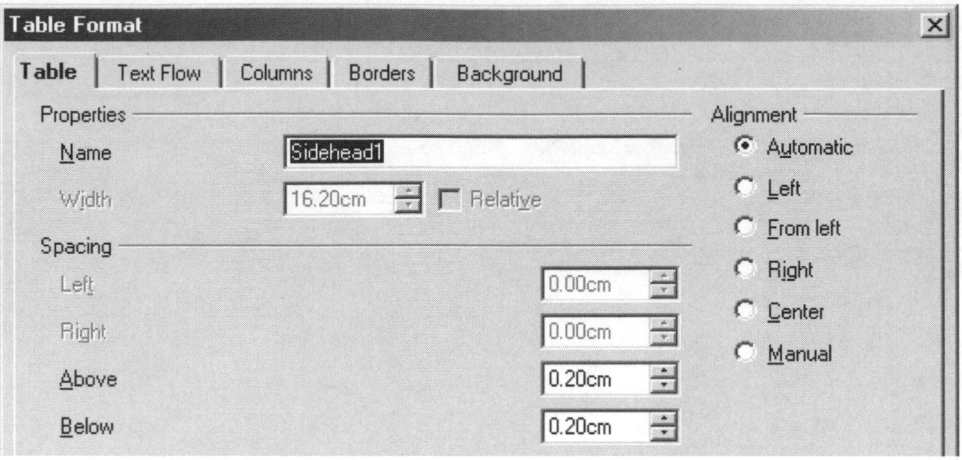

Figure 3-11. Defining the space above and below a table

Tip   If you use this table format often, you may want to save it as AutoText, as
described on page 64.

Using Columns for Page Layout

You can use columns for page layout, and you can switch between single-column and
multiple-column layouts on the same page. Columns can be of equal or unequal widths.
For complex layout purposes, you may find that frames are a better choice, because you
have more control over the placement of text. (See "Using Frames for Page Layout" on
page 56.)

Define the Number of Columns in a Page Style

When you change the number of columns on a page, the change affects all pages in your
document with that page style. Therefore, you need to define a separate page style if you
want some pages to have a different number of columns than the other pages. To define
the number of columns:

1. In the Page Style dialog, go to the Columns tab (Figure 3-12).

    You can also click Format > Columns to reach a different version of this dialog
    (Figure 3-13).

2. Choose the number of columns, and specify any spacing between the columns and
    whether you want a vertical separator line to appear between the columns. Click OK
    to save the changes.

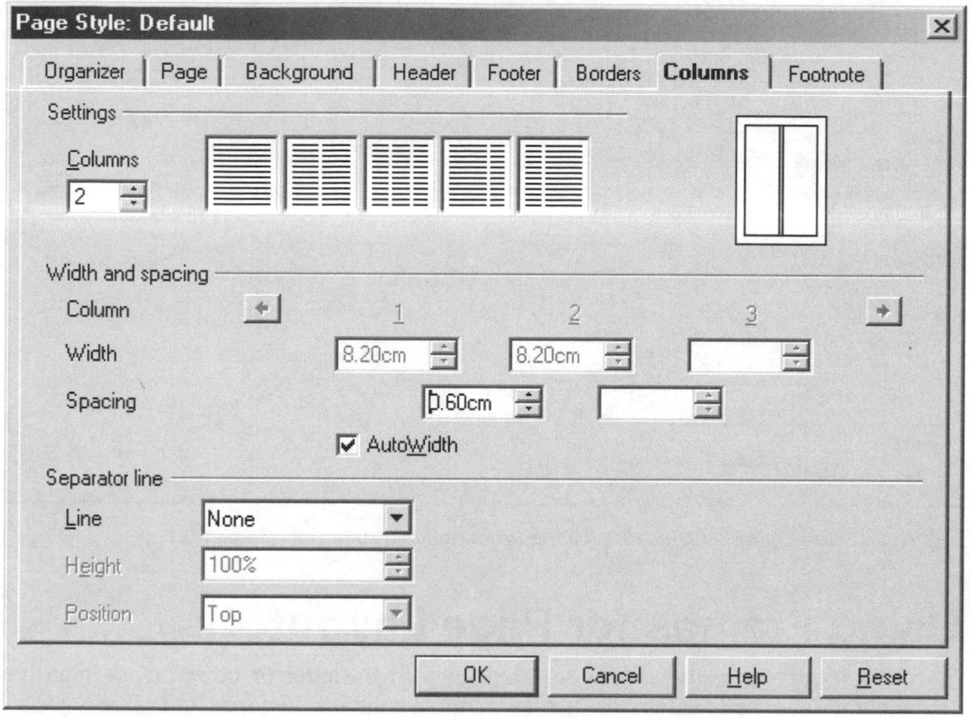

Figure 3-12. Defining the number of columns on a page

Change from One- to Two- Column Layout on a Page

You might want some parts of a page to have one column and other parts of the page to have two or three columns. For example, you might have a page-width headline over a three-column news story. To create this layout, use sections.

1. Position the cursor where you want the three-column section to begin. Click Insert > Section.

2. On the Insert Section dialog, go to the Columns tab, which looks much like Figure 3-12. Make your selections and click OK.

3. As you add text to the section, you'll see that the text flows from one column to the next so that all the columns adjust to the same length. If this is not what you want, click anywhere in the section, then click Format > Columns.

    On the Columns dialog (Figure 3-13), deselect Evenly distribute contents to all columns. Notice that the Apply to box shows Current section; if you change this to Page Style, the Evenly distribute checkbox disappears.

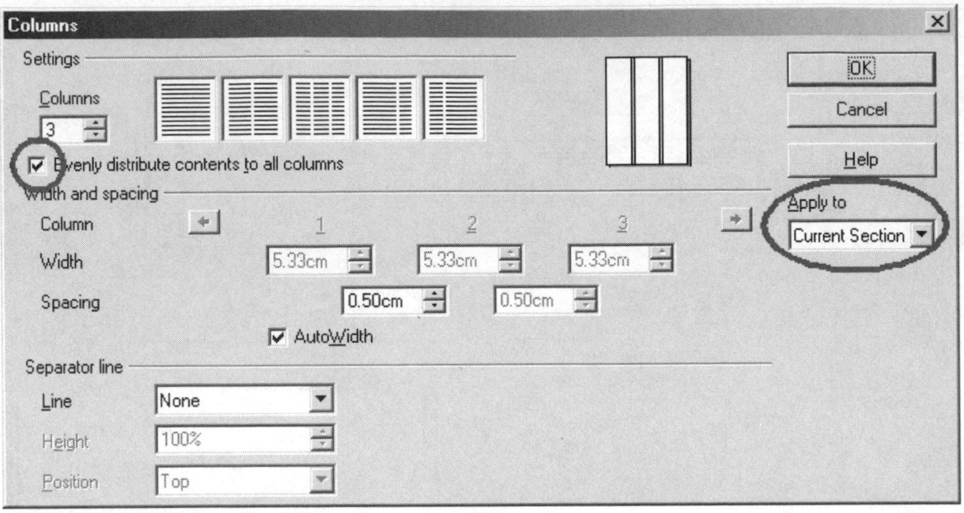

Figure 3-13. Specifying contents distribution among columns in a selected section

Using Frames for Page Layout

Frames can be very useful if you are producing a newsletter or other layout-intensive document. Frames can contain text, tables, multiple columns, pictures, and other objects.

You can link the content of one frame to another, so the contents flow back and forth between them as you edit the text.

You can define and apply frame styles using the Style Catalog and the Stylist. For more information, see "Working with Styles"on page 79.

Tip   The online help for Writer uses the phrase "text frame" for two quite different things with very different characteristics: frames (as discussed here) and text objects, which are drawing objects similar to lines and boxes. Drawing objects are discussed in "Using Writer's Drawing Tools to Create Graphics" on page 164.

Create a Frame Containing Text

You can either insert a blank frame and type the text into it afterward, or you can select existing text and place it into a frame.

Inserting a blank frame

To insert a blank frame, you have two choices. Which one you choose depends on the complexity of your page design and your preferred way of working.

- You can click Insert > Frame and set numerous parameters on the various tabs of the Frame dialog (Figure 3-14).

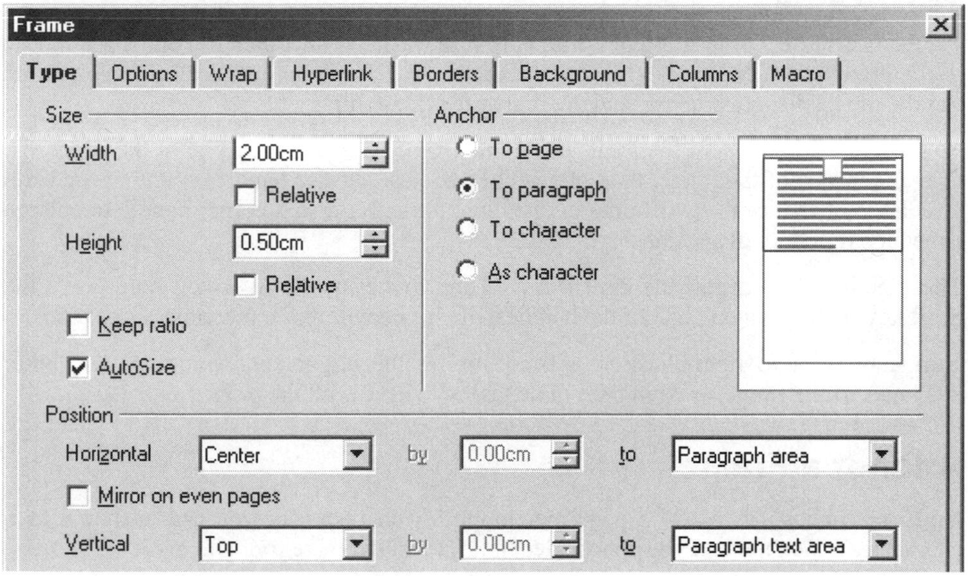

Figure 3-14. Inserting a frame using Insert > Frame

- You can long-click the Insert icon at the top of the main toolbar, move the mouse pointer over the Insert Frame Manually icon, then move the cursor down to select the number of columns you require in the frame, as shown in Figure 3-15.

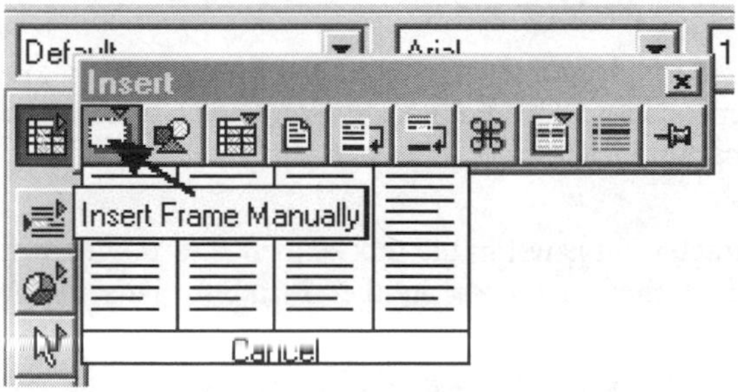

Figure 3-15. Inserting a frame using the Insert icon on the main toolbar

The cursor changes to a cross-hair symbol. Click and drag where you want the frame to appear on the page. Then you need to click Format > Frame (or right-click, and then click Frame on the pop-up menu) to adjust the settings for the frame.

Placing existing text in a frame

To place existing text in a frame, select the text, then use either method described above to create the frame. The selected text is automatically deleted from the normal text flow and inserted into the frame.

Move, Resize, or Change Other Attributes of a Frame

To change the size or location of a frame, first select the frame, then use either the mouse or the Frame dialog (Figure 3-14). Using the mouse is faster but less accurate. You might use the mouse for gross layout and the dialog for fine-tuning.

To change the location of the frame using the mouse, drag and drop one of the edges. To change the size of the frame, drag one of the handles. Drag a handle on one of the sides to enlarge or reduce the text frame in one direction only; drag a corner handle to enlarge or reduce it in both dimensions.

These actions will distort the dimensions of the frame; however, if you hold down the Shift key while dragging one of the handles, the frame will retain the same proportions.

You may want to right-click on a frame to set the alignment, wrapping, and other attributes of the frame, or open the Frame dialog to access all the properties.

Anchor a Frame

You can anchor a frame to a page, paragraph, or character, or you can anchor it as a character. Which method you choose depends on what you are trying to achieve.

To Page
Frame keeps the same position in relation to the page margins. It does not move as you add or delete text. This method is useful when the frame does not need to be visually associated with a particular piece of text. It is often used when producing newsletters or other documents that are very layout-intensive.

To Paragraph
Frame is associated with a paragraph and moves with the paragraph. It may be placed in the margin or another location. This method is useful as an alternative to a table for placing icons beside paragraphs.

To Character
Frame is associated with a character but is not in the text sequence. It moves with the paragraph but may be placed in the margin or another location. This method is similar to anchoring to a paragraph.

As Character
Frame is placed in the document like any other character and therefore affects the height of the text line and the line break. The frame moves with the paragraph as you add or delete text before the paragraph. This method is useful for adding a small icon in sequence in a sentence (but you can insert a graphic this way without using a frame; see page 175).

Link Frames

You can link several frames to each other even when they are on different pages of a document. The contents will automatically flow from one to the next.

1. Select the frame to be linked from.

2. Click the Link icon on the object bar. [icon]

3. Click the next frame in the series.

When a linked frame is selected, any existing links are indicated by a connecting line. You cannot link from a frame to more than one other frame.

The height of a frame that is linked from is fixed; you can change this height using the Frame dialog, but it does not automatically adjust to the contents of the frame (that is, the AutoHeight attribute is disabled). Only the last frame of a chain can adapt its height to the content.

Editing Headers and Footers

You can type in the header or footer areas, or insert cross-references or other fields to include information such as the chapter title, the date, the author, and so on. For more about the use of fields, see Chapter 5.

To insert a page number, click Insert > Fields > Page Numbers (or long-click the Insert Fields icon on the main toolbar and click Page Numbers).

Define the Header and Footer styles to suit the needs of your document. You can also define character styles for individual elements in the header or footer; for example, you could make the font for the page number large and bold, as I've done in this book. For more information on styles, see "Working with Styles" on page 79.

Tips	Avoid using floating pictures in a table in a header or footer—you won't be able to cross-reference to the text in the same header or footer. Put the picture in a frame, anchored to a paragraph in the header or footer.

Putting Portrait Headers and Footers on Landscape Pages

When you define a header and footer on a landscape page, they will be aligned with the long side of the page. If your landscape pages are going to be inserted between portrait pages, you might want the headers and footers to be on the short sides of the landscape pages, so the final printed product looks like the contents of the landscape pages have been rotated 90 degrees on portrait pages.

You can set up portrait headers and footers on landscape pages by using a trick involving frames. These are a bit tedious to set up, but once you have done so, you can copy and paste them to other landscape pages. I have not found a way to make these part of the landscape page style.

1. Calculate the required margins so the text area of the landscape page is the same size as the text area on the portrait pages, taking into account the space for headers and footers on the portrait pages. For example, this book uses the margins shown in the

following table. The extra space used by the header is 1 cm (0.5 cm for the height of the header and a 0.5 cm gap between the header and the main text). The footer takes the same amount of space.

Portrait page (right page)		Landscape page (right page)	
Top margin	1.5 cm	Right margin	2.5 cm
Bottom margin	1.5 cm	Left margin	2.5 cm
Left (inner) margin	2.8 cm	Top margin	2.8 cm
Right (outer) margin	1.8 cm	Bottom margin	1.8 cm

2.   Create the landscape page style as described in "Define Other Page Styles" on page 51.

3.   Measure the distance from the upper and left edges of the page to the upper left-hand corner of the space where you want the footer to appear. Measure the width and length of the space the footer will occupy (to match footers on portrait pages). See Figure 3-16.

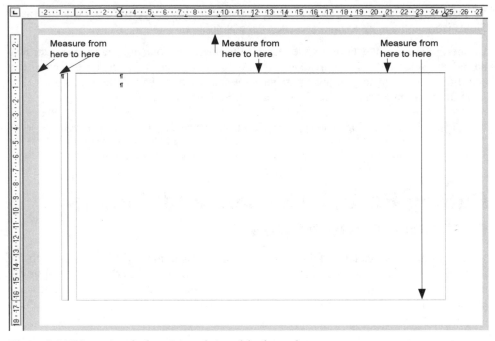

Figure 3-16. Measuring the location and size of the footer frame

4.   In a blank paragraph in the text, type the footer text or insert fields such as the page number or the chapter number and name—to match the footer text and fields on the portrait pages. Assign the Footer style to this paragraph, so the typeface, font size, and tab settings match those of the footers on the portrait pages.

5. Select the text (including the fields) you just entered. Click Format > Character. On the Character dialog, choose the Position tab (Figure 3-17) and set Rotation/ Scaling to 270 degrees. Click OK.

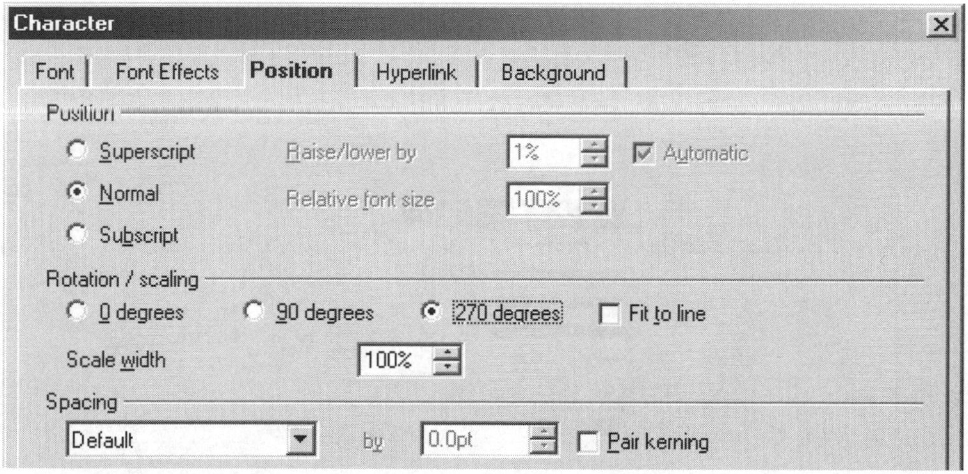

Figure 3-17. Rotating the footer text 270 degrees

6. With the text still selected, click Insert > Frame. In the Frame dialog, choose the Type tab (Figure 3-18) and enter the width, height, and horizontal and vertical position for the footer.

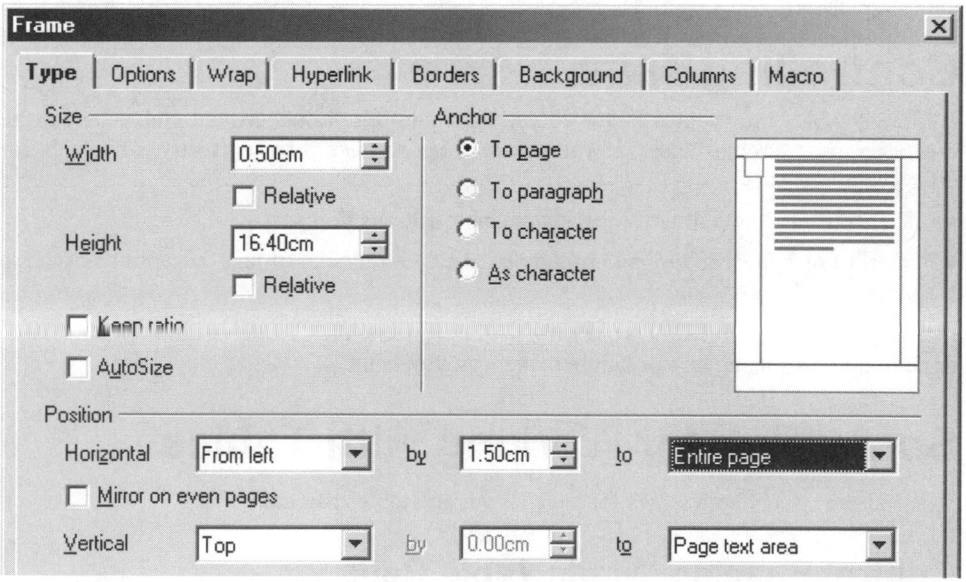

Figure 3-18. Defining the size and position of the footer frame

7. If your footer has a line above the text, as I've done in this book, choose the Borders tab (Figure 3-19), select a right border and specify the line width and spacing to the contents of the frame.

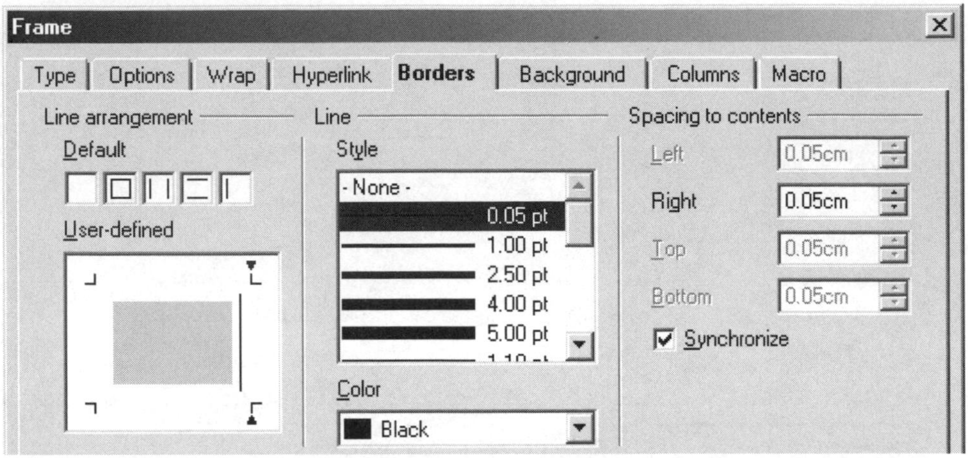

Figure 3-19. Specifying the border position, line width, and spacing to contents for the footer

8. Click OK to save these settings. The footer should now appear in the required position and orientation.

Repeat these steps (using appropriate measurements) to set up a portrait header on the landscape page.

Controlling Tabs

Although tables are often a better choice than tabs for lining up material, tabs can be useful in some circumstances, if you set them up and use them correctly. The rules for effective tab use are:

*   Don't use the default tab stops; set the tab positions yourself.
*   Don't press the Tab key more than once between blocks of text, except to skip a tab setting.

Don't use spaces to line up text; choose the appropriate tab setting—right, left, centered, or decimal—to line up text or numbers the way you want.

Some Tips for Working with Tables

This section covers both tables for page layout and tables of data.

Control Spacing Within Table Cells

Any top or bottom space defined for a paragraph works between paragraphs in the same table cell, but is ignored at the top and bottom of the cell.

To create space between the cell border (whether visible or not) and the text, use the Spacing to Contents section on the Borders tab of the Table Format dialog (similar to Figure 3-6). You may prefer to deselect the Synchronize checkbox, so you can define different distances from different borders.

The Spacing to Contents settings affect every cell in the table. To change the spacing of a single row, column, or cell, you can use the following keyboard combinations.

Alt+Arrow keys	Changes the size of the column or row on the right or bottom cell edge
Alt+Shift+Arrow keys	Changes the size of the column or row on the left or top cell edge
Alt+Ctrl+Arrow keys	Like Alt, but only the active cell is modified
Alt+Ctrl+Shift+ Arrow keys	Like Alt+Shift, but only the active cell is modified

Create a Heading Row in an Existing Table

To create a heading row in an existing table that doesn't have one, you need to apply an autoformat that does have a heading defined. (Here's where having some personalized table formats could come in very handy.) Place the cursor anywhere in the table, and then click Format > AutoFormat. Choose a format. Click OK.

Define a Default Table Style

If you often use one combination of table characteristics, you can specify that combination as the default table style. For example, if you use tables a lot for page layout purposes, you might choose the combination of no borders, no table header, and no number recognition as your default.

1. Click Tools > Options > Text Document > Table.

2. On the Options – Text Document – Table dialog (Figure 3-20), deselect all the checkboxes (Heading, Do not split, and Border) in the Default section, and deselect Number recognition in the Input in tables section. Click OK.

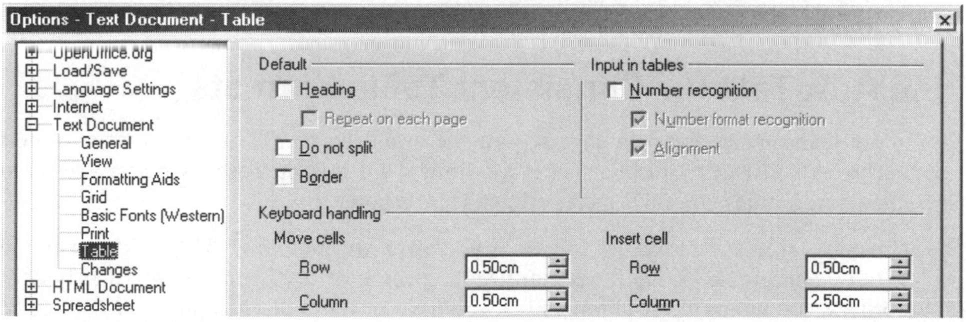

Figure 3-20. Setting a borderless table as the default

Use AutoFormat for Consistent Table Formats

As in Microsoft Word, you can use AutoFormat and AutoText to make your table formats consistent. Additionally, in Writer you are not restricted to the autoformat choices supplied with the program; you can define your own. Here's how:

1. Create a table and manually format it as you wish, including borders, spacing of text from the top and bottom borders, fonts to be used in the table heading and data cells, and background colors.

2. Position the cursor anywhere in the table, and then click Format > AutoFormat.

3. On the AutoFormat dialog (Figure 3-21), click Add.

4. On the Add AutoFormat dialog (not shown), type a name for the new table format. Click OK. The name is added to the list in the AutoFormat dialog.

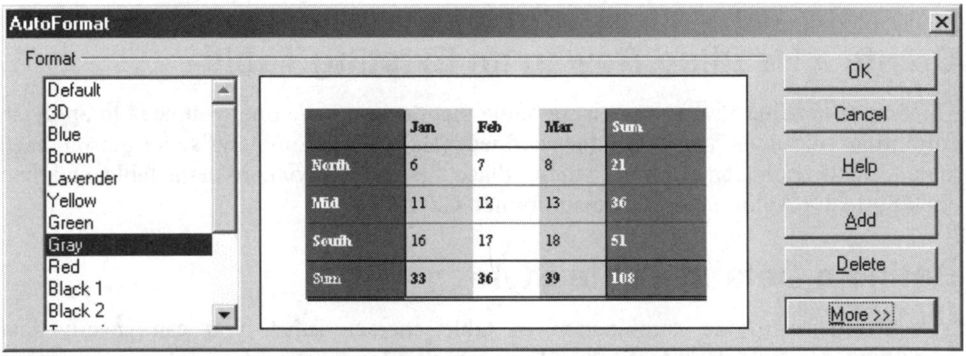

Figure 3-21. Preparing to add a table format to the AutoFormat list

When you insert a table, you can click the AutoFormat button on the Insert Table dialog (Figure 3-9) and choose from the list of predefined table formats.

Tip This technique does *not* include table and column widths in the table format. To insert a table with predefined full formatting, use AutoText, which is described in the next section.

Use AutoText for Consistent Table Formats

If you are using tables for page layout, you will want the number of columns and their spacing to be consistent. AutoFormat is too limited for this purpose. A better way is to save the table formats you need as AutoText. Here's how:

1. Create a table and manually format it as you wish, including table width, column widths, borders (as complex as you need), spacing of text from the top and bottom borders, fonts (and their alignment) to be used in the table heading and data cells, and background colors. Include any text that you want to appear in every table based on this format (you can delete the text after the table is inserted). In this example, I've designed a table that includes the word "Tip."

2. Select the table, and then click Edit > AutoText (or click the Edit AutoText
    icon on the main toolbar).

3. On the AutoText dialog (Figure 3-22), select the category for the entry ("My
    AutoText" in this example), type a name for the new entry ("Tip" in this example),
    and change the suggested shortcut ("T") if you wish.

4. Click the AutoText button and click New. The new AutoText entry is created. Click
    Close.

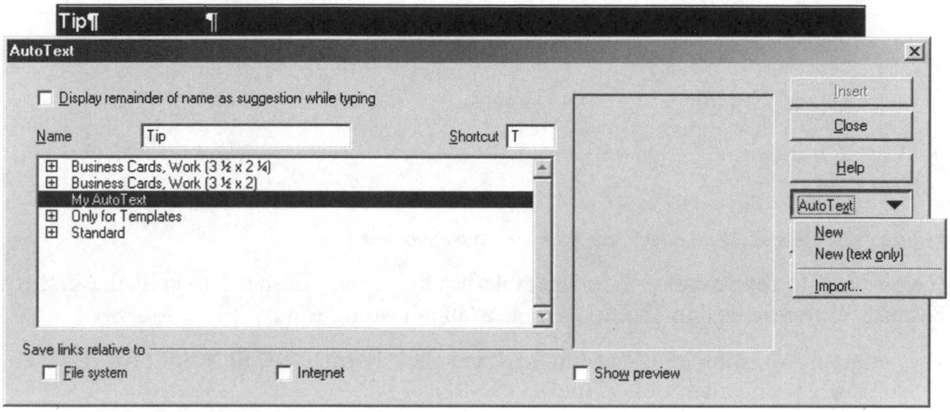

Figure 3-22. Defining a table as an AutoText entry

To insert a new table based on this AutoText entry:

1. Position the cursor where you want the table to appear.

2. Type the shortcut, and then press F3. Note: Shortcuts are *not* case-sensitive.

    If you can't remember the shortcut, you can click Edit > AutoText, select the
    required entry, and click Insert. Then click Close.

Repeat a Table Heading When the Table Continues on Another Page

When you work with a table that flows from one page to the next, you can make the table
heading (if there is one) repeat on the second page.

When inserting a new table, select the Header and Repeat header checkboxes on the
Insert Table dialog (Figure 3-9). (Writer is inconsistent in its terminology, using both
"Table header" and "Table heading" to refer to the same thing.)

For existing tables:

1. Position the cursor in the table and click Format > Table (or right-click on the table
    and click Table on the pop-up menu).

2. Choose the Text Flow tab of the Table Format dialog (Figure 3-23).

3. Select the Repeat heading checkbox. Click OK.

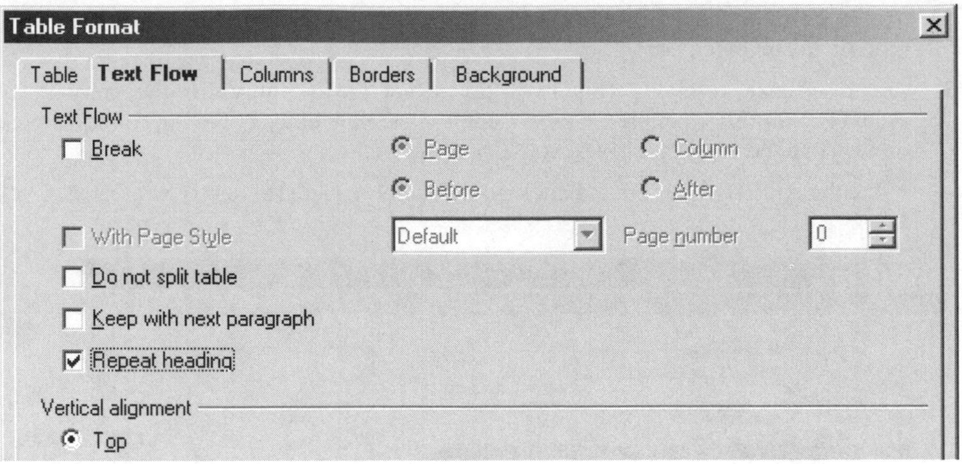

Figure 3-23. Repeating a header row following a page break

If you want to repeat more than one table-heading row, you need to split the first row because Writer treats only the first row as a table-heading row.

1.   Select the existing table-heading row and click Format > Cell > Split (or right-click on the row and click Cell > Split).

2.   In the Split Cells dialog (Figure 3-24), select the Horizontal direction. Enter the number of rows that are to be repeated and confirm your choice by clicking OK.

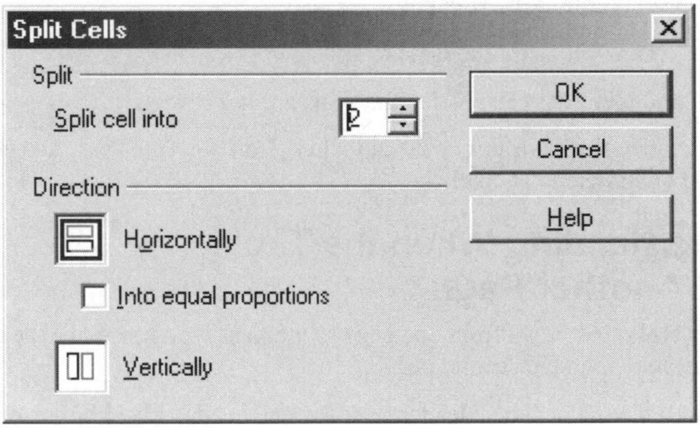

Figure 3-24. Splitting a table row into two rows

All rows at the beginning of the table created in this way will be repeated after a page break if you have Repeat heading selected.

Use the Table Object Bar

When the cursor is in a table, look at the right-hand end of the Formatting object bar. A left-facing arrow icon has appeared. Click on this icon to display the Table object bar (Figure 3-25). You can use the icons on this object bar to quickly access many table-formatting functions. Any formatting applied this way affects the selected table only.

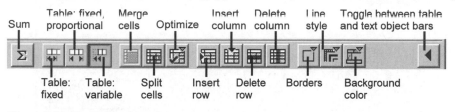

Figure 3-25. The Table object bar

Insert Tabs, Rows, and Columns

If you press the Tab key in a table cell, the insertion point jumps to the next cell. If the cursor is in the right-hand cell of the last row, a new row is inserted after the last row.

To insert a tab into a table cell, press Ctrl+Tab.

You can choose whether to insert new rows above or below the selected row or new columns to the left or right of the selected column. Right-click in the relevant row or column and click Row > Insert (or Column > Insert). You will be prompted to specify the number of rows (or columns) and where to insert them.

Change Tabbed Text into a Table

If you have used tabs to put text into columns, and particularly if some lines have more than one tab between columns (because you used default tab stops instead of defining them explicitly), the formatting can go seriously wrong if something else is changed—for example, the typeface, type size, or line length. To control the layout, you can change columns of text into tables. To do this:

1. Be sure tab marks are visible. (Select Tabs in Tools > Options > Text Documents > Formatting Aids.)

2. Remove any extra tabs; you want only one between each pair of columns. (This may temporarily make the columns not line up.)

3. Select all the tabbed text, including the paragraph markers.

4. Click Tools > Text <-> Table.

5. On the Convert Text to Table dialog (Figure 3-26), select Tabs in the Separate Text At group.

    *   If you want the first row to be a table heading, select the Header checkbox. For a long table, you might also select the Repeat header checkbox.

    *   If you want the table to have a border, select the Border checkbox.

- Note: The text in the resulting table will have the paragraph style of the original tabbed text. You can select an AutoFormat to apply direct formatting to the text, or manually format the text before or after creating the table.

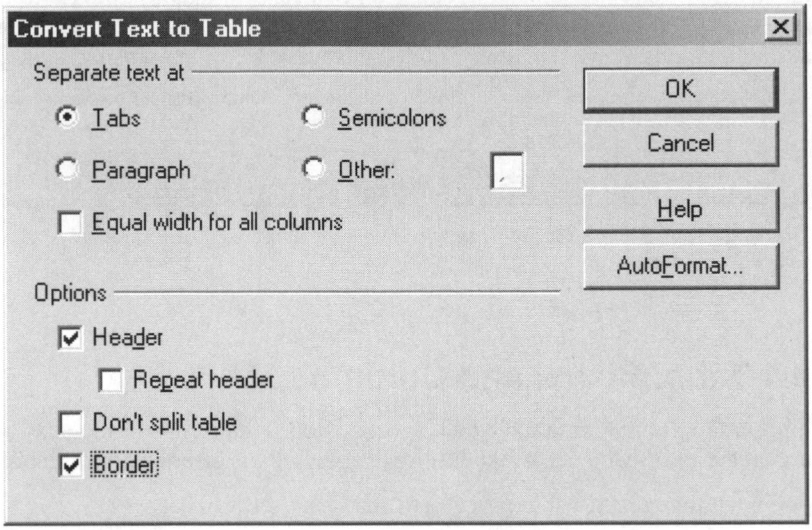

Figure 3-26. Converting text into a table

6. Click OK to finish.

Position Text in a Table Cell

To position text vertically in a table cell: Place the cursor in the text, right-click, and select Cell, then select Top, Center, or Bottom.

To position text horizontally in a table cell: Place the cursor in the text, right-click, and select Alignment, then select Left, Right, Center, or Justified.

Rotate Text in a Table Cell

You can rotate text in a table cell 90 or 270 degrees. Text rotation is useful when you have long headings for narrow columns. Select the text to be rotated, and then click Format > Character > Position tab.

Break Up Rows or Cells into Smaller Units

Don't put several paragraphs in a single cell, especially if you need to line them up with paragraphs in an adjacent cell. This defeats the purpose of using a table for alignment, can cause problems with page breaks, and makes maintenance difficult.

Merge Cells

If you can create the same effect by removing the border between cells, do that instead of merging the cells. Don't merge cells across columns until you are sure the column widths are final because selecting and sizing columns is complicated if any of the cells are merged.

4

Using Templates and Styles Effectively

Templates can store styles, text, graphics, and user-specific setup information such as measurement units, language, the default printer, and toolbar and menu customization.

A *style* is a collection of formatting specifications that is given a name. Writer supports:

- Character styles (typeface, font size, bold, italic, superscript, among others)
- Paragraph styles (line spacing, space before and after, first line indent, borders and shading, plus a character style for the paragraph)
- Frame styles, page styles, and numbering styles, described later in this chapter.

This chapter does not cover everything about templates and styles, but it should be enough to get you started.

Tip	You can get predefined templates from several sources. Check the OpenOffice.org website for links. Save these templates to your hard drive and then import them into the templates folder. See "Import a Template" on page 73.

Working with Templates

All Writer documents are based on templates. If you don't specify a template when you start a new document, the document is based on the default template for text documents. If you have not specified a default, Writer uses the blank template that is installed with the program.

Templates have a file extension of *.stw*. Documents have a file extension of *.sxw*.

Create a New Template

To create a new template:

1. Create a new document, open an existing document, or open an existing template. You can:

    - Set up your styles for pages, paragraphs, characters, frames, and numbering, as described in "Working with Styles" on page 79.

    - Specify a default printer for documents based on this template, as described in "Define a Default Printer for a Template" on page 74.

    - Set up user options such as the language and measurement units, as described in Chapter 1.

2. Click File > Templates > Save.

Tip   Do *not* use File > Save As > Template for the reasons discussed below in "Making your templates sticky."

---

3. In the Templates dialog (Figure 4-1), type a name for the new template, navigate to the required folder in the Categories list, then click OK.

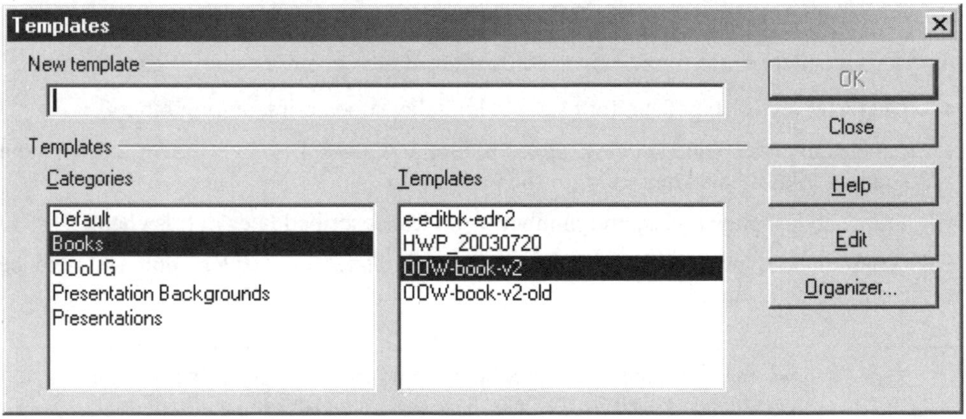

Figure 4-1. Saving a file as a new template

Making your templates sticky

File > Templates > Save creates a template with slightly different characteristics from templates created with File > Save As > Template.

Any document based on a template created using File > Templates > Save will retain an association with the template. I call these "sticky" templates. If you change a sticky template, then the next time you open any document based on that template, you will receive a message that your styles don't match the template, and you can choose to update the document's styles from the template.

If you want your documents to always reflect the latest changes to a template, be sure to save the template this way. Large projects, including master documents (described in "Creating and Using Master Documents" on page 149) and projects with more than one writer, typically make extensive use of templates in this way.

Any document based on a template created using File > Save As > Template will *not* retain any association with the template. Therefore, if you change the template, then the next time you open the document, you will *not* be asked if you want to update the document's styles. You might not want letters that are produced, sent, and then archived to retain an association with the template.

How to tell if a template is sticky

Both types of template have the same file extension, and both otherwise behave the same. The only way to tell if a template is sticky is to create a new document from the template and look in the document's properties to see if the template is listed there, as described in "Determine Which Template is Associated with a Document" on page 76.

Import a Template

You can change a non-sticky template into a sticky template by importing it. You might wish to do this if, for example, you saved the template incorrectly the first time, or you downloaded a template from someone else. To import a template:

1. Click File > Templates > Organize.

2. On the Template Management dialog (Figure 4-2), select a folder in the Templates list, and then click the Commands button and select Import Template.

3. The usual browse dialog opens. Find and select the template you want to import, and then click Open. The imported template is now listed in the selected folder in the Template Management dialog, and it has the "sticky" characteristics.

4. Click Close.

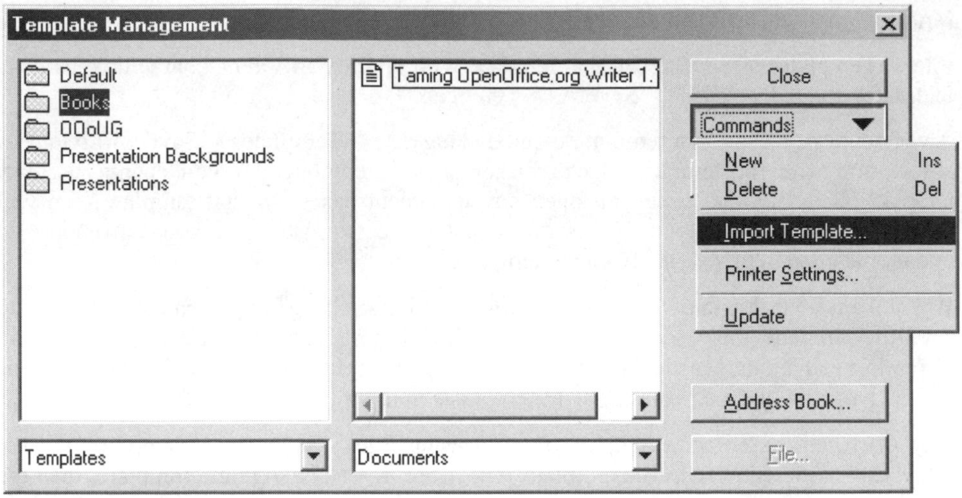

Figure 4-2. Importing a template

Define a Default Printer for a Template

1. Click File > Templates > Organize.

2. On the Template Management dialog, select a template, and then click the Commands button and click Printer Settings.

3. On the Printer Setup dialog (Figure 4-3), select the printer, and then click OK.

4. Click Close on the Template Management dialog.

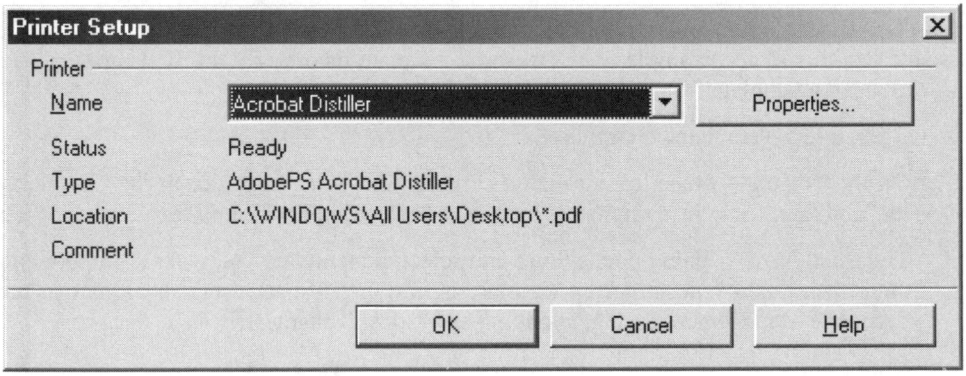

Figure 4-3. Choosing a default printer

Specify Which Template Is the Default for Text Documents

The default template is applied when you click File > New > Text Document or long-click the New icon on the function bar and click Text Document.

You can specify any template to be the default template, and you can change the default at any time. Any change will apply to documents created after the change; it has no effect on existing documents. To specify a default template:

1. If the Template Management dialog is not open, click File > Templates > Organize.

2. In the Template Management dialog, select a template, and then click the Commands button and select Set as default template. Click Close.

Change the Information in an Existing Template

You cannot save changes to a template from within a document. Instead, you need to edit the template directly, or use the Template Management dialog to copy styles from one template to another, as described in "Copy Information Between Templates" on page 75. To edit the template directly:

1. Click File > Templates > Edit. Navigate to the folder containing the required template and open the template from there.

2. Make your changes, then click File > Save (or click the Save icon, or press Ctrl+S). Do *not* use File > Templates > Save because this will create a new template based on the one you've just changed.

Copy Information Between Templates

If you have styles in one template that you want to use in another template, you can copy them from one to the other.

1. Click File > Templates > Organize.

2. In the Template Management dialog (Figure 4-4), set both lists to Templates. Open the folders and find the templates from and to which you want to copy.

3. Double-click on the template name and then the Styles icon to show the list of individual styles.

4. To copy a style from the template on the left to the template on the right, hold down the Ctrl key and drag the name of the style from the left template to the right template. (If you drag a style name without holding down the Ctrl key, the style will be moved, not copied; that is, it will be deleted from the template you are dragging it from.)

5. Repeat for each style you want to copy. When you are finished, click Close.

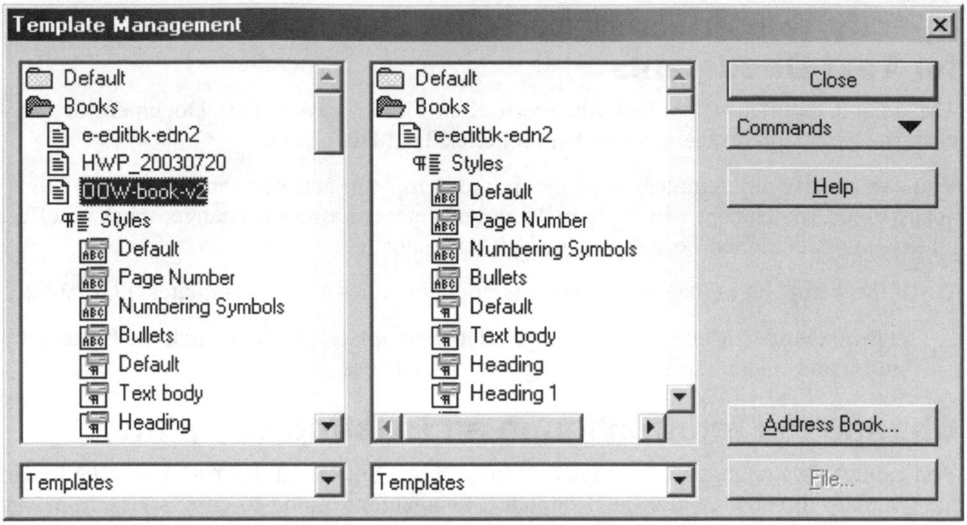

Figure 4-4. Copying styles from one template to another

Create a New Document from a Template

To start a new document from the default template, click File > New > Text Document. The new document opens in the Writer window.

To start a new document from any other template:

1. Click File > New > Templates and Documents.

2. On the Templates and Documents dialog (Figure 4-5), you can display either the document properties for the template or a preview of the first page of the template by selecting one of the icons at the top of the right-hand pane. Select the required template, and then click Open.

    If you cannot see the required template, you may need to use the navigation icons above the Title pane to locate it. It may be in a different folder.

Determine Which Template is Associated with a Document

To determine which template is associated with a document:

1. Open the document in Writer.

2. Click the Files > Properties > General tab. The associated template (if any) is shown near the bottom of the page.

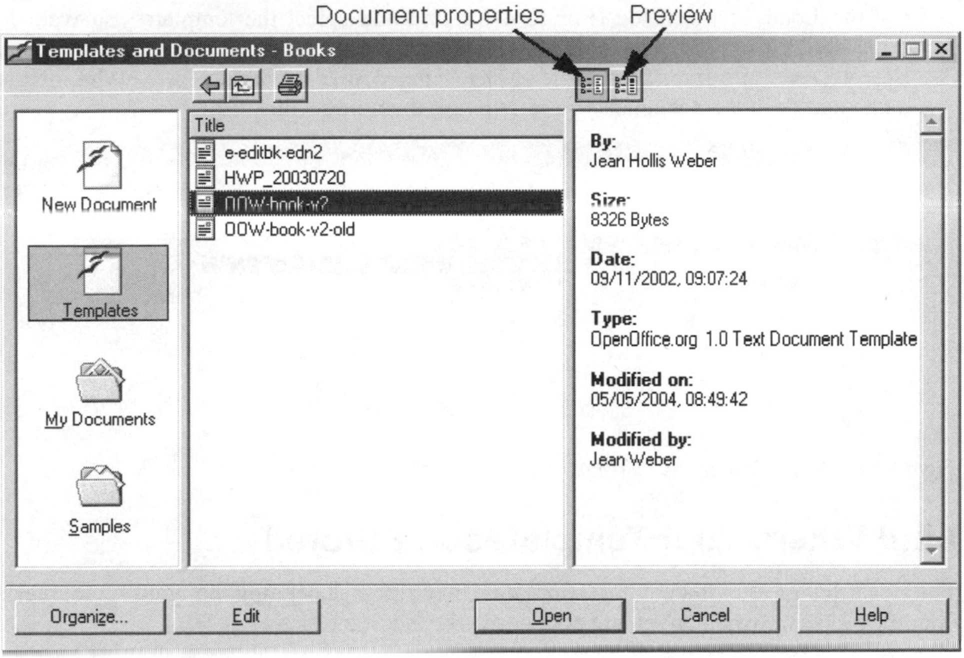

Document properties   Preview

Figure 4-5. Creating a new document from a template

Apply a Different Template to a Document

You cannot apply a different template to an existing document in Writer as you can in Microsoft Word. Here is how to do it in Writer:

1. Start a new document based on the new template, using File > New > Templates and Documents.

2. Delete any text that may be in this new document.

3. Copy the contents of the old document into the new blank document and save it under a new name.

4. Rename the old and new documents if necessary.

Copy Styles from a Template into a Document

You can use Format > Styles > Load to copy the styles from a template into a document. This does not associate the new template with the document, so any changes you make to the template will not be reflected in the document unless you go through the process again.

1. Open the document you want to copy styles into.

2. Click Format > Styles > Load.

3. On the Load Styles dialog (Figure 4-6), find and select the template you want to copy styles from. Select the checkboxes for the categories of styles to be copied. Select Overwrite if you want the styles being copied to replace any styles of the same names in the document you're copying them into. Click OK.

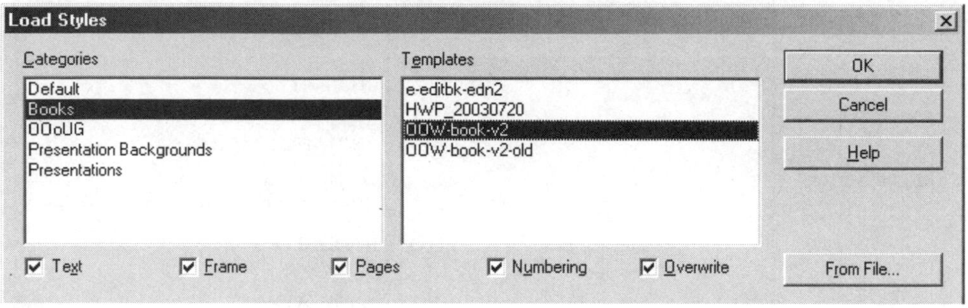

Figure 4-6. Copying styles from a template into the open document

Find Where Your Templates Are Stored

The location of the folders for templates may vary depending on your computer's operating system, whether you are on a network, and other factors.

The easiest way to find out where your templates are stored is to click Tools > Options > OpenOffice.org > Paths and look down the list for Templates. The entry will show the paths to both the shared templates and your personal set of templates. Typically, these paths will be *..\share\template* for the shared templates (which may be on a network) and *..\user\template* for your personal templates (under wherever OpenOffice.org is located on your computer).

You or your network administrator can change these paths and store templates wherever you wish. You can also make any subfolders you want to organize your templates.

Make sure any templates used in shared documents are available to all members of your workgroup—for example, by storing them on a LAN server.

If everyone does not have access to the same templates (for example, not everyone is connected to the LAN all the time, perhaps because they are working from home), some people may need to keep a copy of the templates on their own computers. In that case, make sure the copies are read-only, or you'll end up with a collection of slightly different templates.

Tip   You can store templates in other folders. They won't show up in the Templates and Documents dialog, but you can still use them to create new documents.

Working with Styles

Many people manually format paragraphs, words, tables, page layouts, and other parts of their documents without paying any attention to templates or styles. Other people use styles, but manually change (override) the styles for some paragraphs. When several people are working on the same document, this can result in a mess. Cleaning up the mess can be time-consuming; avoiding it is a better strategy.

A style is a set of formats that you can apply to selected pages, text, frames, and other elements in your document to quickly change their appearance. When you apply a style, you apply a whole group of formats at the same time.

Writer supports the following types of styles:

- Page styles include margins, headers and footers, borders and backgrounds. An example of creating page styles is given in Chapter 3.

- Paragraph styles control all aspects of a paragraph's appearance, such as text alignment, tab stops, line spacing, and borders, and can include character formatting.

- Character styles affect selected text within a paragraph, such as the font and size of text, and bold and italic formats.

- Frame styles are used to format graphic and text frames, including wrapping type, borders, backgrounds, and columns.

- Numbering styles apply similar alignment, numbering or bullet characters, and fonts to numbered or bulleted lists.

Apply a Style to Text

Writer provides three ways for you to select styles to apply. When you first start a document and have not applied any styles to anything, the third method is very limited.

Method 1: Select from the Stylist

This is the most commonly used method.

1. Click the Stylist icon , click Format > Stylist, or press F11. Move the Stylist (Figure 4-7) to a convenient position on the screen.

2. Click on one of the icons at the top left of the Stylist to display a list of styles in a particular category (paragraph, character, page, frame, or numbering).

3. To apply an existing style (except for character styles), position the insertion point in the paragraph, frame, or page, and then double-click on the name of the style in one of these lists. To apply a character style, select the characters first.

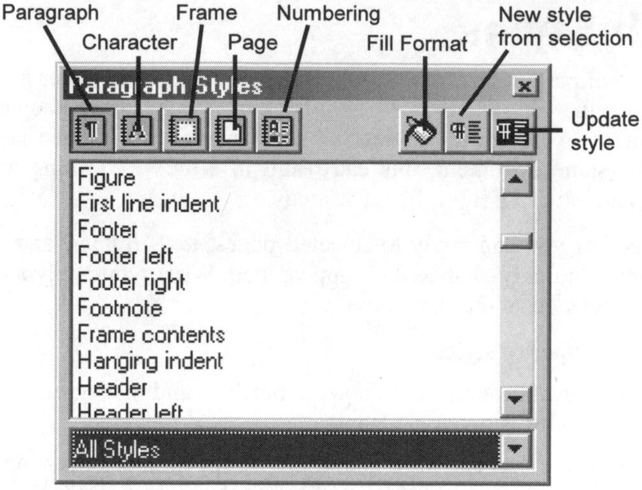

Paragraph   Frame   Numbering   New style
      Character   Page   Fill Format   from selection

Paragraph Styles

Update
style

Figure
First line indent
Footer
Footer left
Footer right
Footnote
Frame contents
Hanging indent
Header
Header left

All Styles

Figure 4-7. The Stylist, showing paragraph styles

Method 2: Use the Fill Format mode from the Stylist

This method is quite useful when you need to format many scattered paragraphs with the same style.

1. Open the Stylist (Figure 4-7) and select the style you want to apply.

2. Click the Fill Format Mode icon.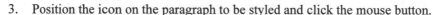

3. Position the icon on the paragraph to be styled and click the mouse button.

   If you are applying a character style, hold down the mouse button while selecting the characters.

4. To quit the Fill Format mode, click the button again or press the Esc key.

   When this mode is active, a right-click anywhere in the document undoes the last Fill Format action. Be careful not to accidentally right-click and thus undo actions you want to keep.

Method 3: Use the Apply Style list on the object bar

After you have used a style at least once in a document, the style name appears on the Apply Style list (Figure 4-8) at the left-hand end of the object bar.

You can open this list and click once on the style you want, or you can use the up and down arrow keys to move through the list, then press Enter to apply the highlighted style.

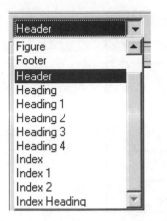

Figure 4-8. The Apply Style list on the Object Bar

Change a Style Definition

Writer comes with many predefined styles. You can redefine existing styles (keeping the same style name), alter an existing style and give the altered style a new name, or create brand new styles.

One good reason to redefine the existing styles, keeping the original names, is that changing templates is easier and more effective if the same style names are used in each template.

Tip	Any changes you make to a style are effective only in the document you're working on. The changes do not go into any associated template.
	If you want to change the styles in a template, you must edit the template. See "Change the Information in an Existing Template" on page 75.

To change an existing style:

1. Do one of the following:

   - In the Stylist (Figure 4-7), right-click on the required style and select Modify from the pop-up menu.
   - Click Format > Styles > Catalog. In the Style Catalog dialog (Figure 4-9), select the required style and click Modify.

2. In this example we're modifying a paragraph style. On the Organizer tab of the Paragraph Style dialog (Figure 4-10), you can change the style on which this style is based, and the default style for the paragraph following this one.

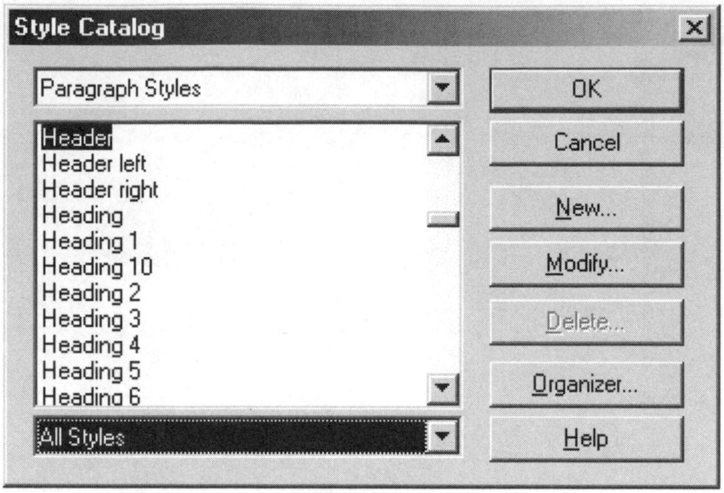

Figure 4-9. The Style Catalog

Do not select the AutoUpdate checkbox. If you do, whenever you manually change any paragraph with this style, all of the paragraphs will change. This will cause havoc. If you want to deliberately update a paragraph style based on your manual changes, use one of the methods described in "Update a Style from a Selection" on page 93.

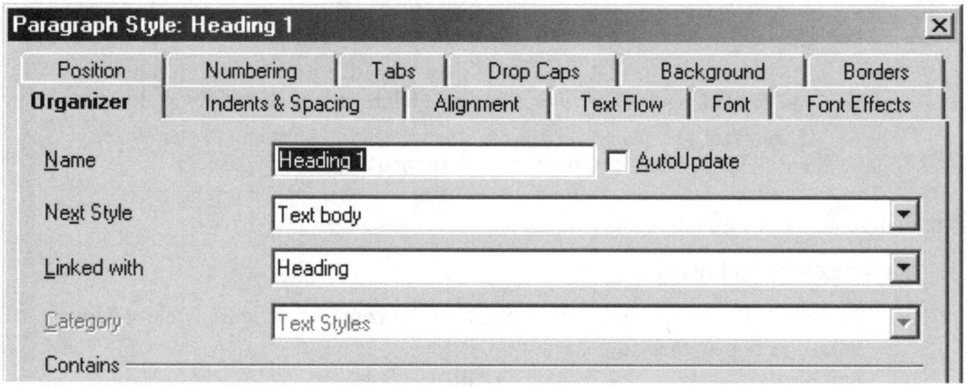

Figure 4-10. The Organizer tab of the Paragraph Style dialog

3. Use the other tabs to change any characteristics you wish. Most of them will be familiar to you or are self-explanatory, so I won't discuss them here.

One set of choices that are a bit different are the page break options on the Text Flow tab. If you want a mandatory page break before every paragraph with this style (as you might with a Heading 1, which is often used for chapter titles), then in the Breaks section select the Enable checkbox, select Page in the Type list and select Before in the Position list. See Figure 4-11.

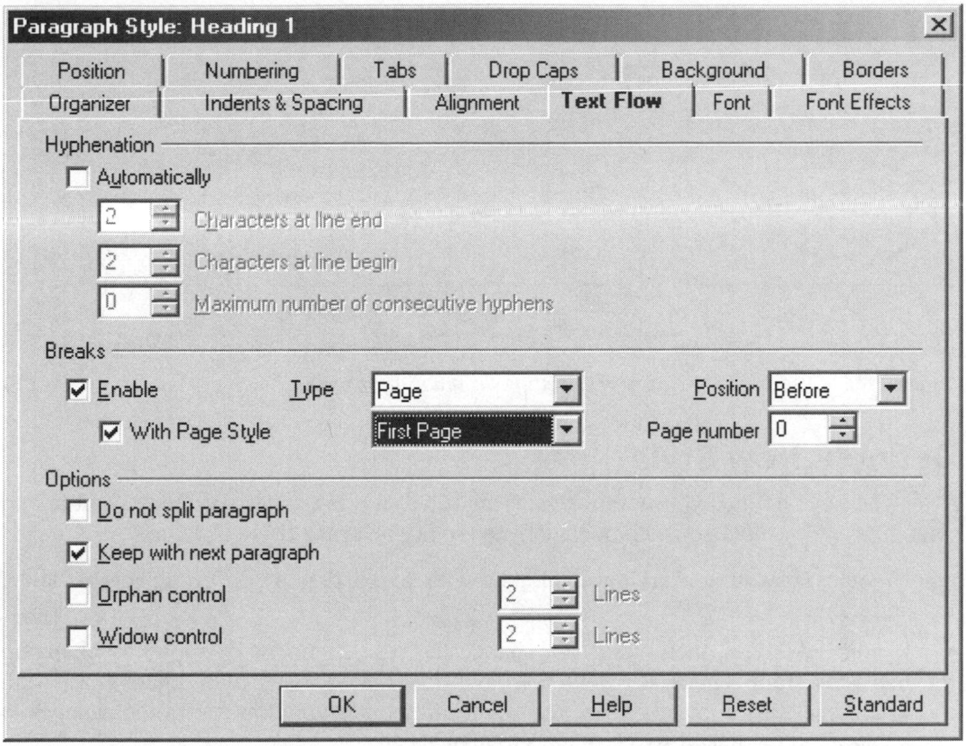

Figure 4-11. Specifying a mandatory page break to a specific page style

If you have defined page styles (as we did in Chapter 3), you might want to specify that this style always starts on a First Page, so you would select the With Page Style checkbox and First Page in the drop-down list. Leave the Page number as 0 so the new page will pick up the next page number automatically.

However, if you do want a page break but you don't want to specify the page style (for example, for a Heading 2, which you always want on a new page, but it could be either a left- or right-hand page), then you would not select With Page Style.

4. Click OK to save your changes. You can now apply this new style as needed.

Tip If spacing between paragraphs seems wrong, see if Register-true is activated on the Indents & Spacings tab of the Paragraph Style dialog (Figure 4-12). If it is selected, deselect it.

Register-true is a typography term used in printing. It refers to techniques used to line up lines of type on the front and back of pages, or in adjacent columns, so they are at the same height on the page. This may cause spacing between some paragraphs to be different from the spacing you have defined.

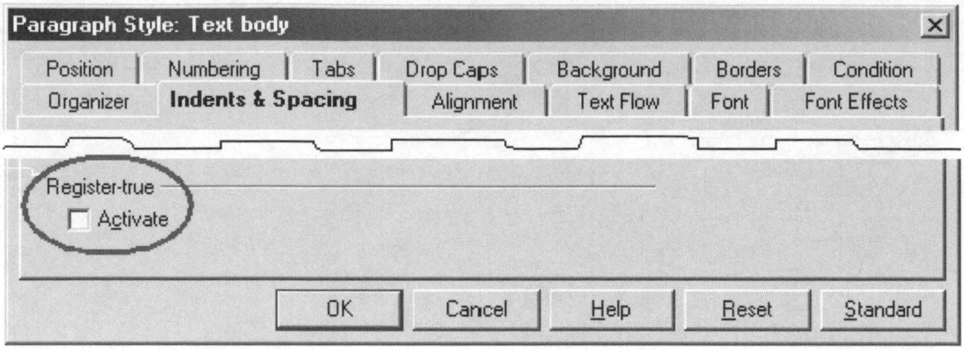

Figure 4-12. Checking the Register-true setting for a paragraph style

Define a New Style

After you have defined your template and modified existing styles, you may want to add some new styles. To do this, click New from the Stylist or the Style Catalog.

- If you want your new style to be linked with an existing style, first select that style, and then click New.

- If you link styles, then when you change the base style (for example, by changing the font from Times to Helvetica), all the linked fonts will change as well. Sometimes this is exactly what you want; other times you don't want the changes to apply to all the linked styles. It pays to plan ahead.

The dialogs and choices are the same for defining new styles and for modifying existing styles.

Use Numbering Styles

You can define the appearance of your lists by using numbering styles, which include styles for bullet lists as well as numbered lists.

After you set up a numbering style, you associate it with one or more paragraph styles. You can use a series of numbering styles to create a hierarchy of numbered paragraphs, and you can define other (unnumbered) paragraphs to fit the indentation or spacing patterns of the numbered paragraphs.

As an example, suppose you want Arabic numbers (1, 2, 3) with no following punctuation, lined up as shown in the illustration below:

8 Example.

9 Example.

10 Example.

1. Click Format > Styles > Catalog. On the Style Catalog (Figure 4-13), choose Numbering Styles in the top box, and either All or Hierarchical in the bottom box.

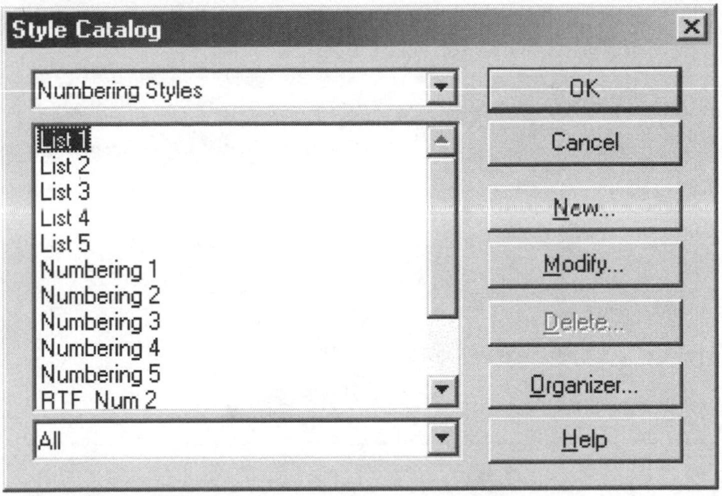

Figure 4-13. Selecting a list numbering style to modify

You'll see a list of styles in the large central box. If you need more styles, or want ones with different (perhaps more descriptive) names, you can click New and define your own. We'll use one of the supplied style names, List 1.

2. Select List 1 and click Modify. On the Numbering Style dialog, you can either choose a predefined style on the Numbering Style tab or design your own on the Options tab. We'll use the Options tab (Figure 4-14).

3. Choose 1, 2, 3 in the Numbering box and delete anything in the Before and After boxes. In the Level box, leave 1–10 (the default) highlighted.

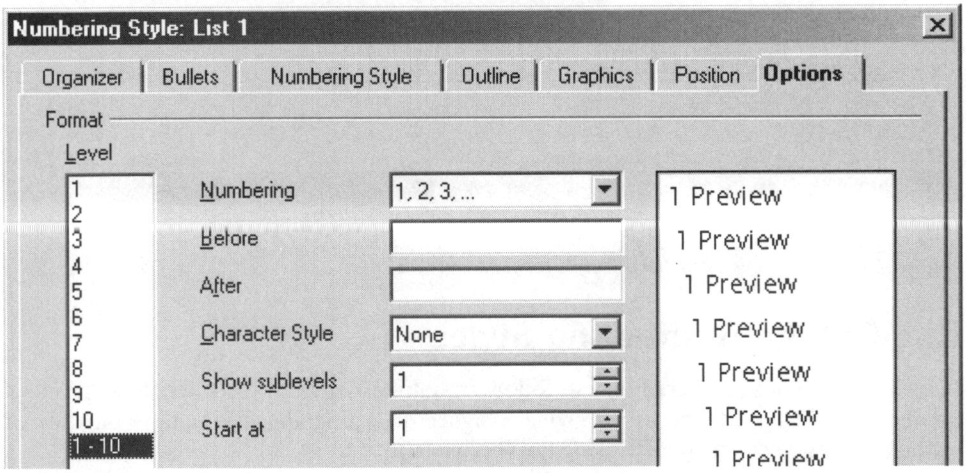

Figure 4-14. Designing a list-numbering style

4. On the Position tab (Figure 4-15), increase Spacing to text from the default, and change Numbering alignment to Right. You might also need to increase the Minimum spacing numbering <–> Text value. I'm not suggesting specific values

because they depend on the typeface, type size, and your personal preference. Try a few combinations to see what works for you. Click OK.

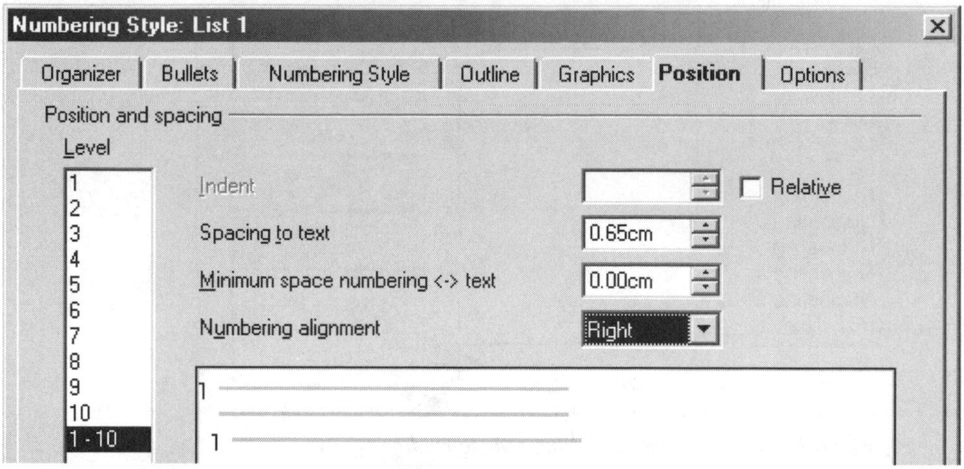

Figure 4-15. Setting spacing and alignment in a list-numbering style

You can apply this numbering style directly to any paragraph, or you can define a paragraph style to use this numbering style.

To define a paragraph style, follow the instructions in "Change a Style Definition" on page 81 or "Define a New Style" on page 84. In addition, go to the Numbering tab (Figure 4-16) and choose the numbering style you just defined. (The name of the paragraph style does not have to match the name of the numbering style, even though I have done it that way in this example.)

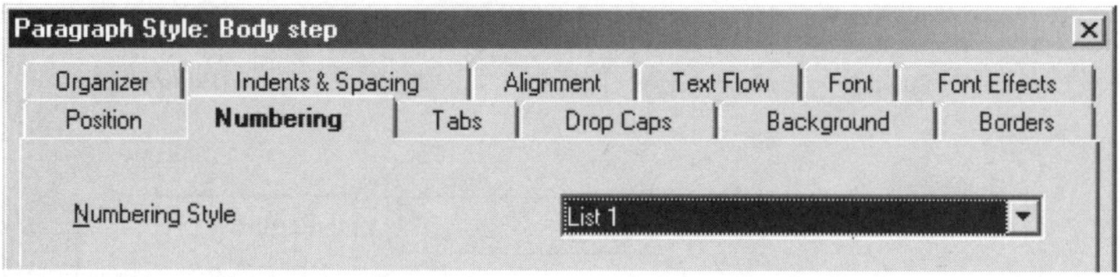

Figure 4-16. Choosing a numbering style for a paragraph style

Use Outline-Numbering Styles

If you require your numbered lists to follow an outline-numbering sequence, you can set up the numbering system using styles assigned to paragraph styles, as you did for ordinary numbered lists, but by using the Outline tab.

Tip   You may find that the selections under Tools > Outline Numbering (described on page 90) are sufficient for your requirements, and you may not need to use outline-numbering styles.

You can modify the predefined styles, or you can define your own. We'll use one of the supplied styles, Numbering 1.

Suppose you want an outline-numbering system to use letters and indents like this:

I. Level-1 list item
   A. Level-2 list item
      i. Level-3 list item
        a) Level-4 list item

1. Click Format > Style > Catalog. On the Style Catalog (Figure 4-13), choose Numbering Styles and select a style such as Numbering 1. Click Modify.

2. On the Numbering Style dialog, go to the Outline tab (Figure 4-17), where you'll find that one style matches your requirements. Click once on that style.

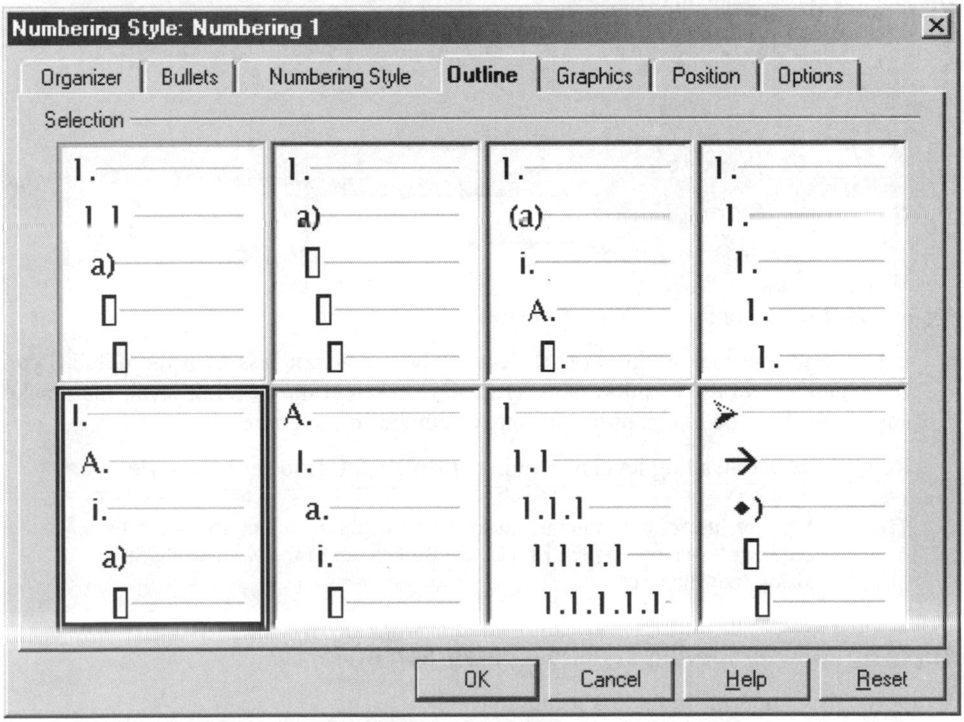

Figure 4-17. Choosing a predefined outline-numbering style

3. If you want to modify the layout of the list, you can use the Options tab (Figures 4-18 and 4-19). Notice that the preview on the right shows the outline you selected. In the Level box on the left, select 1, then 2, 3, and 4, and see how the information in the Numbering and After boxes changes.

    If you want different punctuation (for example, a period after "a" on level 4 instead of a parenthesis), you can change it here.

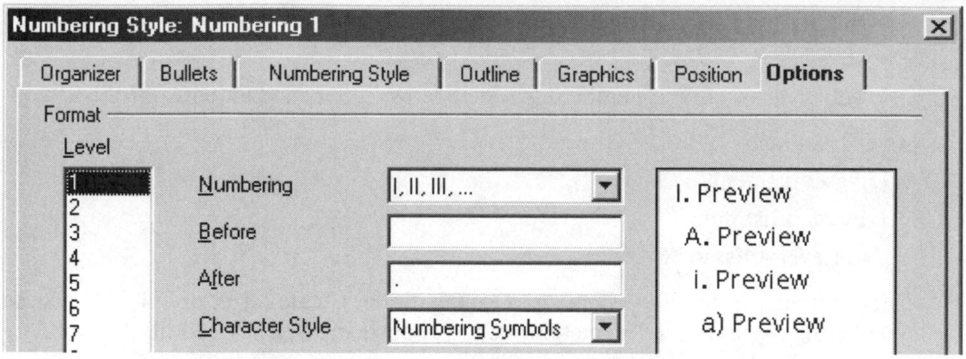

Figure 4-18. Checking the outline numbering, and changing it if necessary, for level-1 list items

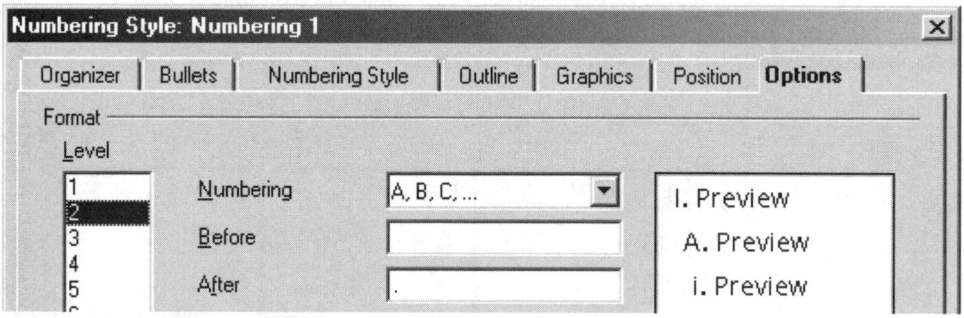

Figure 4-19. Numbering style for level-2 list items

4. If you want the indentation at each level to be greater or less than the default, you can change it on the Position tab (Figure 4-15). Select the heading level, then make any changes in the indentation, spacing, or numbering alignment.

    Repeat for each heading level as required, then click OK to save the style.

Tip   You can use outline numbering to define different bullet styles for the different levels of a bullet list. Use the Bullets tab of the Numbering Style dialog (not shown).

Applying this numbering style to a paragraph style

To apply this numbering style to a paragraph style:

1. Click Format > Style > Catalog, select Paragraph Styles and the paragraph style you want to use for an outline-numbered list (in this example, List 1). Click Modify.

2, Follow the instructions in "Change a Style Definition" on page 81 to set up the font and other required attributes.

    In addition, go to the Numbering tab (Figure 4-16) and choose the numbering style you just defined (Numbering 1, in this example). Click OK to save the style.

Applying the different levels of a list-numbered paragraph style

To apply the different levels of a list-numbered paragraph style:

1. Type the first paragraph and apply the List 1 style. Notice that the level-1 list number is added automatically.

2. Look at the right-hand end of the Formatting object bar. A left-facing arrow icon has appeared. Click on this icon to display the Numbering object bar (Figure 4-20).

3. Press Enter to start the next paragraph. If you want it to be a level-2 list item, click the Down One Level icon on the object bar. You'll see that the number applied to this paragraph has changed to a level-2 number, and the paragraph is indented (if you are using an indented outline style).

4. Continue typing list items, moving each paragraph up or down levels as needed.

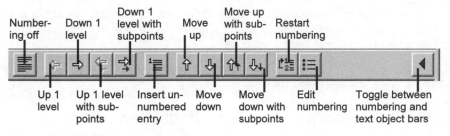

Figure 4-20. The Numbering object bar

Tips   You can enter all the list paragraphs and apply the levels afterward.

You can use keyboard shortcuts to move paragraphs up or down the outline levels. Place the cursor at the beginning of the numbered paragraph and press:

Tab   Down a level
Shift+Tab   Up a level

If you need to insert a tab stop at the beginning of a numbered paragraph (that is, after the number but before the text), press Ctrl+Tab.

Use Frame Styles

You can use frames as containers for text or graphics for a variety of purposes. To provide consistency in the appearance of frames used for similar purposes, you can define styles for frames. For example, you might want photographs to be enclosed in a frame with a drop-shadowed border, line drawings in a frame with a plain border, marginal notes in a frame without a border but with a shaded background, and so on.

Writer provides several predefined frame styles, which you can modify as needed; and you can define other frame styles. The technique for defining and applying frame styles is similar to that for other styles.

Use Character Styles

Use character styles when you want a character, word, or phrase to be consistent, but different from the rest of a paragraph. For example, you might want page numbers in a larger font than the rest of the text in a header or footer; or you might want Internet links underlined and in a particular color (as they appear on many websites). You can also define a style for drop caps (large first letters at the beginning of a paragraph), and many other effects for special purposes.

Character styles can also help you manage change. Suppose your company style uses bold for menu items, commands, and dialog titles. Just before you finish a book, someone decides to change the styles so dialog titles are no longer in bold. If you have defined a character style for dialog titles, you only need to change bold to not-bold in one place and then apply the change to the document.

Writer provides several predefined character styles, which you can modify as needed; and you can define other character styles. The technique for defining and applying character styles is similar to that for other styles.

See "Changing the Default Bullet Character" on page 196 for instructions on how to change the bullet character used for lists.

Number Chapters and Appendixes Separately

If your document contains several chapters and some appendixes, you may want to use automatic chapter numbering. Suppose you want the chapters numbered 1, 2, 3, and the appendixes numbered A, B, C. Here is one way to do this.

Before you take this approach, read "Other things you may need to do" on page 92. You won't be able to bookmark or set a reference to the chapter or appendix number part of the paragraph, so if you plan to use cross-references to specific chapters (for example, "See Chapter 12, Walking your dog"), you'll need to use a different method of numbering chapters and appendixes. See "Using Fields Instead of Outline Numbering for Chapter Numbers" on page 107.

Tip	You must have in your document at least one heading or other paragraph tagged with the style associated with each level of your outline, or these settings will be lost when you close your document. To prevent this problem when developing a new template or document, include a page at the end of the document with sample headings. Delete this final page when the document is complete.

Bug   Writer 1.1.1 has a bug that does not occur in earlier versions, including
1.1.0. This bug is in the default template provided with the program.
Documents based on the default template do not display outline numbers
on paragraphs after you close and reopen a document, even though the
outline numbering dialog retains the settings you have specified. If you
open the document in an earlier version of Writer, the outline numbers are
displayed, and if you create a document based on a template from an
earlier version of Writer, the outline numbers display correctly in Writer
1.1.1.

Set up chapter numbering

1. Click Tools > Outline Numbering.
2. On the Numbering tab of the Outline Numbering dialog (Figure 4-21):
   a) Select Level 1.
   b) Choose Heading 1 from the Paragraph Style list.
   c) Choose 1, 2, 3 from the Number list.
   d) Type Chapter (followed by a space) in the Separator Before box.
   e) Choose a character style for the number if you want it to be different from the
      rest of the paragraph (you'll also need to define the character style).
   f) Type any punctuation you want to appear after the chapter number in the
      Separator After box (you'll probably want at least a space or two there).
   g) Leave the Start at number as 1.

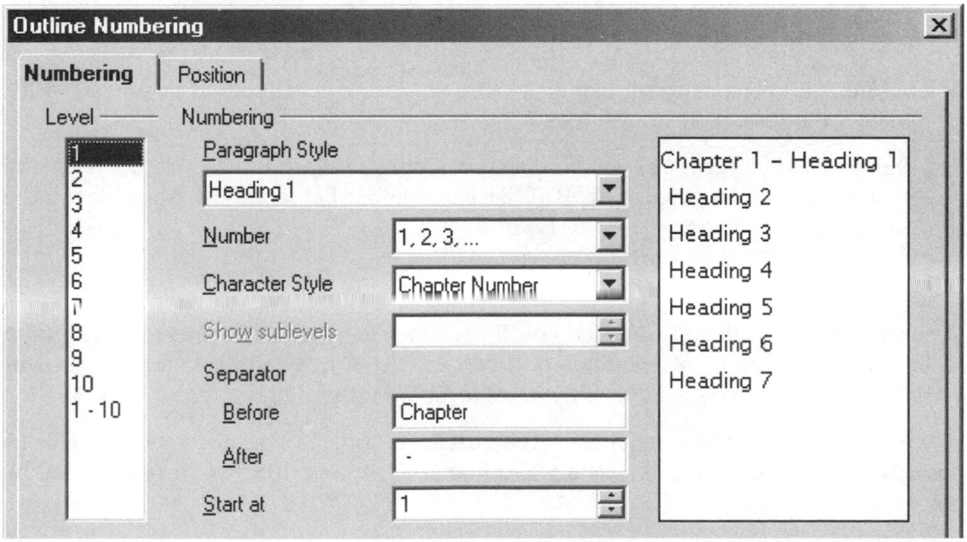

Figure 4-21. Set up automatic chapter numbering

3. Go to the Position tab (Figure 4-22) and make any required changes to the position
   and spacing. For example, if you expect some of your chapter titles to be long and

you want them to wrap to line up in a particular way, you can define the Space to Text to suit your requirements.

4. If you want other headings to be numbered (for example, 1.1 for Heading 2 and 1.1.1 for Heading 3), you can select the relevant level and set the paragraph style, number type, punctuation, and so on as you did for Heading 1. For Heading 2, set the number of sublevels to 2; for Heading 3, set it to 3.

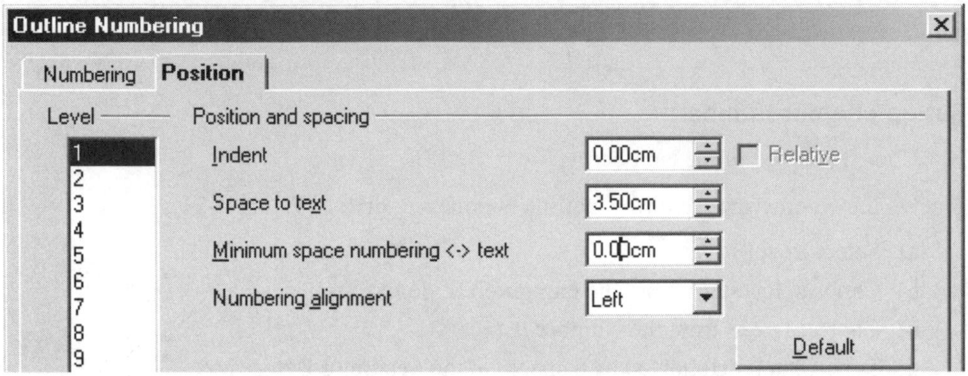

Figure 4-22. Setting up the position and spacing for outline numbers

Set up appendix numbering

To put appendix numbers into your outline-numbering scheme:

1. Define an Appendix 1 paragraph style. Define its characteristics (font, spacing) to match the Heading 1 style, but do not make it "linked with" Heading 1. I suggest linking it to –None–.

2. On the Outline Numbering dialog, choose an outline level that you won't need for another purpose, such as level 6 or 7.

3. Define the numbering as for chapter numbering, but choose Appendix 1 in the paragraph style list; choose A, B, C in the Number list; and type Appendix in the Separator Before box.

Other things you may need to do

When you set up a table of contents, you'll need to specify that the Appendix paragraph style is to be treated at the same table of contents level as Heading 1, as described in "Assign paragraph styles to table of contents levels" on page 120.

If you include the chapter number in the header or footer using a document field, as described in "Using Fields in Headers and Footers" on page 105, you'll need to follow these steps:

1. Define different page styles for pages in chapters and pages in appendixes.

2. When inserting the document field in the header or footer of chapter pages, set the "Layer" field to 1.

3. When inserting the document field in the header or footer of appendix pages, set the "Layer" field to the outline level you've assigned to Appendix 1 style (6 in our example).

4. Just before the first appendix page, insert a manual page break and specify the page style for the first page of an appendix.

Update a Style from a Selection

You can update a style from a selection. Any changes to a style apply only to this document; they will not be saved in the template.

1. Open the Stylist.

2. In the document, select formatted text or a paragraph that has the format you want to adopt as a style.

3. In the Stylist, select the style you want to update (single-click, not double-click), and then click on the Update Style icon.

Create a New Style from a Selection

You can create a new style by copying an existing style. This new style applies only to this document; it will not be saved in the template.

1. Open the Stylist. From the drop-down list, choose the type of style you want to create.

2. In the document, select a page, formatted frame, some text, or a paragraph you want to save as a style.

3. In the Stylist, click the New Style from Selection icon. In the Create Style dialog (Figure 4-23), type a name for the new style. The list shows the names of existing styles of the selected type. Click OK to save the new style.

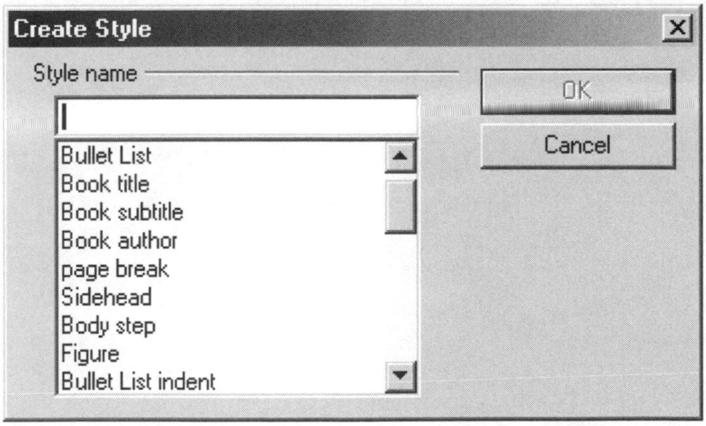

Figure 4-23. Creating a new style from a selection

Remove Unwanted and Unused Styles from a Document

You cannot remove (delete) any of Writer's predefined styles from a template, even if you are not using them.

You can remove any user-defined styles; but before you do, you should make sure the styles are not in use. If an unwanted style is in use, you'll want to replace it with a substitute style. See "Find and Replace Paragraph Styles" on page 36 for instructions.

Replacing styles (and then deleting the unwanted ones) can be very useful if you are dealing with a document that has been worked on by several writers or has been formed by combining several documents from different sources.

To delete unwanted styles, right-click on them (one at a time) in the Stylist and click Delete on the pop-up menu.

Remove Unwanted Character Styles from Selected Text

If some of your text has picked up unwanted character (not paragraph) styles, you can remove those styles. Select the characters, then click Default on the Character Styles page of the Stylist.

5

Getting the Most from Fields

Fields are extremely useful features of Writer. This chapter describes how to use a few of them to solve common business and technical-writing problems. Some more uses of fields are covered in Chapter 7.

Tip   If you have selected the Fields checkbox in the Highlighting section of the Options – Text Document – View dialog (Figure 1-15), fields will have a gray background when viewed onscreen. This gray background will not show when you print the file to hardcopy or a PDF. If you do not want the gray background to show onscreen, then deselect the Fields checkbox.

Using Document Properties to Hold Information That Changes

The Properties dialog for any document contains spaces on the Description tab (Figure 5-1) and the User Defined tab (Figure 5-2) for information that you might want to include in your document, especially if it's information that might change during the course of the project. To display this dialog, click File > Properties.

Later in this chapter I'll show how to use this information in fields. You can return to this dialog at any time and change the information you entered. When you do so, all of the references to that information will change wherever they appear in the document. For example, you might need to change the contents of the Title field from the draft title to the production title.

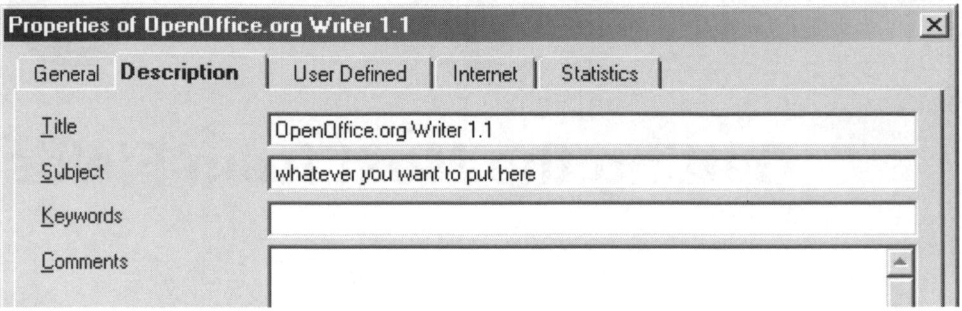

Figure 5-1. The Description tab of the document properties dialog

The User Defined tab provides four fields for you to use as required. You can change the default names for these fields to more meaningful names. The example in Figure 5-2 shows that Info 1 has been changed to ProductName and Info 2 to ShortName.

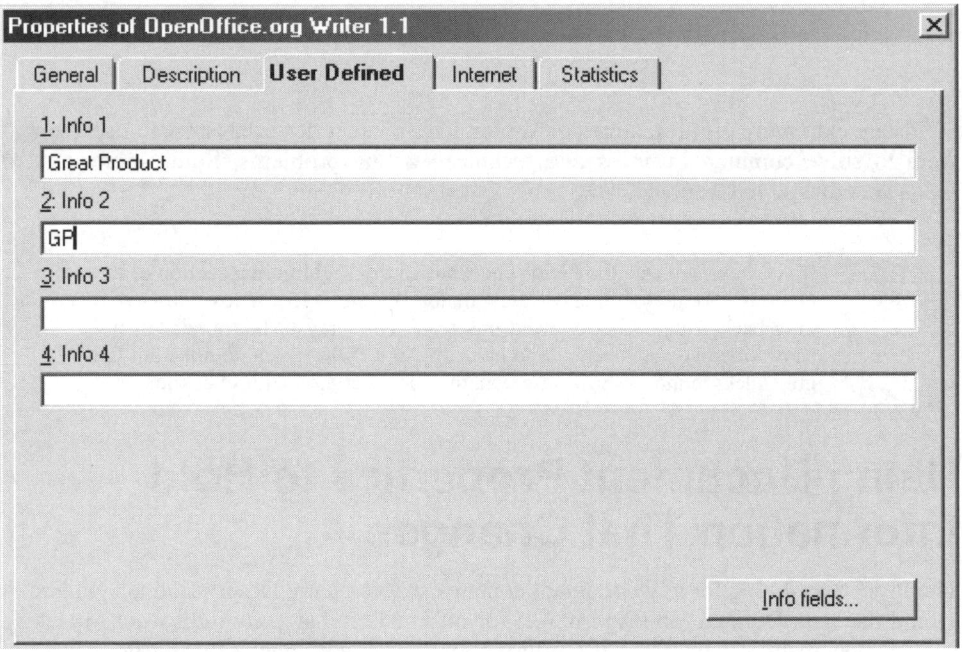

Figure 5-2. The User Defined tab of the document properties dialog

To change these field names, click the Info fields button near the bottom of the dialog. In the small pop-up dialog (not shown), type the field names you want, then click OK.

Using Other Fields to Hold Information That Changes

One way that writers use (or should use) fields is to hold information that is likely to change during the course of a project. For example, the name of a manager, a product, or even your entire company may change just before the document is due to be printed. If you have inserted the changeable information as fields, you can change the information in one place and it will automatically change in all the places where that field occurs.

Writer provides several places where you can store the information referred to by a field. We'll look at some of them here.

Three document properties (Title, Subject, Author) are on the Insert > Fields menu (Figure 5-3). To insert one of these fields, click on it in the menu.

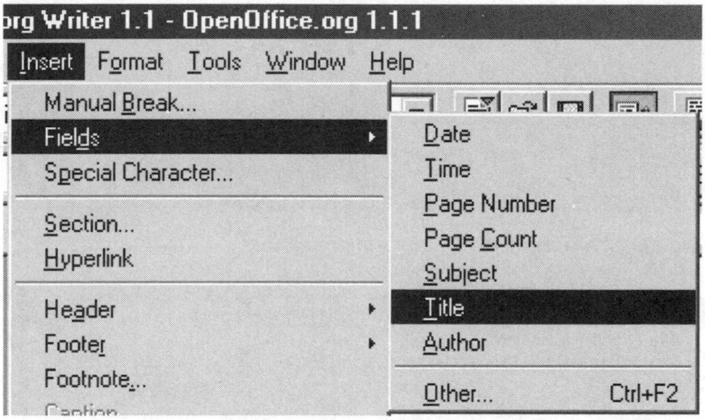

Figure 5-3. Inserting a Title field from the Fields menu

Other document properties are on the DocInformation and Document tabs of the Fields dialog (Figures 5-4 and 5-5), reached by clicking Insert > Fields > Other.

To insert one of these fields, select it in the Type list, then select from the Select and Format lists if choices appear. Finally, click Insert.

Some of these items are picked up from the User Data page of the Options dialog, so make sure the information on that page is correct.

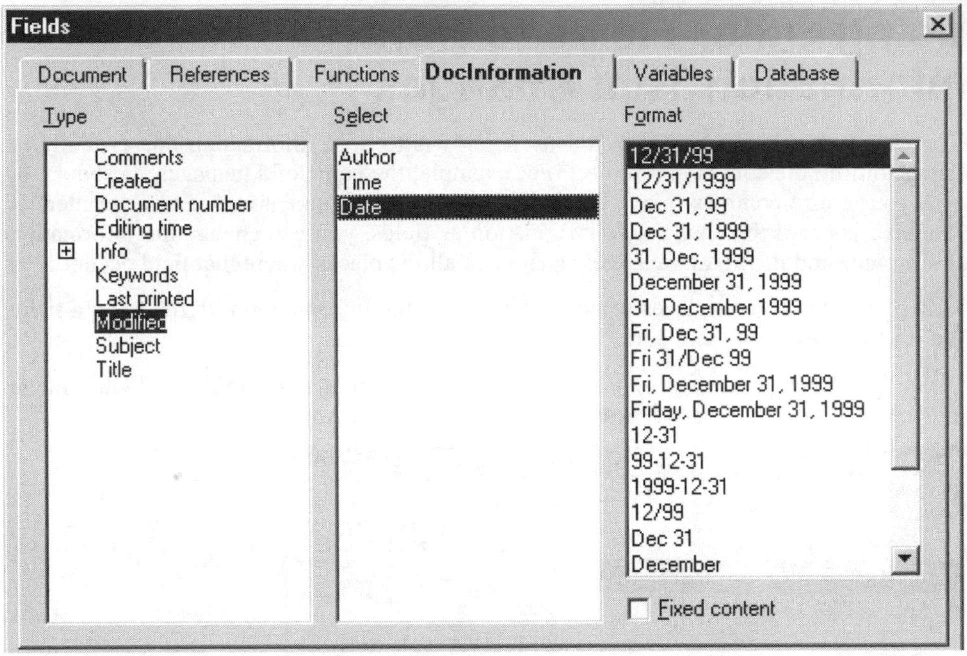

Figure 5-4. Inserting a Date Modified field using the DocInformation tab of the Fields dialog

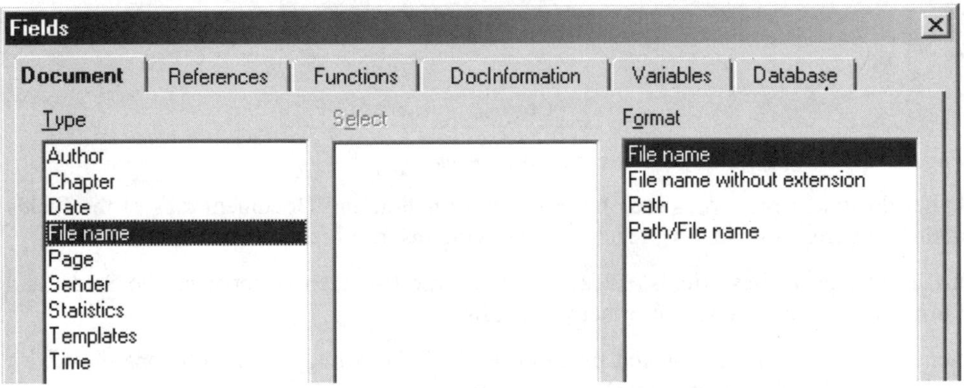

Figure 5-5. Inserting a File name field using the Document tab of the Fields dialog

> **Tip**   Although these fields are often used to hold information that changes, you
> can make the content unchangeable by selecting the Fixed content
> checkbox (visible in Figure 5-4) when inserting the field. If necessary,
> you can come back to this dialog later and deselect this checkbox to make
> the field variable again.

Using AutoText to Insert Often-Used Fields Quickly

If you use the same fields often, you'll want a quick and easy way to insert them. Use AutoText for this purpose. To define an AutoText entry for a field:

1. Insert a field into your document, as described previously.

2. Select the field, and then click Edit > AutoText (or press Ctrl+F3).

3. On the AutoText dialog (Figure 5-6), choose the group where this new entry will be stored (in this example, it's going into My AutoText), type a name for the entry, and change the suggested shortcut if you wish.

4. Click the AutoText button, and click New to have the entry inserted as a field. Do not choose New (text only) or the AutoText entry will be plain text, not a field.

5. Now whenever you want to insert this field at the cursor position, press the shortcut keys, then press F3.

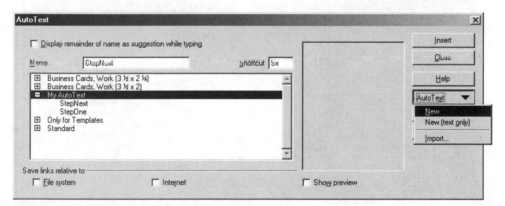

Figure 5-6. Creating a new AutoText entry

Defining Your Own Numbering Sequences

You may want to define your own numbering sequences to use in situations where you don't always want the number at the start of the paragraph, or where you want more control than the built-in numbering choices give you.

This topic describes how to create and use a numbering sequence, using a "number range variable" field.

Create a Number Range Variable

To create a number range variable using Arabic (1, 2, 3) numbers:

1. Place the insertion point in a blank paragraph in your document.

2. Click Insert > Fields > Other and select the Variables tab (Figure 5-7).

    In the Type list, select Number Range. In the Format list, select Arabic (1 2 3). Type whatever you want in the Name field (I've used Step in this example).

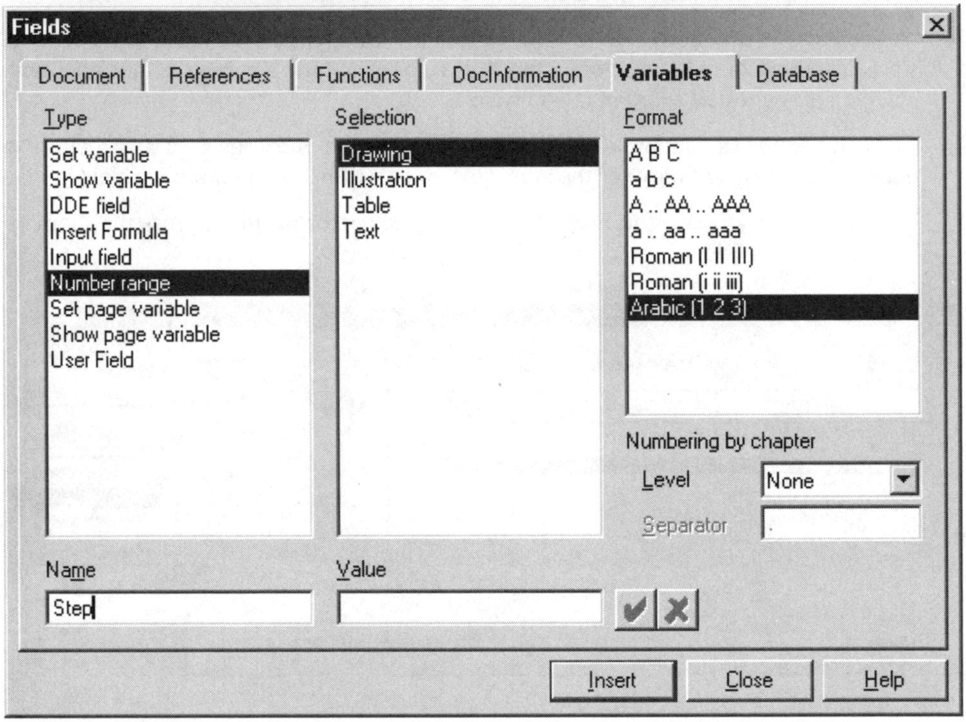

Figure 5-7. Defining a number range variable

3. Click Insert. The name of the variable (Step) now appears in the Selection list, and a number field (showing 1) appears at the insertion point in your document. The Fields dialog remains open, so you may need to move it out of the way to see the field in the document.

    Hover the mouse pointer over this number field and you'll see the field code of Step = Step+1. If you click several more times on the Insert button in the Fields dialog, the numbers 2, 3, 4, and so on will appear in the document.

4. Now you want to create another field, to restart the Step sequence at 1, so you can use the same sequence name more than once in your document (for example, to begin each set of instructions).

To create this new field, open the Fields dialog to the Variables tab. Make sure the variable name Step appears in the Name box. In the Value box, type *Step=1*, as shown in Figure 5-8. Click Insert. Now hover the mouse pointer over the new field in your document and you'll see the field code of Step = Step=1.

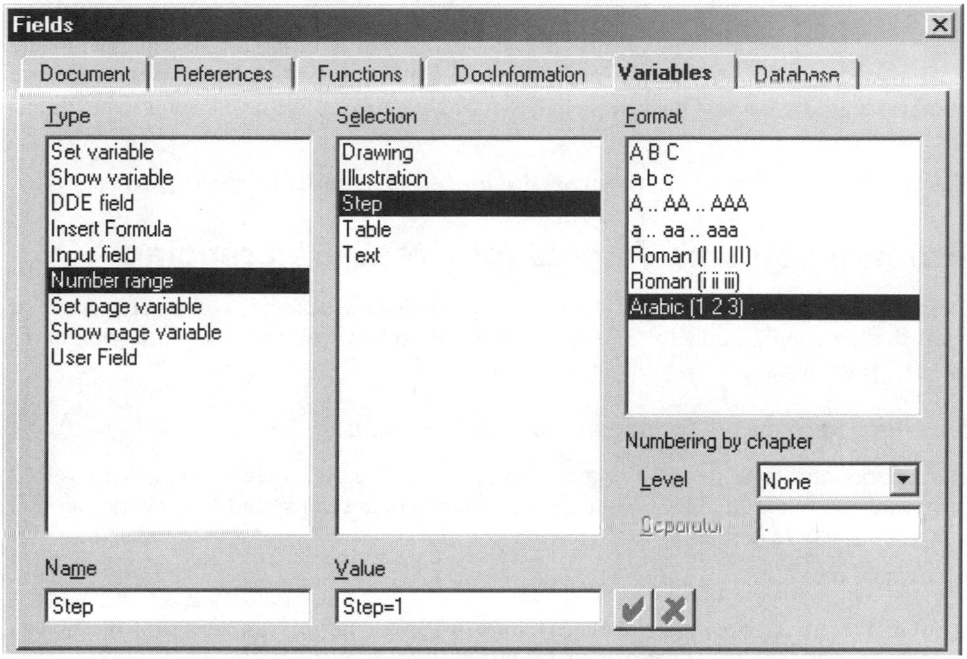

Figure 5-8. Defining a field to restart a number range variable

Use AutoText to Insert a Number Range Field Into a Document

You certainly don't want to go through all of that every time you want to put in a step number. Instead, create two AutoText entries, one for the Step = Step=1 field (call it Step1, for example) and one for the Step = Step+1 field (StepNext). See "Using AutoText to Insert Often Used Fields Quickly" page 99.

You can create similar fields for substeps or other sequences that you want to be numbered with letters (a, b, c), Roman numerals (i, ii, iii), or some other sequence supported by Writer. In the Fields dialog, choose the required format in the Format list when creating the field codes.

Tip

If a user-defined variable is not in use in the document, the [X] icon next to the Value box is active. You can delete the variable by clicking this icon.

Using Automatic Cross-References

If you type in references to other parts of the document, those references can easily get out-of-date if you reword a heading, add or remove figures, or reorganize topics. Replace any typed cross-references with automatic ones and, when you update fields, all the references will update automatically to show the current wording or page numbers. The References page of the Fields dialog (Figure 5-10) lists some items, such as user-defined number range variables. Other items that you might expect to be listed, such as headings, are not shown.

See also "Cross-Reference Between Subdocuments in a Master Document" on page 159.

Prepare Items as Targets for Cross-Referencing

Before you can insert a cross-reference to text such as a heading, you must prepare or "set" that heading as an item to be referenced. To do this, you can either use bookmarks or "set" references.

Inserting bookmarks for use in cross-referencing

Bookmarks are listed in the Navigator and can be accessed directly from there with a single mouse click. In HTML documents, bookmarks are converted to anchors that you can jump to via hyperlink.

1. Select the text you want to bookmark. Click Insert > Bookmark.

2. On the Insert Bookmark dialog (Figure 5-9), the larger box lists any previously defined bookmarks. Type a name for this bookmark in the top box. Click OK.

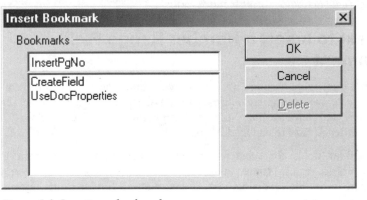

Figure 5-9. Inserting a bookmark

Marking headings or other text to be used in cross-referencing

To mark or "set" some text as an item to be referenced:

1. Click Insert > Cross Reference.

2. On the References page of the Fields dialog (Figure 5-10), click Set Reference in the Type list. The Selection list shows any references that have been defined.

    You can leave this page open while you set many headings as references.

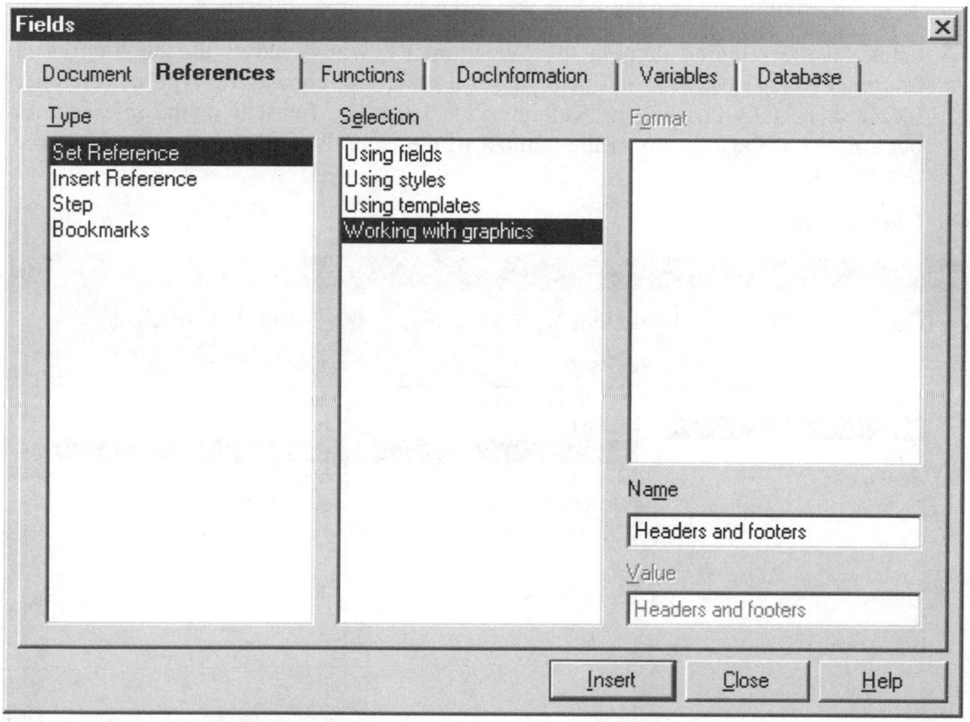

Figure 5-10. Setting text to be used as a target for a cross-reference

3. Click in the document and highlight the text of the first heading to be used as a target for a cross-reference. Click on the Fields dialog. The text of the heading will appear in the Value box in the lower right of the dialog. In the Name box, type some text by which you can identify this heading.

4. Click Insert. The text you typed in the Name box now appears in the Selection list.

5. Repeat steps 3 and 4 as often as required.

Insert Cross-References

To insert a cross-reference to a heading or other text:

1. In your document, place the cursor where you want the cross-reference to appear.

2. If the Fields dialog is not open, click Insert > Cross Reference. On the References tab of the Fields dialog (Figure 5-11), in the Type list, click Insert Reference or Bookmark (depending on how you set your references).

    You can leave this page open while you insert many cross-references.

3. Click on the required item in the Selection list, which shows the bookmarks or references that have been defined. In the Format list, choose the type of reference required. Usually this will be Reference (to insert the full text of the reference or bookmark) or Page (to insert the number of the page the referenced or bookmarked text is on).

4. Click Insert.

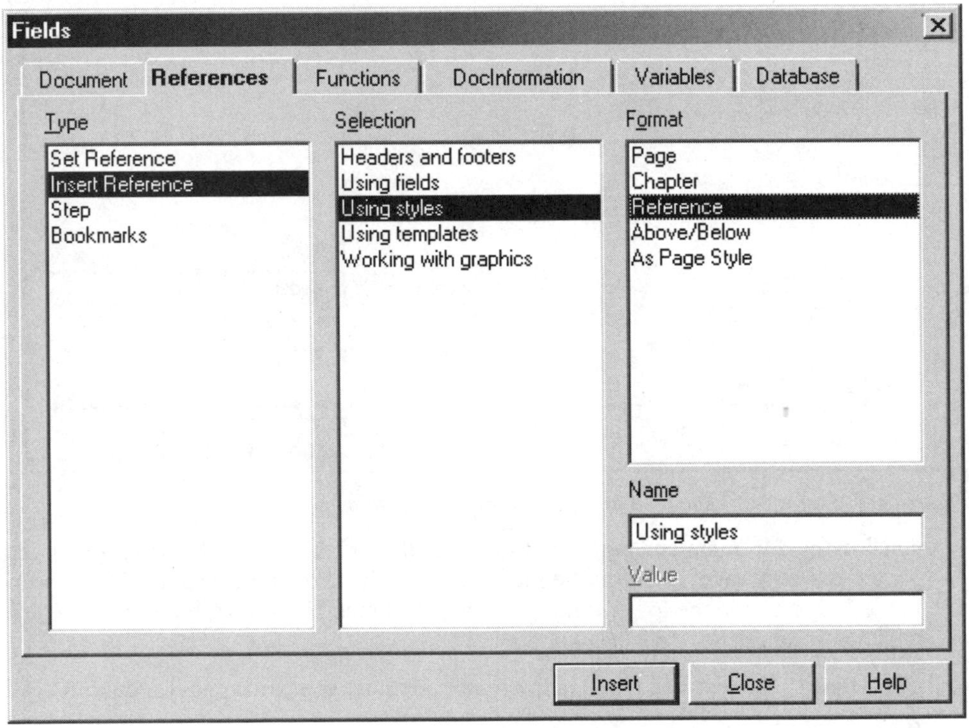

Figure 5-11. Inserting a cross-reference to a heading

To insert a cross-reference to an item (such as a figure caption) that you have previously inserted into the document as a numbering-sequence field:

1. In your document, place the cursor where you want the cross-reference to appear. If the Fields dialog is not already open, click Insert > Cross-reference.

2. On the References tab of the Fields dialog (Figure 5-12), select Figure in the Type list.

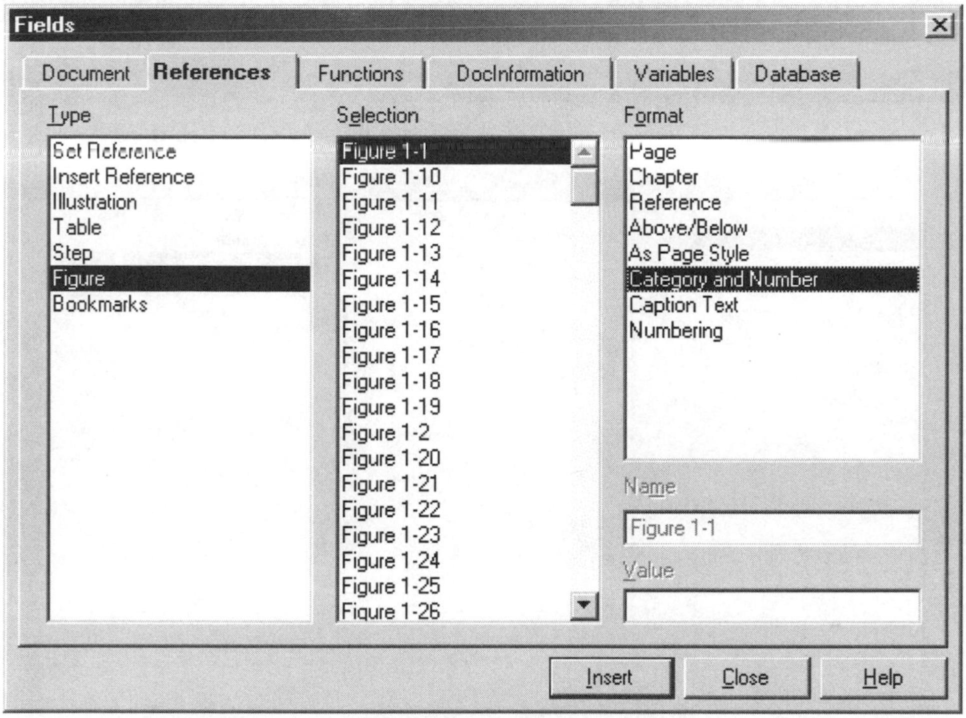

Figure 5-12. Cross-referencing to a figure number

3. Click on the required item in the Selection list, which shows the list of figures that have previously been inserted into the document. The Format list shows different choices from those given for headings. Choose the type of reference required. Usually this will be Category and Number (to insert the word "Figure" and its number), Reference (to insert the word "Figure" with its number and the full text of the caption), or Page (to insert the number of the page the figure is on).

4. Click Insert.

Using Fields in Headers and Footers

You can insert fields into headers or footers, using techniques described earlier in this chapter:

*   To insert a page number, document title, author, creation date and time, current date and time, or total page count field, use document properties (see page 95).

*   You can insert a cross-reference to a bookmark or a set reference.

- If you have used Heading 1 for your chapter titles, you can use a document field to insert the current chapter title, so it changes from one chapter to the next. See Figure 5-13, which calls chapter titles "names." If you have used outline numbering on your Heading 1, you can choose whether to include these numbers in the field.

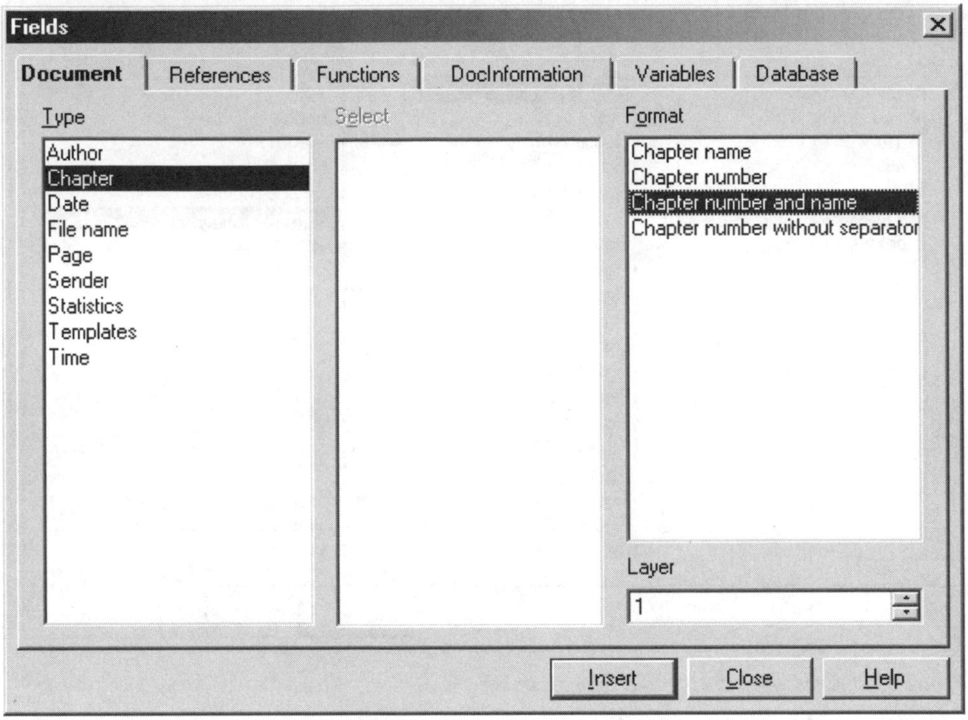

Figure 5-13. Inserting the current chapter name and number into your document

- You can insert cross-references to other heading levels by specifying a value in the Layer box in the lower right of the Document tab of the Fields dialog (Figure 5-13). That is, Layer 1 = Heading 1, Layer 2 = Heading 2, and so on.

  A cross-reference field in the header of a page picks up the *first* heading of that level on the page, and a field in the footer picks up the *last* heading of that level.

  This feature did not work correctly in OOo 1.0, but it does work in Version 1.1.

- To include the chapter number with the page number, position the cursor just before the Page field you inserted. Click Insert > Fields > Other. On the Document tab of the Fields dialog, select Chapter in the Type column and Chapter number without separator in the Format column. Click Insert.

  Go to the header or footer where you inserted this field, type the character you want to appear between the chapter number and the page number—for example, a period or a dash.

  The table of contents won't automatically pick up these chapter numbers, so you'll need to make a change on the Tables and Indexes page, as described in "Modify What the Table of Contents Displays" on page 119.

- You can add a page count to the footer—for example "Page 9 of 12." Type the word "Page" and a space in front of the Page field. Type a space, the word "of," and a space after the Page field. Then click Insert > Fields > Page Count.

Using Fields Instead of Outline Numbering for Chapter Numbers

The technique in "Using Fields in Headers and Footers" on page 105, combined with outline-numbered chapter headings (described in "Number Chapters and Appendixes Separately" on page 90), works well when you want the field to show information for the current chapter. But what if you want to use a cross-reference to refer to a different chapter? You cannot bookmark or set a reference to the chapter number part of a heading created using outline numbering.

Tip	If you use this technique, some other features won't work because Writer doesn't recognize the field as chapter numbers. For example, you won't be able to include chapter numbers with the page numbers in headers or footers, or the table of contents, using the technique described in "Using Fields in Headers and Footers" on page 105.

To have chapter numbers that update automatically and can be used in cross-referencing, use a numbered range field.

1. Define your number range variable, as described in "Defining Your Own Numbering Sequences" on page 99. I've called this variable *Chapter*.

2. To insert the field into your Heading 1, type Chapter <space>. Click Insert > Fields > Other. On the Variables tab, pick Number range, Chapter, Arabic. Click Insert. You'll need to do this manually for each Heading 1.

3. Select the entire text of the first Heading 1, including the word "Chapter" and the chapter number, and set a reference to it.

4. You can now insert a cross-reference to this heading anywhere in your document.

Tip	You can also use this technique for easier management of appendix numbering. Keep your appendix headings in the Heading 1 style, define a separate number range sequence for appendix numbers (choosing "A,B,C" for the number format), and type Appendix <space> <insert appendix number field> in the Heading 1 paragraph. You can then use the same page styles for chapters and appendixes, and the same field in the header or footer of chapters and appendixes.

Tricks for Working with Fields

Keyboard Shortcuts for Fields

Here are some handy keyboard shortcuts to use when working with fields:

Ctrl+F2	Open the Fields dialog.
Ctrl+F9	Show/hide fields.
Ctrl+F8	Field shadings on/off.
F9	Update fields.

Fixing the Contents of Fields

You can specify "fixed content" for many items on the Document and DocInformation tabs so the field contents don't update. For example, you might use a field to insert the creation date of a document, and you would not want that date to change. In another place you might use a date field to show the current date, which you do want to change; in that case, deselect "fixed content" when you insert the field.

Converting Fields into Text

Writer does not provide any easy way to convert field contents into text. To do this, you need to copy the field contents and paste them back as unformatted text. This is not a very good solution if you have hundreds of fields that you want to change, but you could use a macro to automate the process. This book does not cover macros.

Developing Conditional Content

Conditional content is text and graphics that are included or excluded depending on a condition you specify.

A simple example is a reminder letter for an overdue account. The first and second reminders might have a subject line of "Reminder Notice," but the third reminder letter might have the subject "Final Notice" and a different final paragraph.

A more complex example is a software manual for a product that comes in two versions, Pro and Lite. Both product versions have much in common, but the Pro version includes some features that are not in the Lite version. If you use conditional content, you can maintain one file containing information for both versions and print (or create online help) customized for each version. You don't have to maintain two sets of the information that is the same for both versions, so you won't forget to update both versions when something changes.

Choose the Types of Conditional Content to Use

This section describes several Writer features that can help you design and maintain conditional content. You can use one or any combination of these features in the same document.

Conditional text
With conditional text, you can have two alternative texts (a word, phrase, or sentence). One text will be displayed and printed if the condition you specify is met, and the other will be displayed and printed if the condition is not met. You cannot include graphics or edit the text except in the field dialog (not in the body of the document). You also cannot format part of the text (for example, bolding one word but not the others), but you can format the field to affect all of the field contents (for example, bolding all of the words). You cannot include a cross-reference or other field in the text.

Hidden text
With hidden text (a word, phrase, or sentence), you have only two choices: show or hide. If the condition you specify is met, the text is hidden; if the condition is not met, the text is displayed. The disadvantages are the same as for conditional text: you cannot include graphics, edit the text in the body of the document, format part of the text, or include a field.

Hidden paragraphs
Hidden paragraphs are like hidden text, but include entire paragraphs. A blank paragraph can also be hidden—for example, if a database field has no content for the current record. This is very useful when merging an address into a letter: if you allow two lines for the street address and the database record uses only one line, you can prevent the blank line from appearing in your document. The disadvantages are the same as for conditional text and hidden text.

Hidden sections
Hidden sections are often the most useful choice, because you can include graphics, edit the text in the body of the document, format any part of the text, and include fields. A section cannot contain less than a paragraph, so you can't use this method for single words or phrases. The contents of a hidden section behave just like the contents of any other part of the document, but you can specify a condition under which the section is not displayed or printed. You can also choose to display the section but not print it. Finally, you can password-protect a section.

Plan Your Conditional Content

Conditions are what programmers call *logical expressions*. You must formulate a logical expression for each condition, since a condition is always either true (met) or false (not met). You can use the same condition in many places in your document, for different types of conditional content.

To make conditional content work, you need to:

1.   Choose or define a variable

2.   Define a logical expression (condition) involving the selected variable

Choosing or defining a variable

You can use the following variables in your condition:

- User-defined variables
- Predefined OpenOffice.org variables, which use statistical values from the document properties
- User data
- Database field contents—for example from your address book

You cannot use internal variables (for example, page number or chapter name) to formulate conditions.

Defining a logical expression (condition) involving the selected variable

The condition compares a specified fixed value with the contents of a variable or database field.

To formulate a condition, use the same elements as you would to create a formula: operators, mathematical and statistical functions, number formats, variables, and constants. The possible operators are shown in the list of operators in the online help. You can define quite complex expressions, but in most cases a simple condition will do the job.

Create the Variable

To create your variable, click Insert > Fields > Other. You can use choices found on the DocInformation, Variables, and Database tabs.

DocInformation field

"Using Document Properties to Hold Information That Changes" on page 95 described how to set up a user-defined document property. You can use that document property as the variable in your condition statement, or you can create another document property field specifically for conditions.

User-defined variable field

To set up a variable or user field:

1.   Place the cursor where you want the field to be inserted.

2.   On the Fields dialog, select the Variables tab (Figure 5-14).

3.   Select Set variable in the Type list and Text in the Format list.

Type a name for the variable in the Name box, and a value in the Value box. I've chosen "ProLite" for the name (to remind me that this variable is related to the two product versions), and I set the value as "Lite" because I can remember "If it's the Lite version, then this text should be hidden."

4. Select Invisble so the field does not show in the document. Click Insert, then click Close.

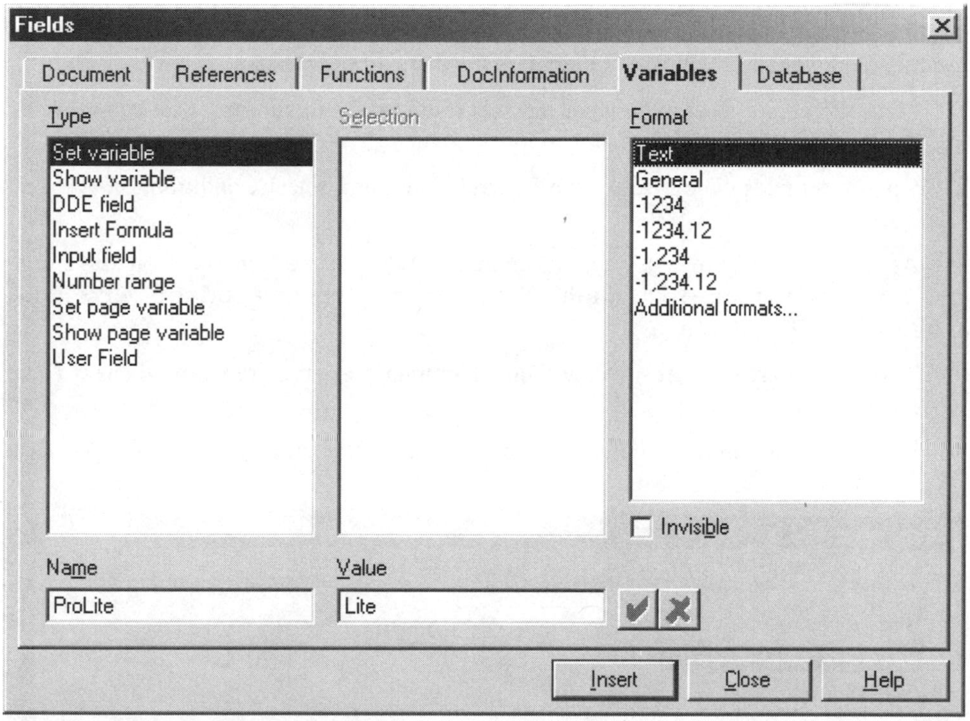

Figure 5-14. Defining a variable to use with conditional content

5. A small gray mark should be visible where you inserted the field. Hover the mouse pointer over this mark and you'll see the field formula *ProLite = Lite*. We'll come back to this field later.

Tips   Because the gray mark is so small, you may have trouble finding it again, especially if you have other fields in the document. You may prefer to leave the variable field visible while you work, and change it to invisible just before you create final copy.

At any time you can place the insertion point just before the field and click Edit > Fields (or right-click on the field, and then click Fields on the pop-up menu). On the Edit Fields dialog (Figure 5-18), select or deselect the Invisible checkbox.

Apply the Condition to the Content

Now that you have defined the variable, you can use it in a condition statement. We'll go through some of the possibilities.

Conditional text

First, let's set up some conditional text that will insert the word "Great Product Lite" into the Lite version and "Great Product Pro" into the Pro version of the manual. You would use this field whenever you want to mention the name of the product.

1. Place the cursor where you want one of these phrases to appear. (You can move or delete it later, if you wish.)

2. Open the Fields dialog, select the Functions tab, and select Conditional text in the Type list.

3. As shown in Figure 5-15, type `ProLite EQ "Lite"` in the Condition box, `Great Product Lite` in the Then box, and `Great Product Pro` in the Else box.

   These fields are case-sensitive, and quotation marks are required around a text value such as Lite.

4. Click Insert to insert the field, then click Close. You should see *Great Product Lite* in your text.

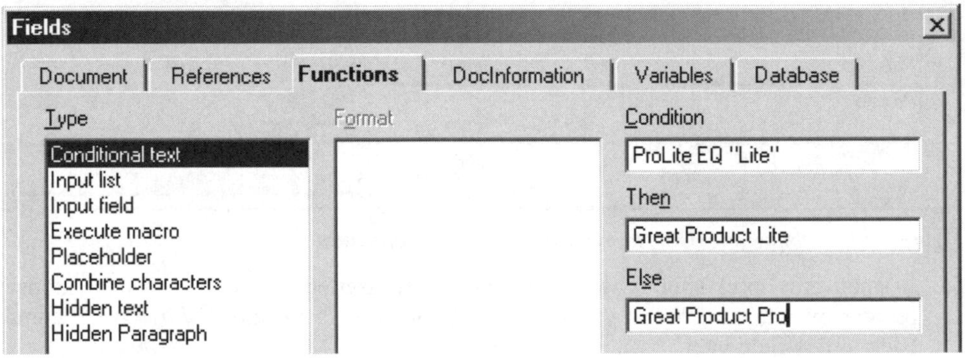

Figure 5-15. Inserting conditional text

Tip   If you want to insert this field into your text in many places (as you probably would for a product name), create an AutoText entry for it. See "Using AutoText to Insert Often-Used Fields Quickly" on page 99 for instructions.

Hidden text

You might use hidden text for words or short phrases that describe features of Great Product Pro that aren't found in the Lite version. You can reuse the same field in several places in your document—for example, by copying and pasting it.

To create a hidden text field:

1. Click Insert > Fields > Other and select the Functions tab.

2. Select Hidden text in the Type list, as shown in Figure 5-16.

3. Type ProLite EQ "Lite" in the Condition box, and enter the required text in the Insert text box. Remember, this is the text that is *hidden* if the condition is true.

4. Click Insert to create and insert the field.

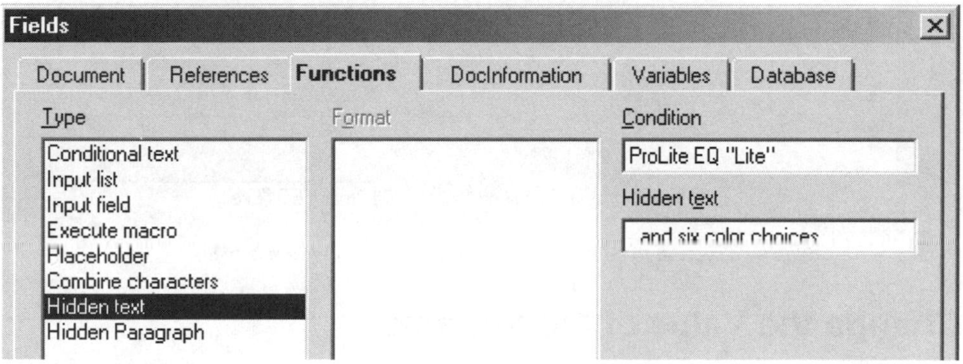

Figure 5-16. Creating a condition for hidden text

Hidden sections

A conditional section is hidden if the condition is true. To create a conditional section:

1. Select the text that you want to be included in the conditional section. (You can edit this text later, just as you can edit any other text.)

2. Click Insert > Section. On the Insert Section dialog (Figure 5-17), select Hide and enter the condition in the With condition box. You can also give the section a name, if you wish. Click Insert to insert the section into your document.

To show the hidden section so you can edit or remove it:

1. Click Format > Sections.

2. On the Edit Sections dialog (not shown), select the section from the list.

3. Do one of the following:

   • Deselect the Hide checkbox, and then click OK. You can now edit the contents of the section. Afterwards, you can click Format > Sections again and select the Hide checkbox to hide the section again.

- Click Undo to remove the section markers (but not the contents of the section). Click OK. The contents of the section are now a normal part of the document.

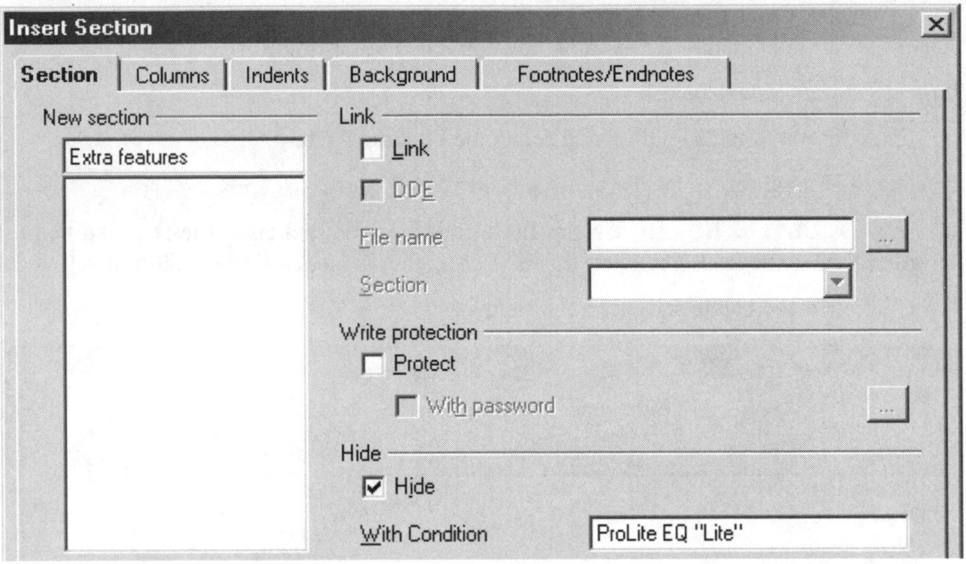

Figure 5-17. Creating a section to be hidden when a specified condition is met

Change the Value of the Variable

1. Find the variable field you created in "Create the Variable" on page 110.

2. Click once just in front of this field, then right-click and click Fields on the pop-up menu.

3. On the Edit Fields dialog (Figure 5-18), change the value of the variable to Pro.

If you have set fields to update automatically, all of the conditional and hidden text that uses this variable as a condition will change.

| Tip | To turn on automatic updating of fields, click Tools > Options > Text Document; on the General tab (Figure 1-13 on page 13), select Fields under Update Automatically. |

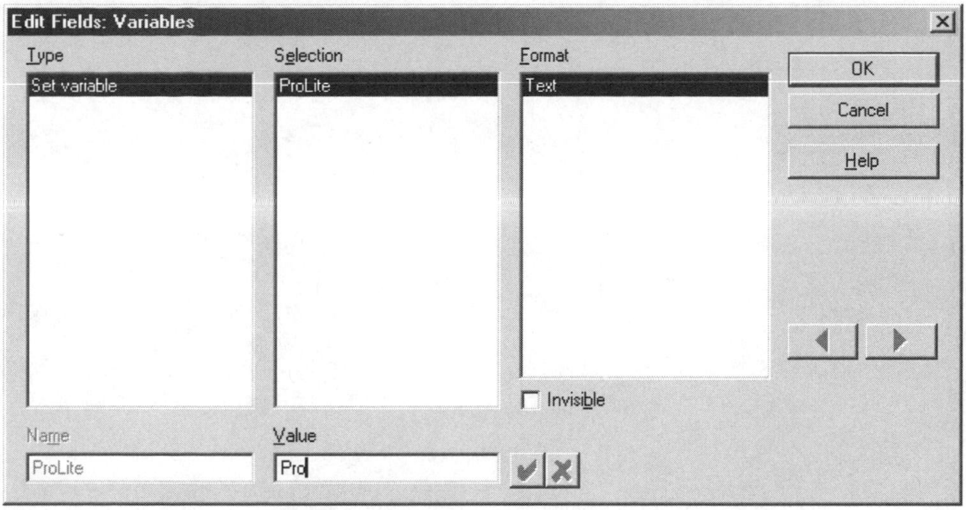

Figure 5-18. Changing the value of the variable

6

Tables of Contents, Indexes, and Bibliographies

This chapter describes how to use Writer's features for developing tables of contents, indexes, and bibliographies. Academic and technical writers, and anyone who produces long or complex documents often require one or more of these features.

Creating a Table of Contents

A table of contents is usually generated from text marked as headings (or other styles specified by the author) in the document. If generated within a master document, the table of contents covers all the linked subdocuments.

Creating a table of contents involves these steps:

1. Define the format and styles to be included in the table of contents.

2. Modify what the table of contents displays.

3. Generate or regenerate the table of contents.

Define the Format and Styles to Be Included in the Table of Contents

To define the format of the table of contents:

1. Place the insertion point where you want the table of contents to appear.

2. Click Insert > Indexes and Tables > Indexes and Tables.

3. On the Insert Index/Table dialog (Figure 6-1), type the heading for your table of contents in the Title box, and choose Table of Contents in the Type list.

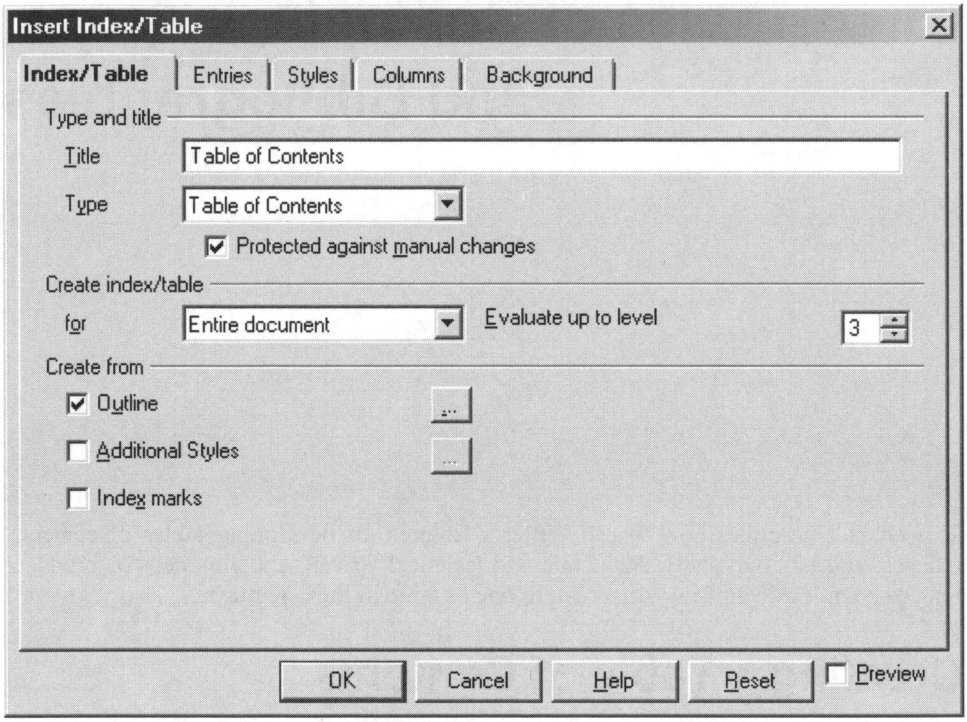

Figure 6-1. Defining the format of a table of contents

Choose whether to protect the table of contents against manual changes. Note that if you do make manual changes to a table of contents, and then update the table of contents, all of your manual changes will be lost.

Choose whether to create a table of contents for the entire document or for a single chapter in a document that has multiple chapters. (A "chapter" in Writer usually starts with a Heading 1, so a single-chapter table of contents would include entries from the current Heading 1 until just before the next Heading 1.)

In the Evaluate up to level box, choose the number of heading levels to be included in the table of contents. For example, you may use five heading levels in the document but only want the first three levels in the table of contents.

To preview what the resulting table of contents will look like, select the Preview checkbox at the bottom right of the dialog. The window will expand to include a preview pane on the left (not shown here).

4. To change which styles are included in the table of contents, select Additional Styles and click the [...] button. On the Assign Styles dialog (Figure 6-2), select the style you want to add, then click the >> button to move that style name to the required level.

In this example, we have used Heading 9 for the Appendix title (equivalent to a Chapter title, but in a different number sequence), so we want the Appendix titles to appear at the same level (1) in the table of contents as the Chapter titles.

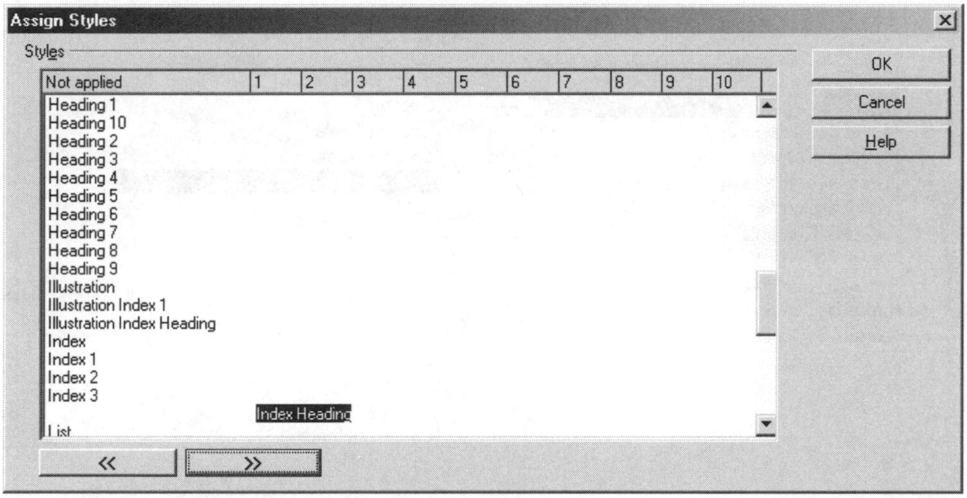

Figure 6-2. Assigning a style to a table of contents level

5. Click OK to return to the Insert Index/Table dialog (Figure 6-1), then click OK again to generate and insert the table of contents.

Modify What the Table of Contents Displays

You can modify the presentation of the generated table of contents in several ways:

- Define styles for table of contents levels, as described in Chapter 4. In most cases, you'll want to define the Contents styles to look the way you want, rather than defining new styles.
- Assign paragraph styles to table of contents levels (see page 120)
- Specify the content and presentation of table of contents levels (see page 121)
- Create hyperlinks from page numbers (see page 122)
- Assign character styles to components of table of contents entries (see page 123)
- Change the appearance of hyperlinks in the table of contents (see page 124)

Assign paragraph styles to table of contents levels

The usual assignment is: Level 1 entries are formatted by the Contents 1 paragraph style, Level 2 entries by the Contents 2 style, and so on. You can change these style assignments.

To assign a style to a table of contents level:

1.   On the Styles tab of the Insert Index/Table dialog (Figure 6-3), select the table of contents level in the left-hand list.

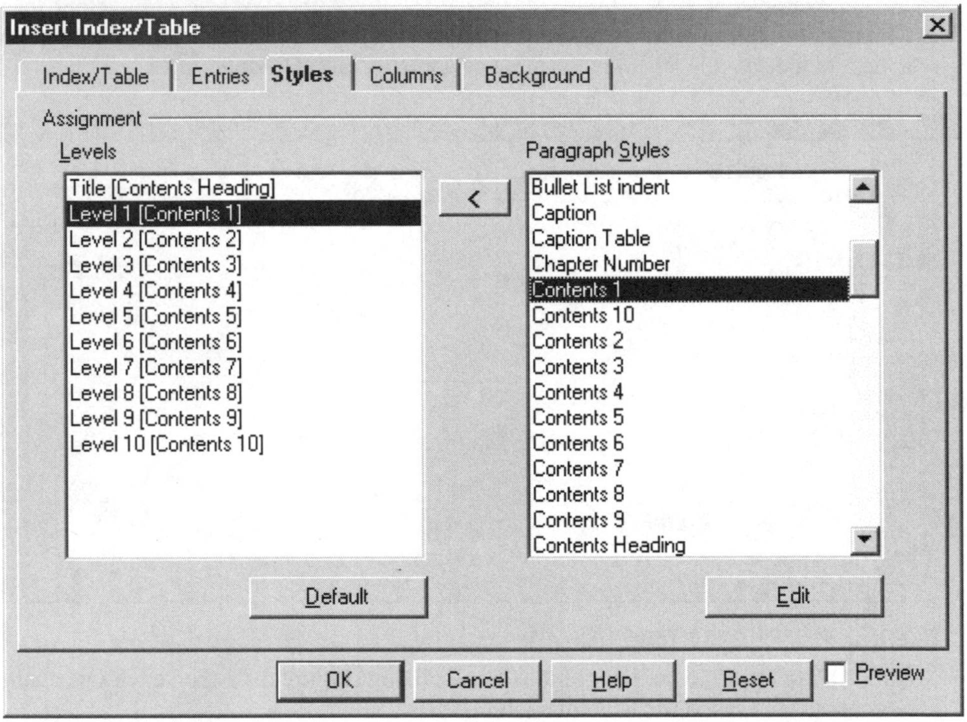

Figure 6-3. Assigning styles to table of contents levels

2.   Select the style in the right-hand list. If the selected style is not available to be assigned to a table of contents level, the arrow button between the lists is not active.

3.   If the arrow button is active, click it. The style listed for the table of contents level will change in the left-hand list.

4.   Continue to the next section, or click OK to save your changes and insert the table of contents.

Specify the content and presentation of table of contents levels

You can change the content and presentation of the table of contents entries on the Entries tab of the Insert Index/Table dialog (Figure 6-6). For example, you might want one or more levels to not include page numbers, or you might want the page numbers or the text to be hyperlinked to the corresponding headings in the document.

You can also assign character styles to components of entries and change the fill character and tab stop position.

To include chapter numbers with page numbers:

1.   On the Entries tab of the Insert Index/Table dialog (Figure 6-4), select 1 in the Level list.

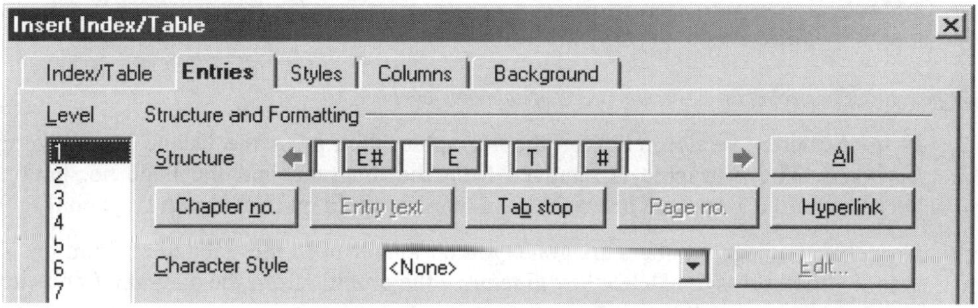

Figure 6-4. The Entries tab of the Insert Index/Table dialog

2.   In the Structure section, click in the space between the T (tab) and the # (page number), then click the Chapter no. button. A new graphic labelled E# (for Chapter number) will appear between the T and the #. (The E graphic is for entry text.)

3.   Click in the space between the E# and the # and type the required separator—for example, a hyphen. The Structure section will now look like Figure 6-5.

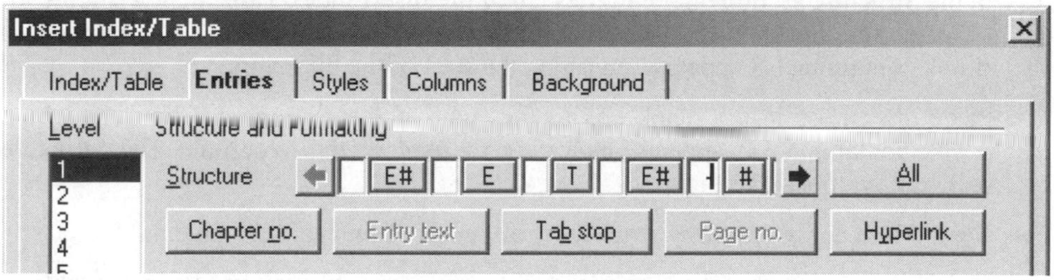

Figure 6-5. Including the chapter number with the page number

4.   Click the All button to apply this change to all levels of the table of contents.

5.   Continue to the next section, or click OK to save your changes and insert the table of contents.

Suppose you want Heading 4 entries to have no page numbers shown in the table of contents. To remove page numbers from a heading level:

1. On the Entries tab of the Insert Index/Table dialog (Figure 6-6), select 4 in the Level list.

Figure 6-6. Specifying the content of table of contents levels

2. In the Structure section, click on the # graphic, then press the Delete key on your keyboard. The # graphic is removed from the diagram, and the Page no. button becomes active. (You can insert the page number again by clicking on Page no..)

3. Now that the page numbers are gone, you no longer need the Tab, so click on the T graphic, then press the Delete key to remove the graphic from the diagram. (You can insert the Tab again by clicking on Tab stop.)

4. Continue to the next section, or click OK to save your changes and insert the table of contents.

Create hyperlinks from page numbers

Suppose you want page numbers at all levels to be hyperlinks.

1. In the Structure section on the Entries tab of the Insert Index/Table dialog (Figure 6-6), place the cursor in the blank box to the left of the # graphic. Click Hyperlink. A box containing LS appears, indicating the start of the hyperlink.

2. Place the cursor in the blank box to the right of the # graphic. Click Hyperlink. A box containing LE appears, indicating the end of the hyperlink. The Structure section now looks like Figure 6-7.

3. Click All to apply this entry structure to all levels of the table of contents.

4. Continue to the next section, or click OK to save your changes and insert the table of contents.

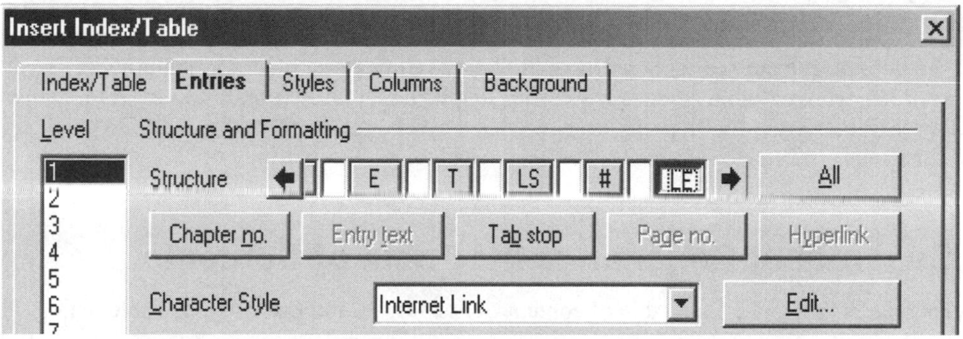

Figure 6-7. Table of contents structure after inserting hyperlinks

Assign character styles to components of table of contents entries

You can assign a character style to each component of a table of contents entry if you want to override the style set for the entry as a whole. For example, you might want the page number in a different font or type size. Click on each element in the structure diagram and select the character style from the list.

You can also change the fill character and tab stop position.

1. Click on the T in the structure diagram. Two extra fields appear below Character style, as shown in Figure 6-8.

2. To change the fill character, choose from the list or type a character of your own choice in the box.

3. To change the tab stop position, first deselect Align right to activate the position setting. Click OK to save your settings and insert the table of contents.

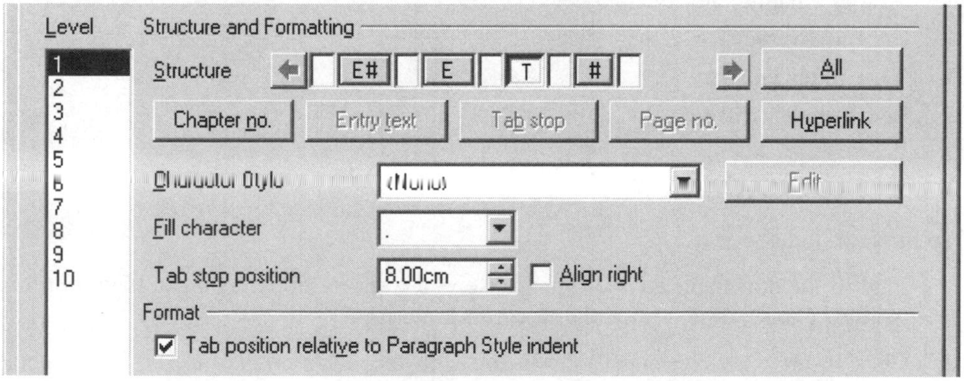

Figure 6-8. Changing the fill character and tab stop position for a table of contents entry

Note   Tabs defined in the styles for table of contents entries are ignored by OOo when inserting the table of contents. You must specify the tab stops in the Insert Index/Table dialog, as described in this section.

Change the appearance of hyperlinks in the table of contents

The default appearance of hyperlinks in OOo documents is blue and underlined. If you want hyperlinked table of contents entries displayed as normal text, you need to change the character style for hyperlinks. Note that any change to this style will affect all the hyperlinks in your document. Refer to "Change Formatting of Hyperlinks in a Document" on page 194 for instructions.

Generate or Regenerate the Table of Contents

To generate and insert the table of contents, click OK on the Insert Index/Table dialog.

To regenerate (update) an existing table of contents, position the cursor in the ToC, right-click, and click Update Index/Table on the pop-up menu.

To change the formatting of a ToC, position the cursor in the ToC, right-click, and then click Edit Index/Table on the pop-up menu. This action displays the Insert Index/Table dialog, where you can make any necessary changes and then click OK to regenerate the table of contents.

Creating an Alphabetic Index

An alphabetic index is generated from index entries that you insert into the relevant pages of the document, either manually or by using a concordance file.

Creating an index includes these steps:

1. Insert the index entries.
2. Define the format of the index.
3. Modify what the index displays.
4. Generate or regenerate the index.
5. View index entries.
6. Edit an index entry.

Insert the Index Entries

To insert an index entry:

1. Find in the document the word or phrase you want to index. You can highlight this word or phrase, or just place the cursor in front of it.
2. Click Insert > Indexes and Tables > Entry, or long-click on the Insert icon and click Insert Index Marker, as shown in Figure 6-9.
3. On the Insert Index Entry dialog (Figure 6-10), the word or phrase you highlighted is shown in the Entry box. Type or make your selections, then click Insert. The illustration shows an entry marked as a main entry. See page 125 for more information about the fields on this dialog.

Figure 6-9. Choosing Insert Index Marker from the Insert menu

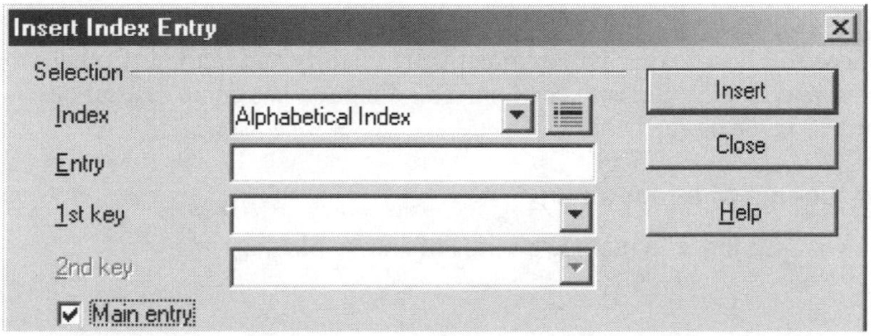

Figure 6-10. Inserting a main index entry using the Insert Index Entry dialog

4. You can leave this dialog open and continue to insert other index entries. Click in the document, select another word or phrase to be indexed, then click on the dialog, make any changes, and click Insert.

5. When you have finished inserting index entries, click Close.

Tip Be careful not to include trailing spaces, or you'll end up with different keys or entries when you want them to be combined in the index.

Fields on the Insert Index Entry dialog

Index
In addition to creating entries for alphabetic indexes, you can use this dialog to create extra entries for a table of contents or entries for user-defined indexes or lists of almost anything. For example, you might want an index containing only the scientific names of species mentioned in the text, and a separate index containing only the common names of species.

1st key
A "key" is a level-1 index entry that has no associated page number and several subentries (level 2) that do have page numbers. Keys are useful ways of grouping related topics. See "Example of the use of an index key" below.

2nd key
You can have a three-level index, where some of the level-1 keys have level-2 entries that are also keys (without page numbers). This degree of index complexity is not often necessary.

Main entry
When the same term is indexed on several pages, often one of those pages has more important or detailed information on that topic, so it is the main entry. Other entries may be of less detail or importance. The online help says you can make the page number for the main, or most important, entry stand out by selecting this checkbox and then defining the character style for the page number of a main index entry to be bold, for example. I've been unable to get this to work.

Apply to all similar texts
If you check this box, Writer will automatically identify and mark any other word or phrase that matches the current selection. This function has some restrictions, which are described in the online help.

Example of the use of an index key

Let's say you want the index to include a series of entries like this:

index
   creating 5
   editing 6
   entries, marking 4

In this example, the key is the term *index* and the entries are *creating*, *editing*, and the inverted phrase *entries, marking*. To insert this index entry:

1. Go to the location of one of the topics; in this case it might be written in the text as *marking entries*. Highlight the phrase *marking entries*, or position the cursor just before this phrase.

2. Click Insert > Indexes and Tables > Entry or long-click the Insert icon and click Insert Index Marker, as shown in Figure 6-9.

3. On the Insert Index Entry dialog (Figure 6-11), type "entries, marking" in the Entry box and "index" in the 1st key box. Click Insert.

4. Repeat for the other entries.

Figure 6-11. Inserting an index entry associated with a key

Define the Format of the Index

You can have a lot of control over the appearance (format) and contents of the index. To define the format of the index:

1. Place the insertion point where you want the index to appear.

2. Click Insert > Indexes and Tables > Indexes and Tables.

3. On the Index/Table tab of the Insert Index/Table dialog (Figure 6-12), type the heading for your index in the Title box, and choose Alphabetic Index in the Type list. Choose whether to protect the index against manual changes. Note that if you do make manual changes to an index, and then update the index, all of your manual changes will be lost.

   Choose whether to create an index for the entire document or for a single chapter in a document that has multiple chapters. (A "chapter" in Writer usually starts with a Heading 1, so a single-chapter index would include entries from the current Heading 1 until just before the next Heading 1.)

   To preview what the resulting index will look like, select the Preview checkbox at the bottom right of the dialog. The window will expand to include a preview pane on the left (not shown here).

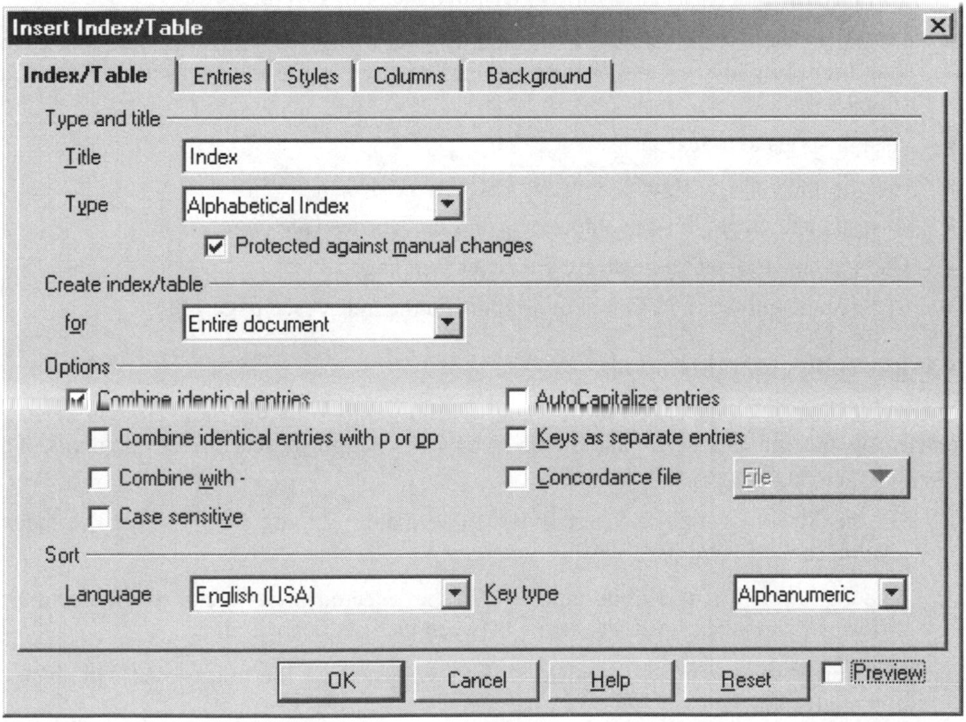

Figure 6-12. Defining the format of an alphabetic index

4. Make other selections to suit your requirements. For example:

> *Combine identical entries*
> Indexes for printed documents would normally combine identical entries; that is, the index would show one entry with several page numbers for each word or phrase indexed. You can choose some variations on how identical entries are formatted. For example, Combine with – produces a range (12–16).
>
> *AutoCapitalize entries*
> If you produce indexes in which each entry starts with a capital letter, you can save a lot of manual work by selecting this option. Writer will automatically capitalize the index entries, even if the highlighted word or phrase does not start with a capital letter.
>
> *Concordance file*
> A concordance file is a list of terms to be automatically indexed. Using a concordance file can speed up production of an index, but unless the words are very carefully selected and you edit the index afterwards, the resulting index can be full of entries for minor mentions of a term.

Modify What the Index Displays

You can modify the presentation of the generated index in several ways:

- Define styles for index levels. In most cases, you'll want to define the Index styles to look the way you want, rather than defining new styles. Define styles as described in Chapter 4.
- Assign styles to index levels.
- Specify the content of index entries (see page 129).
- Assign character styles to components of index entries (see page 131).
- Change tab stop position and fill character (see page 131).
- Specify the number and format of columns in the index (see page 131).

Assign styles to index levels

The usual assignment is: Index level 1 entries are formatted by the Index 1 style, level 2 entries by the Index 2 style, and so on. You can change these style assignments. To assign a style to an index level:

1. On the Styles tab of the Insert Index/Table dialog (Figure 6-13), select the index level in the left-hand list.

2. Select the style in the right-hand list. If the selected style is not available to be assigned to an index level, the arrow between the lists is not active.

3. If the arrow button is active, click it. The style listed for the index level will change in the left-hand list.

4. Click OK (not shown in picture) to save your changes and insert the index.

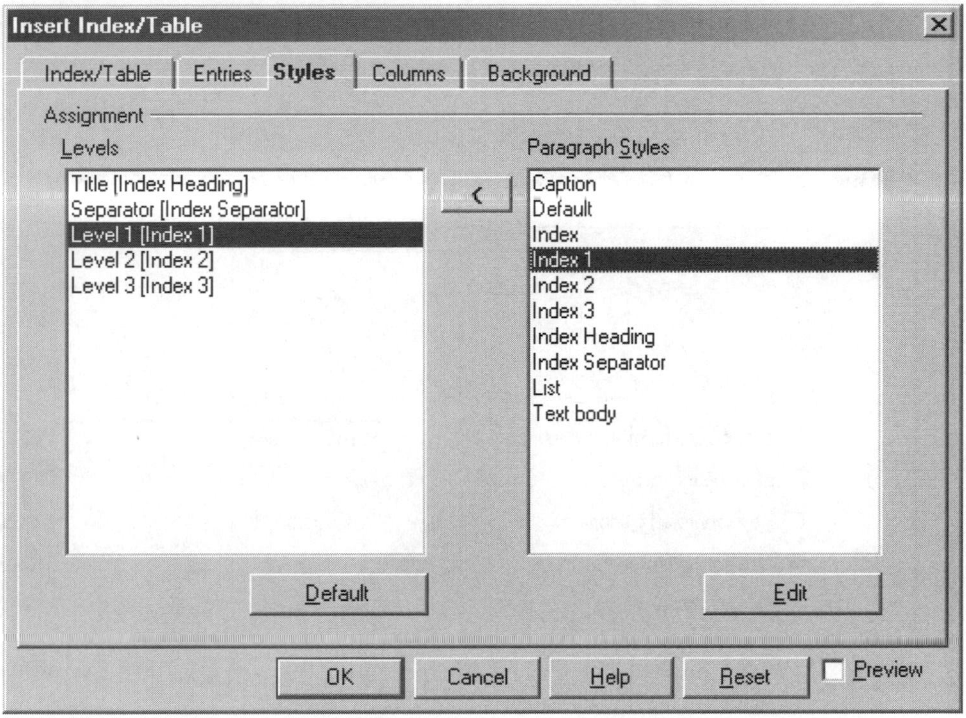

Figure 6-13. Assigning styles to index levels

Specify the content of index entries

You can change the usual content of the index entries on the Entries tab of the Insert Index/Table dialog (Figure 6-14). For example, you might not want any punctuation between the text of the entry and the page number; or you might want a tab, a comma and a space, just a space, or some other punctuation.

You can define different formatting for level-1, level-2, and level-3 index entries, but in most cases you'll probably want all levels formatted the same.

1. On the Entries tab of the Insert Index/Table dialog (Figure 6-14), look at the graphic in the Structure section, which shows E (entry text), T (tab stop), and # (page number).

    - To remove the tab stop, click once on the T, and then press Delete on your keyboard.

    - To insert a comma and a space between the entry and the page number, click once on the blank space after the E and type a comma and a space.

    - You cannot insert hyperlink markers for an index like you can for a table of contents.

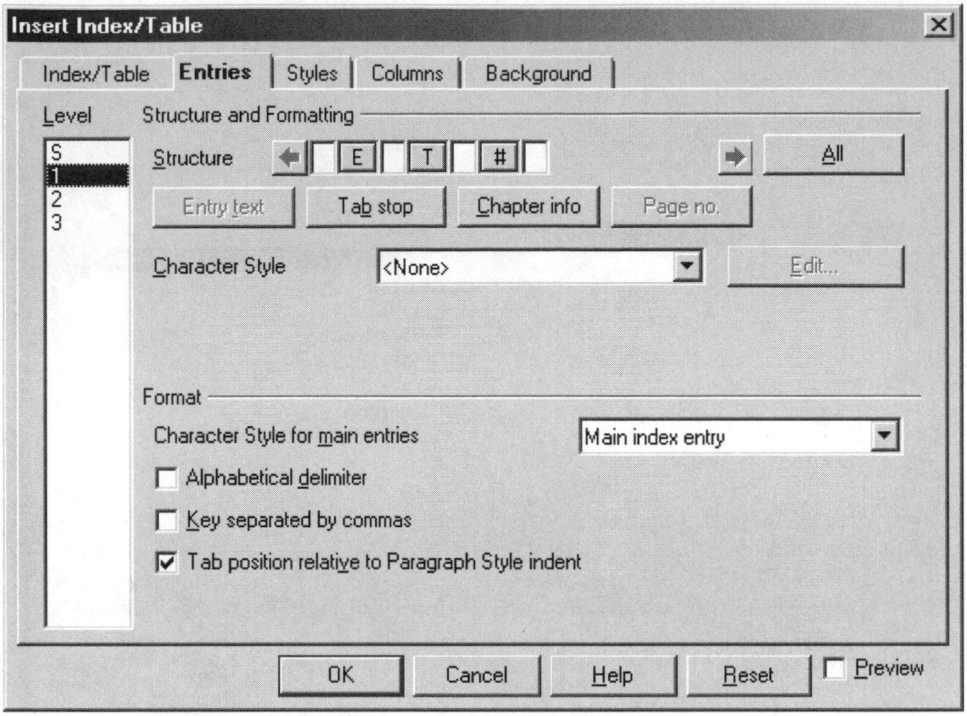

Figure 6-14. Defining the content and formatting of the index entries

2. Are you numbering by chapter? If so, you probably want the chapter number and a dash or other punctuation to appear before the page number. Click on the blank space before the # in the graphic and click the Chapter info button. CI appears in the space, and another blank space appears between CI and #. Type a hyphen in that space. (See Figure 6-15.)

    Click on the CI graphic to display the Chapter entry field, where you can choose what information to include; usually this will be the chapter number without any text, so you would select Number range only.

    In the Format section of this tab, you can specify a character style for the page numbers of main index entries, and you can choose whether to include alphabetic delimiters (also known as "group separators" or "index headings")—the larger letters at the beginning of each group of index entries starting with that letter.

3. Click OK to save your changes and insert the index.

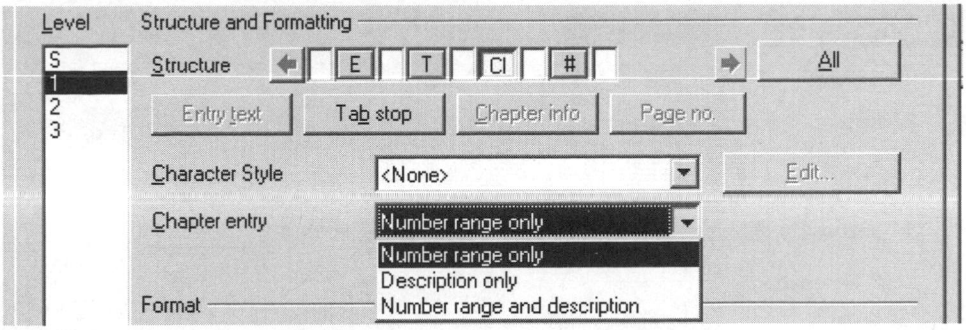

Figure 6-15. Inserting a chapter number before the page number in an index

Assign character styles to components of index entries

You can assign a character style to each component of an index entry if you want to override the style set for the entry as a whole. For example, you might want the page number in a different font or type size. Click on each element in the structure diagram and select the character style from the list.

Change tab stop position and fill character

You can also change the fill character (also known as a *leader*) and the tab stop position. Click on the T in the structure diagram. Two extra fields appear, similar to those shown in Figure 6-8. Choose the fill character from the list, or type a character of your own choice in the box. To change the tab stop position, first deselect Align right.

Note   Tabs defined in the styles for index entries are ignored by OOo when inserting the index. You must specify the tab stops in the Insert Index/Table dialog, as described in this section.

Specify the number and format of columns in the index

On the Columns tab of the Insert Index/Table dialog (Figure 6-16), choose the number of columns, their size and spacing, and whether they should be separated by a vertical line. Click OK to save your changes and insert the index.

Generate or Regenerate the Index

To generate and insert the index, click OK on the Insert Index/Table dialog.

To regenerate (update) an existing index, position the cursor in the index, right-click, and then click Update Index/Table on the pop-up menu.

To change the formatting of an index, position the cursor in the index, right-click, and then click Edit Index/Table on the pop-up menu. This action displays the Insert Index/Table dialog, where you can make any necessary changes. Click OK to regenerate the index.

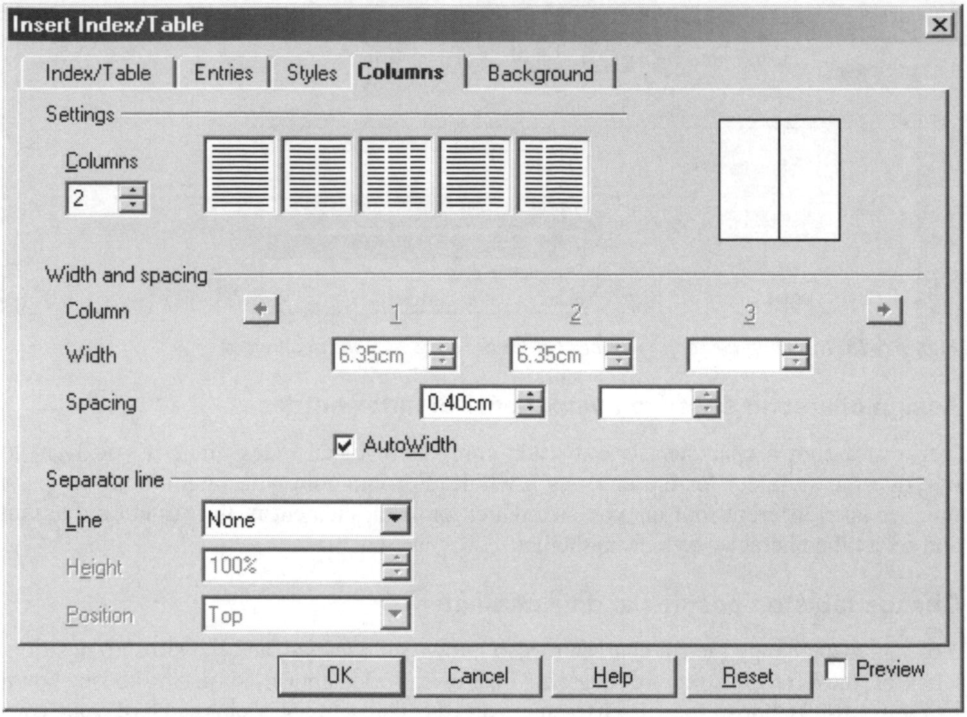

Figure 6-16. Specifying two columns for the index

View Index Entries

To view index entries:

1. Make sure Help Tips are active. (You can activate them from the Help menu.) Make sure highlighting of index entries is selected on the Tools > Options > Text Document > View dialog.

2. To view a specific index entry, hover the mouse pointer over the gray index marker in the text.

    To view all index entries, open one entry as described in "Edit an Index Entry," then use the arrow buttons to move between all of the entries.

If you have trouble finding the small gray markers, use this trick:

1. Click on the small dot at the bottom of the vertical scroll bar (marked "1" in Figure 6-17). The navigation toolbar appears.

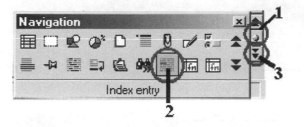

Figure 6-17. Navigation toolbar with Index entry selected

2. On the navigation toolbar, click on the Index Entry icon (2) to activate it.

3. Click the double down arrow (3) to jump to the next index entry. The cursor will be positioned correctly for viewing the entry in the pop-up tip, or for editing the entry as described below.

Unfortunately, you cannot search for a specific index entry.

Edit an Index Entry

When you review the index, you'll find some entries that should be changed, combined, deleted, or added.

To edit an index, you need to edit the individual index entries, not the generated index. Any changes you make to a generated index will be lost when the index is generated again. To prevent changing a generated index, protect it against manual changes (see Figure 6-12).

To edit an index entry:

1. Find the entry in the text of your document, place the cursor just to the right of the gray bar and click Edit > Index Entry (or right-click, and then click Index Entry on the pop-up menu).

2. On the Edit Index Entry dialog (Figure 6-18), make any changes you require.

3. You can move through the index entries by clicking on the arrow keys on this dialog. The highlighting in the document moves too, so you can see each index entry in context.

4. When you have finished editing index entries, click OK.

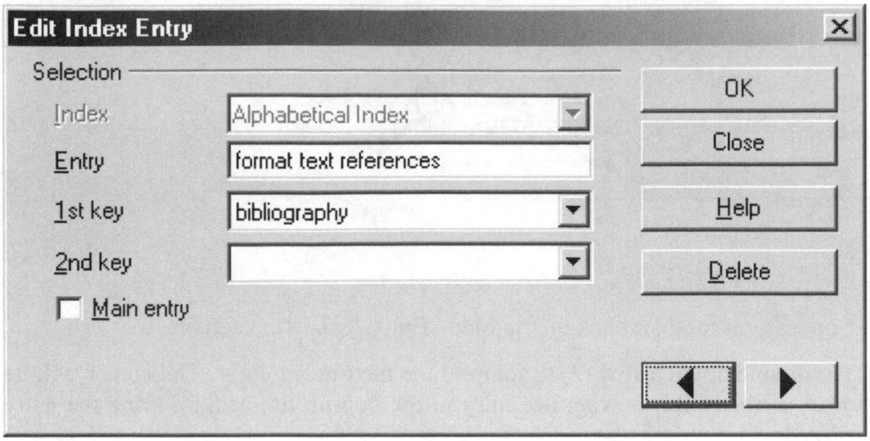

Figure 6-18. Editing an index entry

Creating Lists of Figures, Tables, Equations, and Other Items

You can create lists (indexes) of figures, tables, equations, and other items that are part of a numbered series defined in your document. Writer provides several built-in choices, and you can also define your own index.

1. On the Insert Index/Table dialog (Figure 6-19), select the required index type from the Type list.

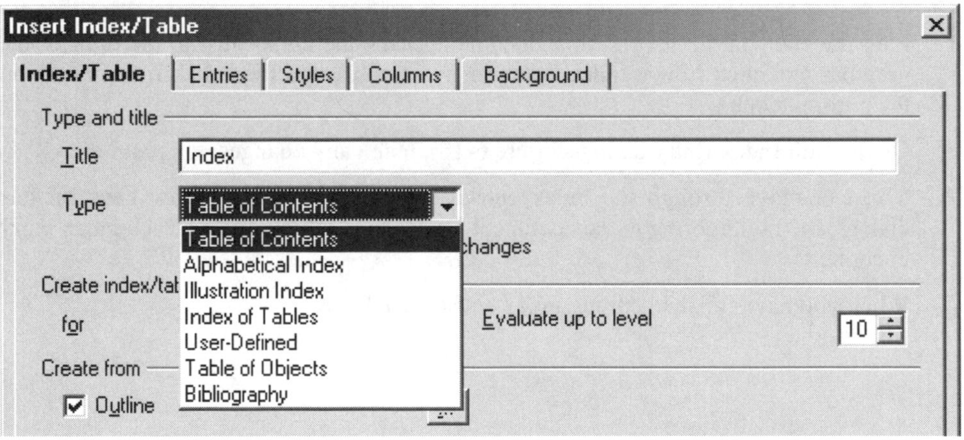

Figure 6-19. Choosing an index type

2. Different index types provide different choices at the bottom of the dialog. Illustration Index and Index of Tables have the choices shown in Figure 6-20.

Use the same methods to format and generate these lists as for alphabetic indexes. The choices on the various tabs of the dialog are similar to those for alphabetic indexes, so I won't describe them in detail.

See "Creating and Using Bibliographies" on page 135 for more information about the Bibliography type.

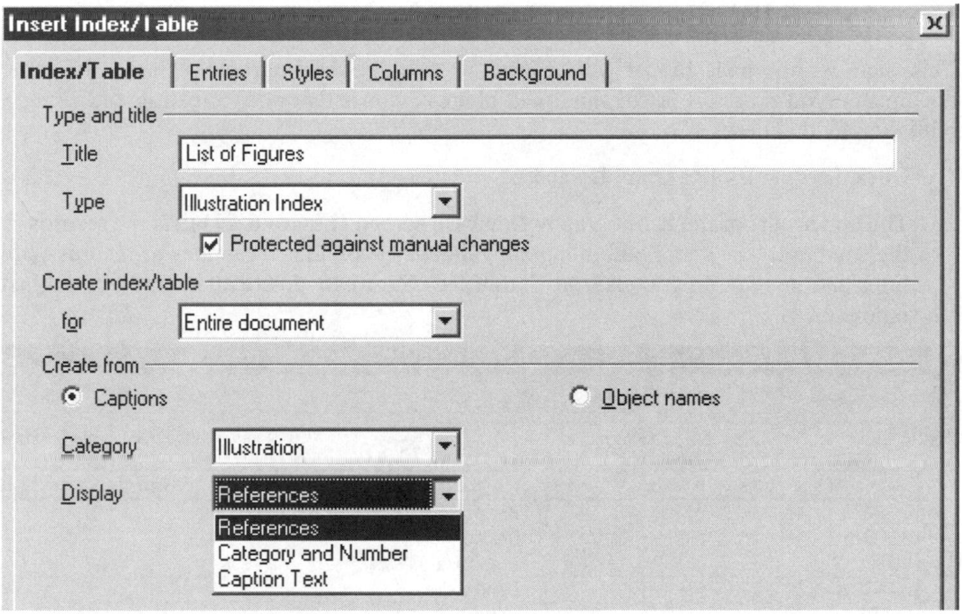

Figure 6-20. Inserting a list of figures

Creating and Using Bibliographies

A bibliography is generated from bibliographic entries that you insert into a bibliography database associated with the document or directly into the document itself. Creating a bibliography involves these steps:

1. Create a bibliographic database.

2. Create entries in the bibliographic database.

3. Change the fields in the bibliographic database.

4. Insert bibliographic references (citations) into text.

5. Define the format of references and the bibliography.

6. Generate or regenerate the bibliography.

Tip   You can use the techniques described in this section to create more than one database. You can also link other existing databases to OpenOffice.org and use them through the dialogs described here. Linking to other databases is not covered in this book.

Create a Bibliographic Database

This step is optional, but if you expect to use the bibliographic entries in other documents, you'll save a lot of time (and improve consistency) by creating and using a bibliography database.

1. Click Tools > Bibliography Database.

2. The upper part of the Bibliography Database screen (Figure 6-21) lists the records in the database. The supplied bibliography database contains a number of records with information regarding books on StarOffice. You can delete these records or just ignore them.

Bibliography Database

File   Edit   Insert   Tools   Window   Help

Table biblio   ▼   Search Key [   ]   ⟱ ▽ ⤳ Column Arrangement Data Source

	Identifier	Type	Address	Annote	Author	Booktitle	Chapter	Edition	Editor	H
▷	BOR02a	1			Borges, Ma					
	BOR02b	1			Borges, Ma					
	BUS00	1			Busch, Da					
	DAN00	1			Dandenell,					
	FAC01	1			Facundo A					
	GAE02	1			Gäbler, Re					
	HAB00	1			Habraken,					
	JON00	1			Jones, Floy					
	MOL02	1			Molla, Rica					
	RAP00	1			Rapion, Ar					
	RIN01	1			Rinne , Ka					
	WAR01a	1			Warner, N.					
	WAR01b	1			Warner, N.					
✳										

Record 1   of   13 |◄ ◄ ► ►| ✳   ◄

Figure 6-21. Records in the bibliography database (you can scroll to the right to see many more fields)

3. The lower part of the Bibliography Database screen (Figure 6-22) contains many entry fields. The first field, labeled Short name, is the same as the field labeled Identifier in the list of records.

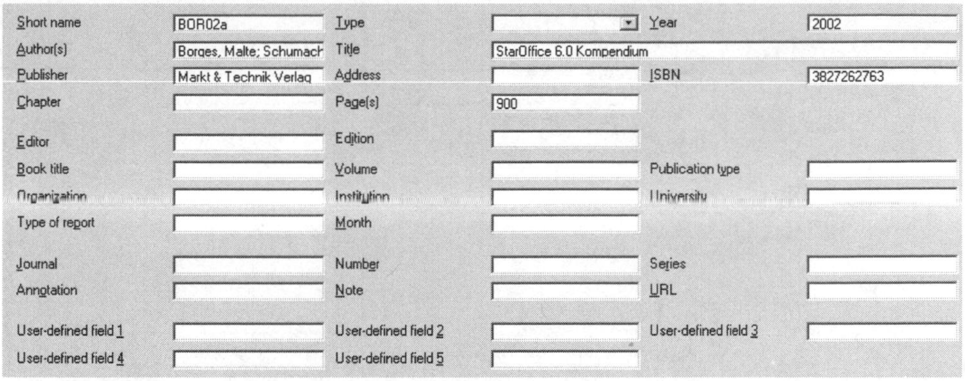

Figure 6-22. The entry fields for the bibliography database

Create Entries in the Bibliographic Database

1. To enter a new record into the Bibliography Database, type a unique identifier in the Short Name field at the bottom of the screen, then fill in any other fields that are appropriate for the item. Press Tab to move from one field to the next. As you fill in the fields in the bottom part of the screen, the information will appear in the new record in the top part of the screen.

2. To finish entering a record, click in the next blank record in the list at the top of the screen.

Tip   If you plan to use the [Name, date] style for references within the text, be sure to use that style for the Short Name. If you number references within the text (for example, [1]), you can use any short-name convention you prefer.

Change the Fields in the Bibliographic Database

If some of the fields in the bibliographic database are too short, you can change the size of those fields.

1. Open any document and press F4 to display the data sources window (Figure 6-23) at the top of the screen.

2. In the directory tree on the left-hand side of the data sources window, click the + signs until you see Tables > Biblio.

3. Right-click on Biblio and choose Edit Table from the pop-up menu. The Table Design dialog (Figure 6-25) is displayed.

4. Select a field in the list at the top of the dialog. The properties of the selected field appear in the boxes at the bottom of the dialog.

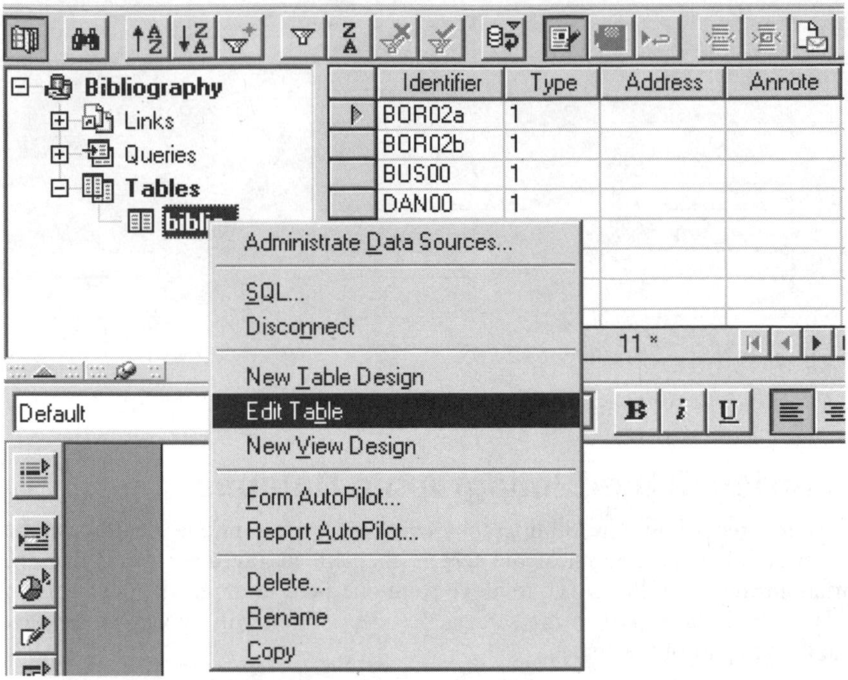

Figure 6-23. Preparing to edit the fields in the bibliographic database

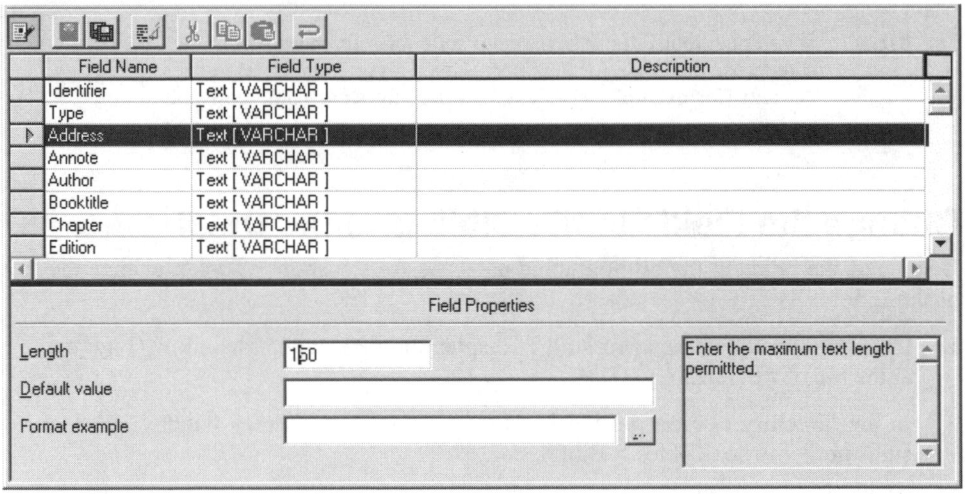

Figure 6-24. Editing a field in the Table Design window

5. Change the field properties as needed.

6. When you close the Table Design window, a message will pop up, asking if you want to save your changes. Click Yes.

Insert Bibliographic References (Citations) into Text

To insert bibliographic references (citations) into the text of your document:

1. Position the cursor where the reference is to appear. Click Insert > Indexes and Tables > Bibliographic Entry.

2. On the Insert Bibliography Entry dialog (Figure 6-25), choose From bibliography database and select the short name from the drop-down list. When you select a short name, the name of the author and the title of the work appear in the dialog (if you have included these in the database).

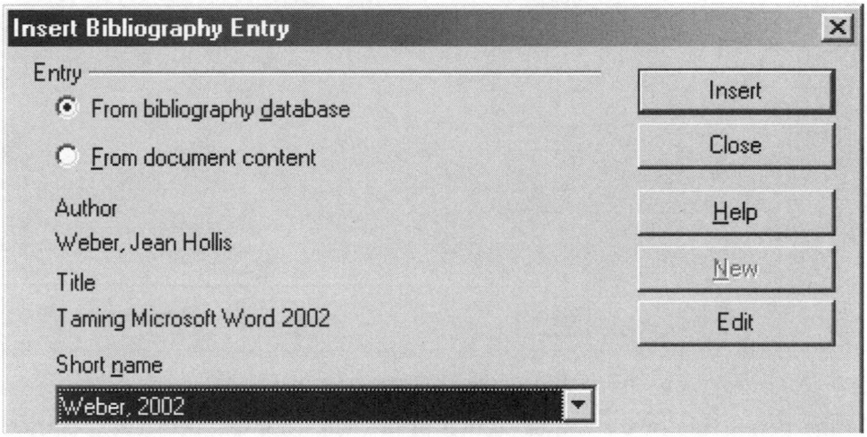

Figure 6-25. Inserting a bibliographic reference (citation) into a text document

3. Click Insert. The format of the inserted reference is as defined for the bibliography; see "Define the Format of References and the Bibliography" for more information.

Tip   Unless you are sure you will not be using a particular reference in other documents, do *not* use From document content or click the New button in the Insert Bibliography Entry dialog. Instead, define new entries in the Bibliography Database and refer to them from here.

Define the Format of References and the Bibliography

To define the format of the text references and the generated bibliography:

1. Position the insertion point where you want the generated bibliography to appear.

2. Click Insert > Indexes and Tables > Indexes and Tables.

3. On the Index/Table tab of the Insert Index/Table dialog (Figure 6-26), choose Bibliography from the Type list.

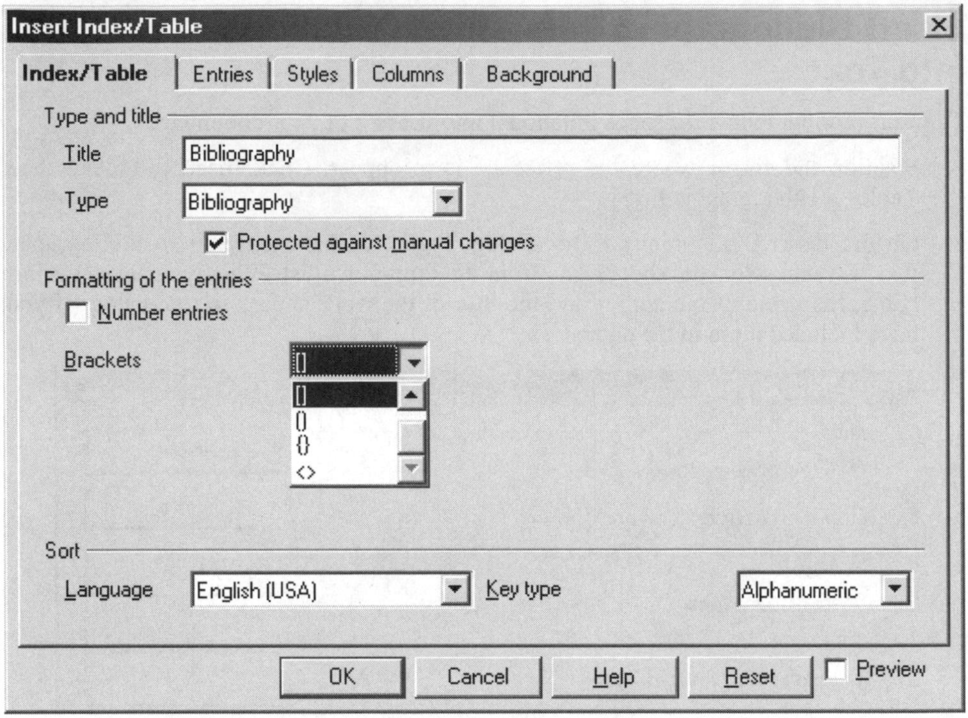

Figure 6-26. Formatting the bibliographic entries that appear in the text

4. In the Formatting of the entries section of this tab, choose whether text entries will be numbered (for example, [1]), and what character to use for the brackets. If you do not select the Number entries checkbox, then text citations will use the short names defined for the records in the Bibliography database.

5. The Entries tab of the Insert Index/Table dialog (Figure 6-27) provides many choices for formatting the entries in the generated bibliography itself, to match the requirements of the referencing system you are using.

    You'll need to go through each type of reference (for example, article or book) and set up the appropriate sequence and presentation. This works in a manner similar to defining the structure of an index or table of contents entry. The choices available depend on the fields defined in the bibliographic database for each type of entry.

Tip   You can define the format of references and the bibliography before you insert any bibliographic references into the text, and then update the bibliography later.

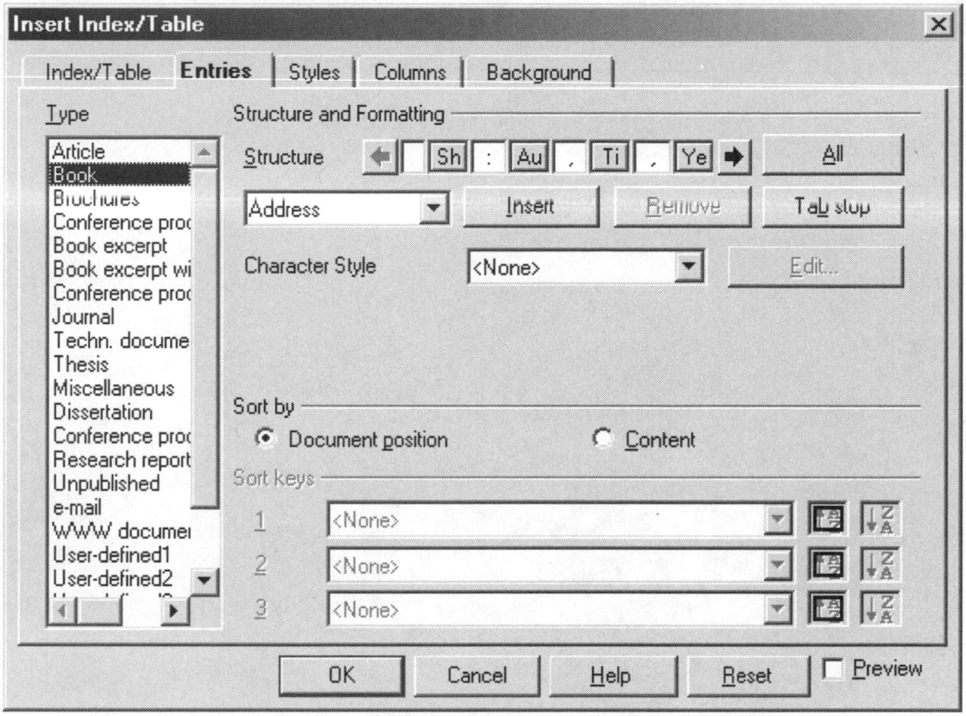

Figure 6-27. Formatting the entries in the generated bibliography

Generate or Regenerate the Bibliography

To generate and insert a bibliography, click OK on the Insert Index/Table dialog.

To edit and regenerate a bibliography, position the cursor in the bibliography, right-click, and then click Edit Index/Table on the pop-up menu. This action displays the Insert Index/Table dialog, where you can make any necessary changes and then click OK to regenerate the bibliography.

To update a bibliography (because you have added new text references to the document) position the cursor in the bibliography, right-click, and then click Update Index/Table from the pop-up menu.

7

Working with Large or Complex Documents

This chapter describes some techniques to help you use Writer effectively when working with large or complex documents—for example, reports or books containing multiple chapters. Many of these techniques build on the use of fields, discussed in Chapter 5.

Strategies for Working with Large or Complex Documents

When working with large or complex documents, you have two choices: keep the entire document in one large file, or break it up into a series of smaller files. Each approach has its advantages and disadvantages. You can often combine smaller files into one large file at the end of the project and thus get the benefits of both approaches.

Some questions to consider when deciding whether to use one file or several:

- Do different people (writers, editors, or reviewers) work on different parts of the document, or are the chapters edited or reviewed separately? Using separate files can make team writing easier.

- Have you had problems with Writer working slowly, saving too frequently, or crashing when you are editing a large, complex document? Using separate, smaller files might solve those problems.

- Do you use material that is common to several documents—for example, legal notices?

Inserting or Linking to Other Files

If you use the same material in more than one document, you'll want to maintain it in one place rather than make changes to several different files. For example, your company may have a standard legal statement that needs to go in each document, or you may be compiling contracts with standard parts in them.

You can include one document (B) in another document (A) in two ways:

- Use Insert > File to insert the contents of document B, which then become part of document A. This technique is similar to copying and pasting the contents of document B, and breaks any connection between the two documents. If you make changes to document B, those changes will not show up in document A.

- Use Insert > Section and link document A to document B, as described below.

If the linked file (document B) is itself divided into sections, you can choose to include a selected section in document A. For example, you can create a file containing all the standard parts of a contract, each in a separate section, and then choose which sections to include in document A, in which order.

Inserting a section linked to a file

1. Place the insertion point where you want the included material to appear.

2. Click Insert > Section. On the Insert Section dialog (Figure 7-1), give the new section a meaningful name, select the Link checkbox, and type the name of document B in the File name box (or click the Browse button and select the file).

    If the included file is divided into sections, you can choose which section to include. At this point you'll discover why it's important to give sections meaningful names instead of leaving them as the default Section 1, Section 2, and so on.

    You'll probably want to select the Protect checkbox under Write protection, and you may want to password-protect the section. If you click on the With password checkbox (or on the Browse button next to it), an Enter Password dialog pops up. Note that passwords must have at least five characters.

3. Click Insert. The contents of the file will be visible in document A.

| Tip | Links will update if you have Always Update Links when Loading selected in Options > Text Document > General (Figure 1-13 on page 13), or if you have On request selected and then answer Yes when prompted after opening the file. |

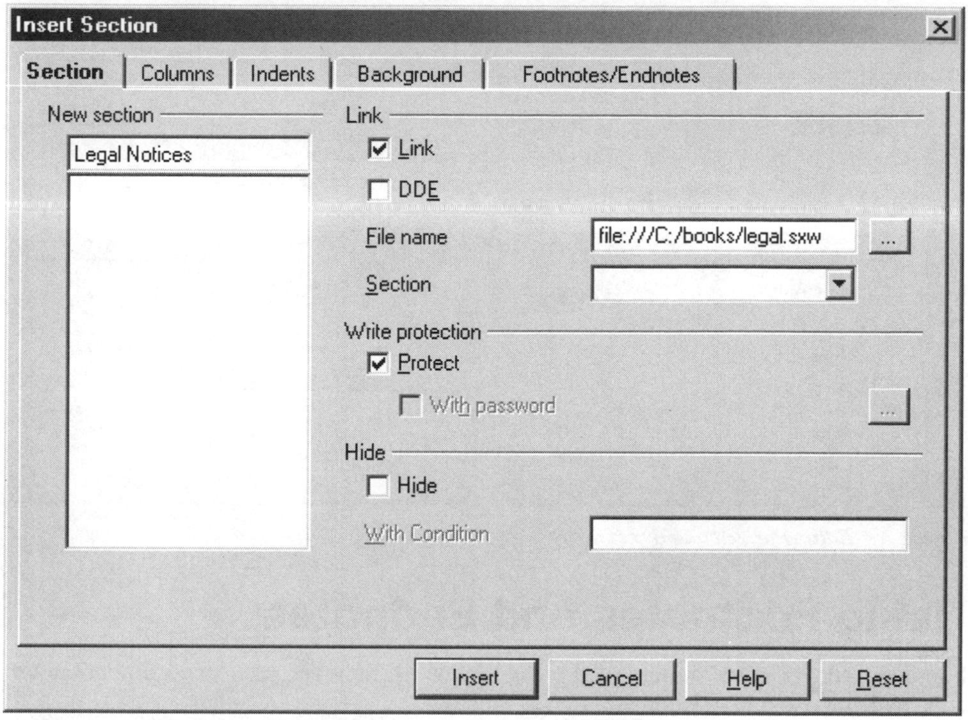

Figure 7-1. Inserting a linked and write-protected section

Removing a section

Removing a section does not remove the *contents* of the section. Instead, the contents become part of the document itself.

To remove a section from your document:

1. Place the cursor in the section.

2. Click Format > Sections.

3. On the Edit Section dialog (Figure 7-2), select the section from the list and click Undo. If the section is password-protected, a dialog will pop up for you to enter the password.

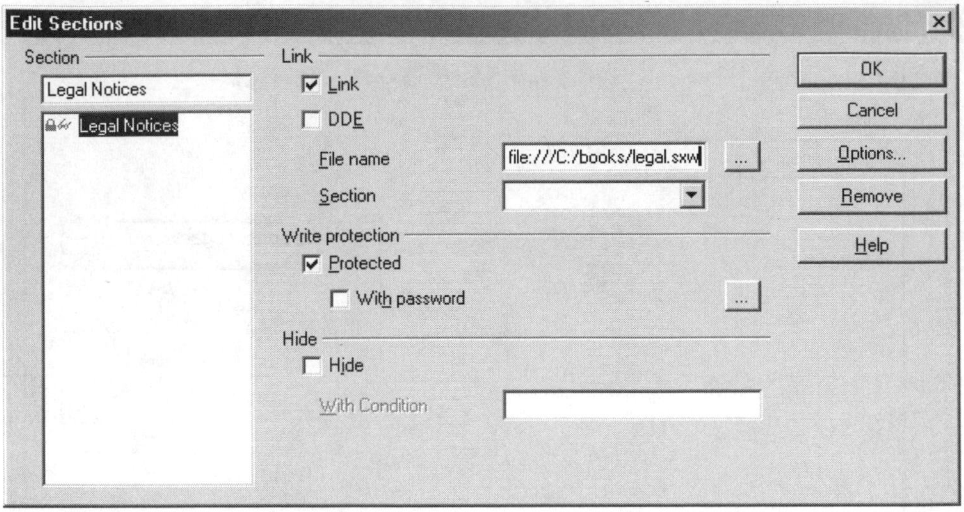

Figure 7-2. Editing or deleting a section

Using Footnotes and Endnotes

Footnotes appear at the bottom of the page on which they are referenced. Endnotes are collected at the end of a document.

To work effectively with footnotes and endnotes, you need to:

- Define the location of footnotes on the page
- Define the formatting of footnotes
- Insert footnotes

Define the Location of Footnotes on the Page

Define the location of footnotes in the page style. If you use more than one page style in your document, be sure to define the footnote location in each page style.

1. Right-click anywhere on the page, and then click Page Style from the pop-up menu.

2. On the Page Style dialog, choose the Footnote tab (Figure 7-3).

3. The settings on this tab should be self-explanatory, so I won't go through them in detail. Choose settings as required, then click OK.

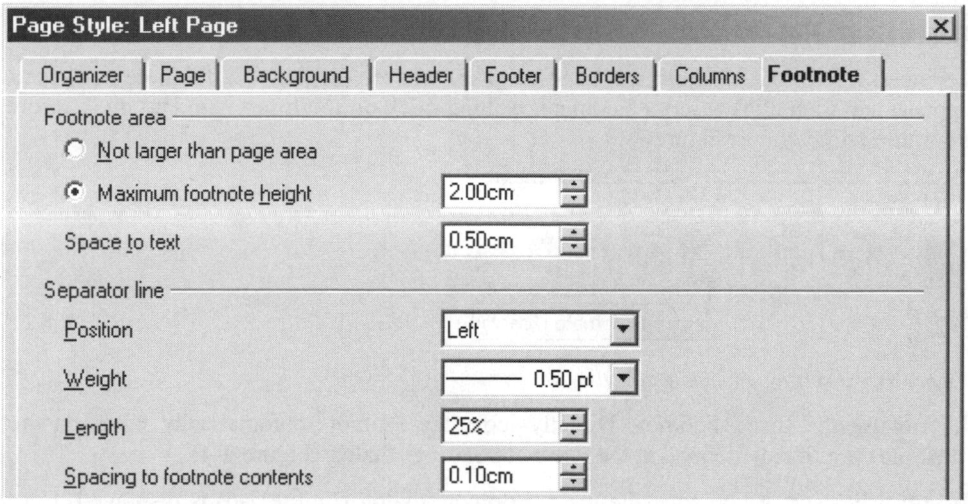

Figure 7-3. Defining how footnotes are displayed on the page

Define the Formatting of Footnotes

To format the footnotes themselves, click Tools > Footnotes. On the Footnote Settings dialog (Figure 7-4), choose settings as required. The Endnotes tab has similar choices.

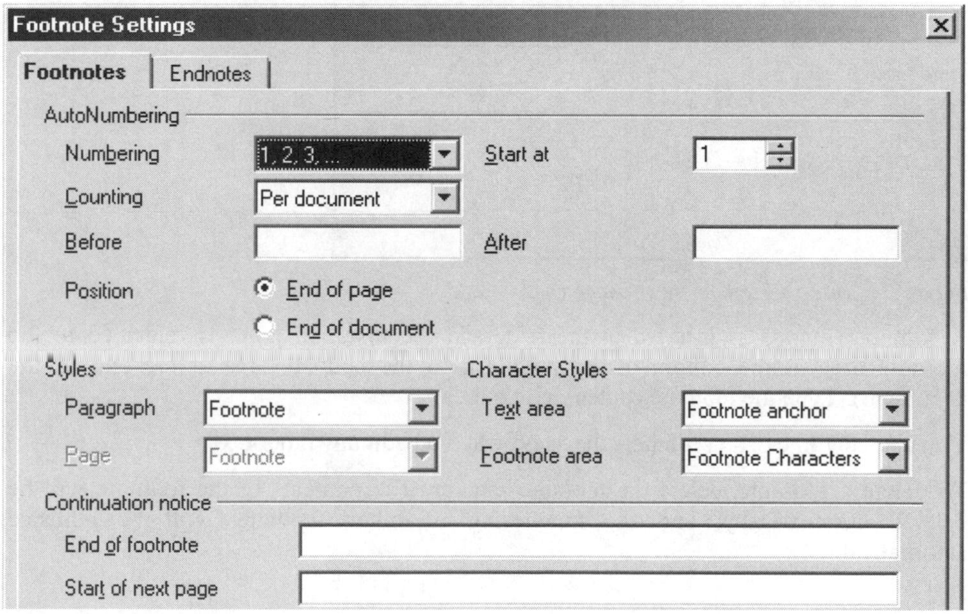

Figure 7-4. Defining footnote formatting

Insert Footnotes

To insert a footnote, position the insertion point where you want the footnote marker to appear, and then click Insert > Footnote, or long-click on the Insert icon and click Insert Footnote Directly (see Figure 7-5).

Figure 7-5. Inserting a footnote directly

If you use the Insert Footnote Directly icon, the footnote automatically takes on the attributes previously defined in the Footnote Settings dialog (Figure 7-4).

If you use Insert > Footnote, the Insert Footnote dialog (Figure 7-6) is displayed. Here you can choose whether to use the automatic numbering sequence specified in the footnote settings, and whether to insert the item as a footnote or endnote.

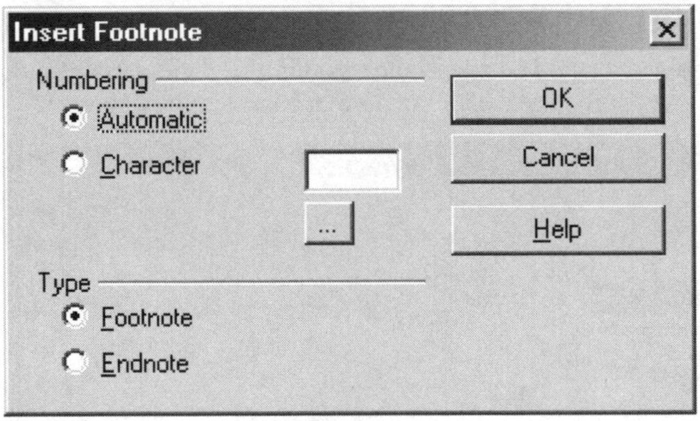

Figure 7-6. Inserting a footnote or endnote

A footnote marker is inserted in the text, and the insertion point is relocated to the footnote area at the bottom of the page (or to the endnote area at the end of the document). Type the footnote content in this area.

You can edit an existing footnote the same way you edit any other text.

To delete a footnote, delete the footnote marker. The contents of the footnote will be deleted automatically, and the numbering of other footnotes will be adjusted automatically.

Creating and Using Master Documents

Master documents are typically used for producing long documents such as a book, a thesis, or a long report, especially when graphics, spreadsheets, or other included material causes the file size to become quite large. Master documents are also used when different people are writing different chapters or other parts of the full document, so you don't need to share files.

Yes, master documents do work in Writer. However, their use is full of traps for inexperienced users. Until you become familiar with the traps and how to avoid (or work around) them, you may think that master documents are unreliable or difficult to use.

You can use several methods to create master documents. Each method has its advantages and disadvantages. Which method you choose depends on what you are trying to accomplish. Depending on the state of your document when you decide to create a master document, here are the three most common scenarios:

- You have one existing document (a "book") that you want to split into several subdocuments ("chapters") that will be controlled by the master document.

- You have several existing documents (chapters) that you want to combine into one book that will be controlled by the master document.

- You have no existing documents but intend to write a long book containing several chapters.

We will look at each of these scenarios in turn.

Split one document into a master document and subdocuments

Use this method when you have one existing document that you want to split into several subdocuments to be controlled by the master document. If the original document uses only the Default page style, is numbered sequentially from the first page, and uses the Heading 1 style to identify the start of each chapter, this method will work well.

Advantages: This method is quick and easy. Although cleanup work may be necessary, once you have done the cleanup, the document will behave itself.

Disadvantages: If the original document was complex, you may have major cleanup work to do because some formatting will be lost—for example, page styles, page breaks, restarted page numbering. If the original document included cross-references between chapters, you'll need to recreate them.

How to do it: Open the document and click File > Send > Create Master Document to split the document. You'll find that each of the subdocuments begins with a Heading 1 and the file names are all *maindocnameX.sxw*, where *X* is 1, 2, 3, and so on. If you have a Preface or other "chapter" starting with a Heading 1 before Chapter 1, the file names will not directly correspond to the chapter numbers.

Combine several documents into a master document

This method works best if all of the documents were created from the same template, but you can also use it if the documents were created from different templates. It can also be quite useful if you need to include one chapter in several different master documents. However, if the master documents use different styles, then you may find that changes you make to the individual chapters do not appear in the master document quite as you expect. This book does not attempt a full discussion of the tips and tricks to deal with this situation.

Use one of the techniques described in "Starting with no existing documents" to create a blank master document and insert the other documents as subdocuments of the master document.

Start with no existing documents

The ideal situation is to start with no existing documents because you can do everything correctly right from the beginning. Writer provides three ways to create a master document:

Method 1. Quick and easy, but not recommended

Method 2. Not too complicated, but with restrictions

Method 3. Complete control

In each case, you need to have a disciplined approach to make sure the master document works correctly and reliably. Each method below describes the steps to take. Be sure to do them in the order given.

Method 1. Quick and easy, but not recommended

Writer provides a quick and easy way to create a master document, but I do not recommend using it because the master document is not associated with a template, so changes to styles and formatting are difficult to apply reliably.

How to do it: Click File > New > Master Document.

Method 2. Not too complicated, but with restrictions

This method works well if you want to use sequential page numbering throughout the final document (not restarting at page 1 at any point), and each chapter starts with a Heading 1 on a new page. If you want to restart page numbering anywhere in the document, use Method 3.

How to do it: Follow the instructions in the next section ("Method 3. Complete control"), but don't put in the text sections between the subdocuments or try to change the page numbering.

Method 3. Complete control

This method gives you complete control over complex documents with several page styles or restarted page numbering. It's a bit more work to set up, but works reliably.

For complete control over your master documents follow these steps:

Step 1. Plan the project.

Step 2. Create a template.

Step 3. Create the master document and subdocuments from the same template.

Step 4. Insert subdocuments into the master document.

Step 5. Add a table of contents, bibliography, or index to the book.

Step 1. Plan the Project

Although you can make changes at most steps in this process, the more you can plan before you start, the less work you'll have to do to correct any problems later. Here are some things you need to plan:

- Parts of book or report required, and the page numbering to be used in different parts of the book. I will use as an example a book with these parts:

Part of book	Number of pages	Page-numbering style
Title (cover) page	1 page	No page number
Copyright page	1 page (back of title page)	No page number
Table of Contents	Unknown length	Start with i
Preface (Foreword)	2 pages	Continue from ToC
Chapters 1 to 8	Unknown length	Start with 1
Appendixes A, B	Unknown length	Continue from Chapter 8
Index	Unknown length	Continue from Appendix B

- What pages will be in the master document and what will be in the subdocs. The ToC and Index must be in the master document. A typical arrangement would be:

Title (cover) page	In master document
Copyright page	In master document
Table of Contents	In master document
Preface (Foreword)	Subdocument
Chapters 1 to 8	Subdocuments
Appendixes A, B	Subdocuments
Index	In master document

- Page, paragraph, character, frame, and numbering styles. See Chapters 3 and 4 for instructions on how to create or modify styles. Some styles for my example book are as follows.

Page styles

Name	Characteristics	Next page style
Title page	No header, footer, or page numbers; layout different from other pages	Copyright page
Copyright page	No header, footer, or page numbers; layout different from other pages	Front matter first page
Front matter first page	No header; page number in footer, Roman numerals (i, ii, iii); layout different from following pages	Front matter left page
Front matter left page	Header and footer, one containing the page number (Roman)	Front matter right page
Front matter right page	Margins mirrored from Front matter left page; Roman page number	Front matter left page
First page	No header; page number in footer, Arabic numbers (1, 2, 3); layout same as Front matter first page	Left page
Left page	Layout as for Front matter left page, but Arabic page numbers	Right page
Right page	Layout as for Front matter right page, but Arabic page numbers	Left page

Paragraph styles

Use Heading 1 for Chapter titles. Define a heading level to use for Appendix titles. A handy style is Page Break, defined as 6 pt, no space before or after, page break before. Others: whatever suits your requirements.

- Fields and AutoText entries as required. See earlier chapters for ideas.

Step 2. Create a Template

You can create your template from an existing document or template that contains some or all of the styles you want for this document, or you can create the template from a blank document. For more about templates, see Chapter 4.

If you use an existing document or template, I recommend that you delete all the text from it except for fields in headers and footers before saving it as the template for this project. It will still have all the styles you defined, even if the text is not there.

The general method for creating a template is described in "Create a New Template" on page 72. Be sure to use File > Templates > Save when creating the template. You can change the styles in the template as your project develops.

Step 3. Create the Master Document and Subdocuments from the Same Template

If you are starting a new project, you must ensure that you create the master document and all the subdocuments from the same template. It doesn't matter what order you use to create the master and subdocuments, and you don't have to create all the subdocuments at the same time, when you're starting the project. You can add new subdocuments at any time, as you need them—as long as you always create them from the same template.

Create the master document

I recommend you follow this process to create the master document. You can use other methods, but each method (including this one) has its drawbacks.

1. Open a new document from the template you created in Step 2. Be sure the first page of this new document is set to the page style you want for the first page of the final document; if it isn't, change it. In our example, the style for the first page is Title Page.

2. If any text or page breaks came into this document from the template, delete the text. (Fields in headers and footers can stay.)

3. Click File > Send > Create Master Document. Save the master document in the folder for this project, not in the templates folder. We'll return to this master document later. For now, you can either leave it open or close it, as you prefer.

Create subdocuments

A subdocument is no different from any other text document. It becomes a subdocument only when it is inserted into a master document and opened from within the master document. Some settings in the master document will override settings in a subdocument, but only when the document is being printed or otherwise manipulated by the master document.

Create a subdocument in the same way as you would any ordinary document:

1. Open a blank document based on the project template (very important).

2. Delete any unwanted text, and set the first page to whatever page style you specified for the first page of a chapter.

3. Click File > Save As. Give the document a suitable name and save it in the folder for this project.

If you already have some of the chapters written, the files are probably not based on the template you just created for this project. You will need to change the template attached to the existing file. As mentioned in Chapter 4, the only way to do this is:

1. Open a blank document based on the project template.

2. Copy the contents of the original document into this new document.

3.   Click File > Save As and save the new document in the project folder under a suitable name.

4.   Rename the original chapter file so you don't use it by mistake.

Step 4. Insert Subdocuments into the Master Document

The instructions in this step use the page-numbering requirements given in Step 1. If your book has different requirements, change these instructions to suit.

These instructions are fairly tedious, but once you have the master document set up, you shouldn't have to change it, and with a bit of practice it doesn't take long to set it up.

1.   Open the master document. Make sure paragraph marks, text limits, and sectiion limits are showing. (If necessary, set them in Tools > Options > Text Document > View, as described in "Formatting Aids Options for Text Documents" on page 14, or click the Nonprinting characters icon.) Display the Navigator (click Edit > Navigator, press F5, or click the Navigator icon).

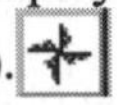

2.   Type the contents of the title page (or leave placeholders and fill in later). With the insertion point in the last blank paragraph on the page, click Insert > Manual Break. On the Insert Break dialog (Figure 7-7), select Page break and the page style for the second page (Copyright page in our example), and leave the Change page number checkbox unselected. Click OK.

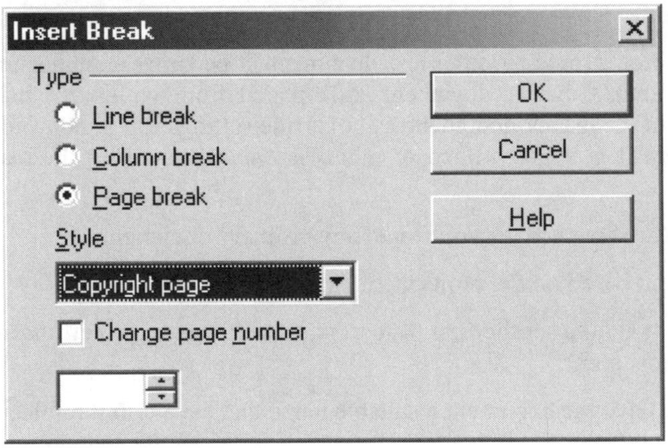

Figure 7-7. Inserting a page break between the title page and the copyright page

3.   Type the contents of the copyright page (or leave placeholders). Insert another manual page break, this time setting the page style to Front matter first page. Select the Change page number checkbox and choose 1 in the box below that, as shown in Figure 7-8. This number 1 will show in your document as i, because the page style is defined to use Roman numerals.

Figure 7-8. Inserting a page break before the first page of the Front matter

4. Let's assume the third page is for the Table of Contents. Leave a blank paragraph or two on this page and insert another page break, with the next page again set to the Front matter first page style, which we want to use for the first page of the Preface. Because we want the page numbering for the Preface to continue from the page numbers of the Table of Contents, we do *not* select the Change page number checkbox this time. Notice that the Navigator shows one item, labelled Text.

5. At last we're ready to add the first subdocument, which is the Preface. On the Navigator, select Text, then long-click on the Insert icon and click File (see Figure 7-9).

Figure 7-9. Inserting a subdocument into a master document using the Navigator

A standand File Open dialog will appear. Select the required file (which you created in Step 3) and click OK. Wait while Writer loads this document.

You'll see that the inserted file is listed in the Navigator *before* the Text item, as shown in Figure 7-10. You do not want it there; you want it after the text. Select Text and then click the Move Up icon.

Check whether the first page of the master document has the correct page style. If not, change it.

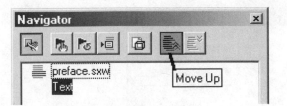

Figure 7-10. Moving text to before a subdocument

Scroll to the place where the subdocument begins (Figure 7-11). You'll see that it has a blank paragraph at the top of the page; this was inserted as part of the manual page break. Set this paragraph to the PageBreak style you created in Step 2.

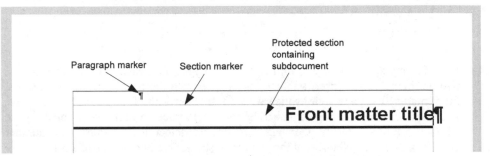
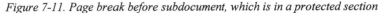

Figure 7-11. Page break before subdocument, which is in a protected section

You'll also notice that the document you just inserted is in a protected section. That means you can't change any of the contents of this subdocument from within the master document. See "Edit Subdocuments" on page 159.

6. Save the master document file before you do anything else.

    Now you want to add the next subdocument, which in our example is Chapter 1. In the Navigator, select the Preface file you just inserted. Long-click on the Insert icon and click File. Select the required file for the first chapter and click OK. Wait while OOo loads the file.

    You'll see that it comes into the master document before the Preface, which again is not what you want. Select the new file and click the Move Down icon to move the new file to be after the Preface.

7. Now place the cursor in the master document itself and scroll around until you find the beginning of Chapter 1 (Figure 7-12). You'll find that it is on the same page as the end of the Preface, and there is no paragraph marker between the section markers for the end of the Preface and the beginning of the chapter, so you can't insert a page break.

Figure 7-12. Two sections of a master document with no text area between them

To fix this, go back to the Navigator. Select the last file in the list (which should be Chapter 1), then long-click on Insert and click Text. A blank paragraph appears in the master document between the two section marks.

Click on this blank paragraph and insert a page break, specifying the First Page style and the page number to start at 1. Click OK.

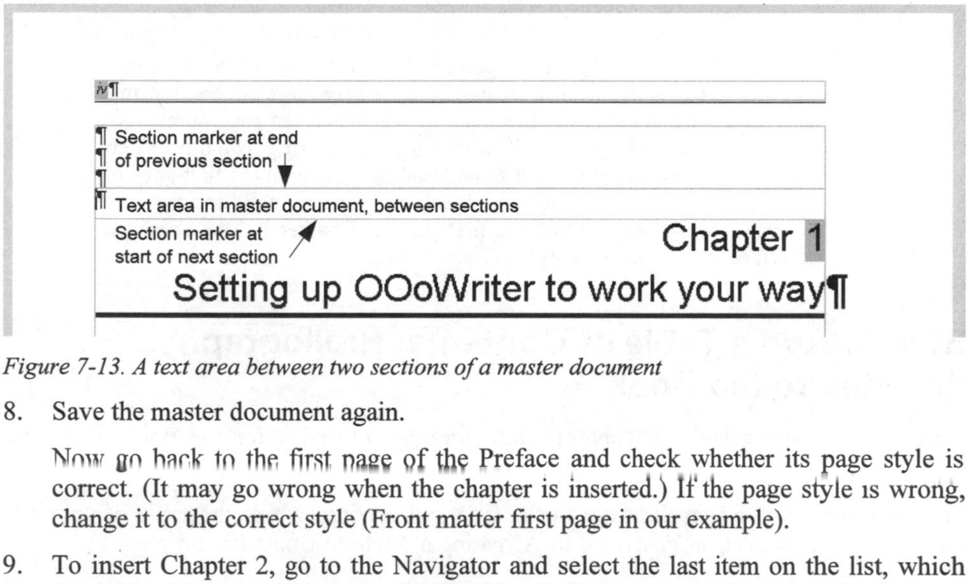

Figure 7-13. A text area between two sections of a master document

8. Save the master document again.

    Now go back to the first page of the Preface and check whether its page style is correct. (It may go wrong when the chapter is inserted.) If the page style is wrong, change it to the correct style (Front matter first page in our example).

9. To insert Chapter 2, go to the Navigator and select the last item on the list, which should be Chapter 1. Insert the file for Chapter 2, move it to the end of the list, and insert a page break as described earlier. Repeat until all the subdocuments have been added to the list.

    The Navigator will now look something like Figure 7-14.

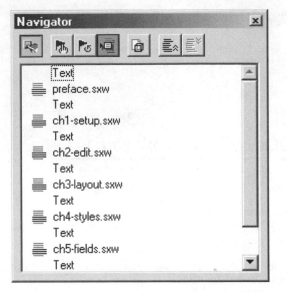

Figure 7-14. The Navigator showing a series of files in a master document

Tip   You can define your Heading 1 paragraph style to start on a new page, and thus avoid inserting manual page breaks between chapters, but this causes a page-numbering problem if you want to restart page numbering at the beginning of Chapter 1. To restart page numbering, you must insert a manual page break; but because the Heading 1 style on the first page of Chapter 1 forces yet another page break, you end up with one or more unwanted blank pages before the first page of Chapter 1. The technique described in this chapter avoids this problem.

Step 5. Add a Table of Contents, Bibliography, or Index to the Book

You can generate a table of contents, bibliography, or index for the book using the master document. You must insert these items into a text section in the master document.

Put the insertion point on the page in the first text section, where the table of contents will go. Create the ToC as described in "Creating a Table of Contents" on page 117.

If you do not have a Text section at the end of the master document, insert one before the last subdocument, then move it down so it is after the last subdocument. Now, if you have included bibliographic entries in your subdocuments, you can put the insertion point on the page in this last text section, where the bibliography will go. Create the bibliography as described in "Creating and Using Bibliographies" on page 135.

If you have included index entries in your subdocuments, put the insertion point on the page in the last text section where the index will go. Create the index as described in "Creating an Alphabetic Index" on page 124.

Editing a Master Document

After creating a master document, you may want to change its appearance or contents.

Change the Appearance of the Document

You can change the styles in the template as your project develops. Don't make changes to styles in the master document or in any of the subdocuments—do it in the template.

To update the master document (and all of the subdocuments) with changes to the template, just open the master document. You'll get two messages: the first, asks if you want to update all links; the second asks if you want to apply the changed styles. Answer Yes to both of these messages.

Edit Subdocuments

You cannot edit a subdocument from within the master document. Instead, you must open the subdocument, either by double-clicking on it in the master document's Navigator, or by opening it from outside the master document. Then you can edit it just as you would any other document. Just one rule: if you make any changes to the styles while editing a subdocument, you must copy those changed styles to the template so they are available to all of the subdocuments and to the master document.

Cross-Reference Between Subdocuments in a Master Document

The process to create cross-references between subdocuments is tedious, but it works.

1. Set references in each subdocument, just as you would when you are cross-referencing within a single document. When you do this, keep a list of what you've named the reference fields, and be sure every name is unique. One way to keep track of this information is by putting it in a separate text file or a spreadsheet.

    The field names are case-sensitive. You can check the field name by hovering the mouse pointer over the referenced item. In our example (Figure 7-15), the heading has the field name "word count."

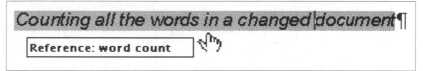

Figure 7-15. Finding the field name for a heading

2. Open the master document. In the Navigator (Figure 7-16), select a subdocument and click the Edit icon (or right-click and choose Edit from the pop-up menu). The subdocument opens for editing.

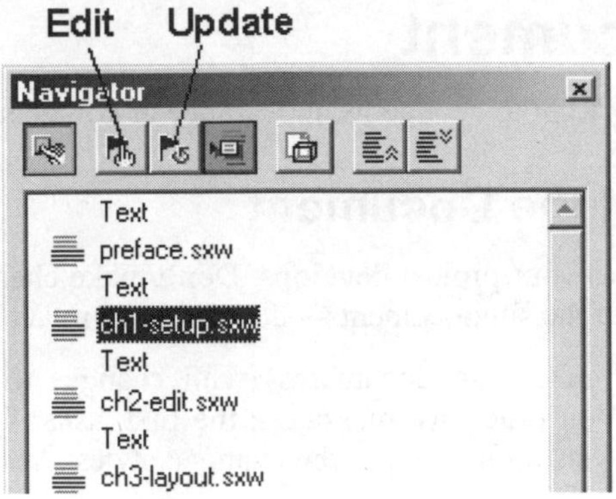

Edit   Update

Figure 7-16. Selecting a subdocument in the Navigator

3. In the subdocument, place the cursor where you want the cross-reference to appear. Click Insert > Cross Reference.

4. In the Fields dialog, on the References page, select Insert Reference in the Type list on the left-hand side (Figure 7-17). The Selection list in the middle column shows only the reference field names for the subdocument you're using, so ignore that list and check the list you created manually in step 1.

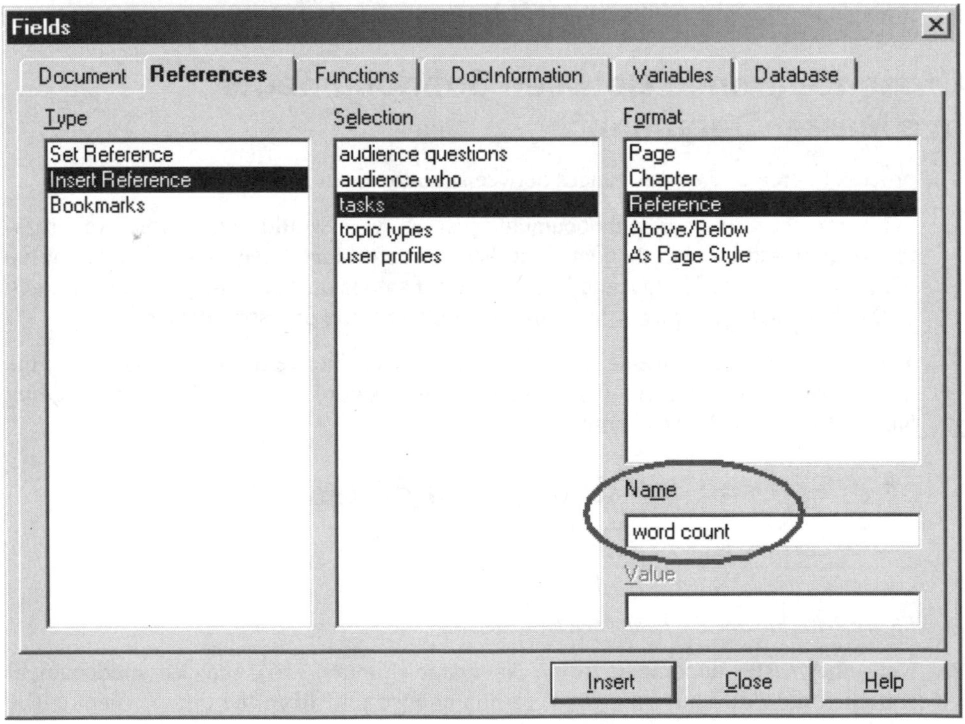

Figure 7-17. Fields dialog showing manual entry of field name

5. In the Name field in the lower right-hand column, type the name of the reference you set in the subdocument you're referring to. In our example, the reference is in Chapter 3, and its name is *word count*.

6. Click Insert. Nothing will appear in the subdocument except a tiny gray bar indicating a field. If you hover the mouse pointer over this field, you should see the field name (Figure 7-18).

Figure 7-18. Viewing the field name

(You can turn on the display of field codes by clicking Tools > Options > Text Document > View and selecting the Field Codes checkbox. The two fields shown as gray lines in Figure 7-18 now look like Figure 7-19.)

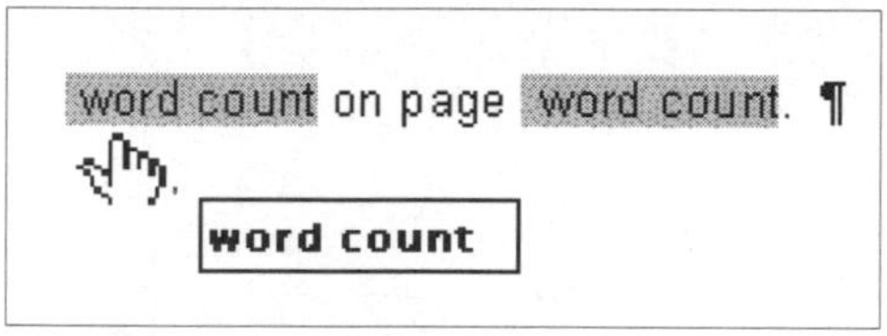

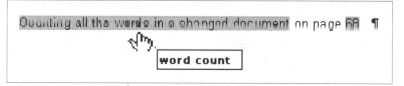

Figure 7-19. Displaying field codes

7. After you have inserted all the cross-references required in the subdocument, save and close it and return to the master document window.

Within the master document, navigate to the page of the subdocument on which you inserted the cross-reference field. You should now see the text of the cross-reference appear in the spot where you inserted it (Figure 7-20) because within the master document, the subdocument can find the target of that field reference.

Figure 7-20. Field contents showing where the cross-reference was inserted in the file

This technique also works if you open a subdocument directly in step 2 (that is, not from within the master document) and insert a cross-reference field.

8

Working with Graphics in Writer

Writer distinguishes between graphics created in another program (including those produced by OOoDraw) and *drawing objects* (graphics created using Writer's drawing tools). Writer treats the two types of graphics differently:

- Graphics created in another program are separate files, even when embedded in a Writer file.
- Drawing objects created using Writer's drawing tools cannot be saved to a separate graphics file; they are part of the Writer file.

This chapter briefly covers a few issues related to working with graphics in Writer. It does not cover the use of other programs to create graphics, you'll need to consult the documentation for those programs. Save or export graphics from other programs in one of the main file types (formats): GIF, JPG, BMP, or PNG.

Creating Graphics and Screen Captures Using Other Programs

For background information on creating graphics and screen captures, I recommend several articles on the TECHWR-L website:
www.raycomm.com/techwhirl/magazine/technical/screencapgraphicshomepage.html.

163

This page links to the following articles:

> *Computer Art Primer, by Steve Hudson*
> Introductory concepts in graphics design using computer technology.
>
> *Screen Captures 102, by Sean Brierley*
> Extensive hands-on information about working with screen captures in a Microsoft Windows environment.
>
> *Understanding Graphic File Formats, by Eric J. Ray*
> Summary of the various kinds of graphic formats and how to use each of them when they're the most appropriate for the situation.

Using Writer's Drawing Tools to Create Graphics

You can use Writer's drawing tools to create graphics such as simple diagrams using rectangles, circles, lines, text, and other objects. Group the drawing objects to make sure they stay together the way you intended.

You can use the drawing tools to place drawing objects directly on a page in your document, or you can insert the drawing objects into a frame. See "Use Frames to Place Graphics on the Page" on page 177 for more information.

You can also use the drawing tools to annotate photographs, screen captures, or other illustrations produced by other programs, but this is not recommended for these reasons:

- You cannot include graphics in a group with drawing objects, so they may get out of alignment in your document.
- If you convert a Writer document to another format, such as HTML, the drawing objects and the graphics will not remain associated; they will be saved separately.

Instead, use OOoDraw or another graphics program to annotate illustrations.

Create Drawing Objects

To begin using the drawing tools, display the Draw Functions toolbar (Figure 8-1):

1. Long-click on the Show Draw Functions icon on the main toolbar (normally found on the left-hand side of the Writer window).
2. If you are planning to use the drawing tools repeatedly, you can tear off this toolbar and move it to a convenient place on the window.

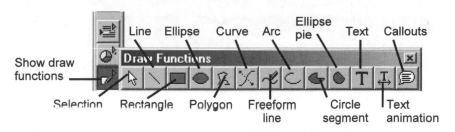

Figure 8-1. Displaying the Draw Functions toolbar

To use a drawing tool:

1. Click in the document where you want the drawing to be anchored. (You can change the anchor later, if necessary; see "Placing Graphics Where You Want Them on the Page" on page 175.)

2. Select the tool from the Draw Functions toolbar (Figure 8-1). The mouse pointer changes to a drawing-functions pointer, a cross-hair with a symbol for the selected tool.

3. Move the cross-hair pointer to the place in the document where you want the graphic to appear, and then click and drag to create the drawing object. Release the mouse button. The selected drawing function remains active, so you can draw another object of the same type.

4. To cancel the selected drawing function, press the Esc key or click on the selection icon (the arrow) on the Draw Functions toolbar.

5. You can now change the properties (fill color, line type and weight, anchoring, and others) of the drawing object using either the Draw Objects toolbar (Figure 8-2) or the choices and dialogs reached by right-clicking on the drawing object.

Set or Change Properties for Drawing Objects

To set the properties for a drawing object before you draw it:

1. On the Draw Functions toolbar (Figure 8-1), click the Selection tool.

2. The object bar changes to look like Figure 8-2. Click on the arrows next to each property and select the value you want for that property.

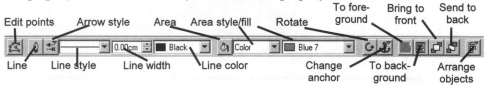

Figure 8-2. Drawing object bar

3. For more control, or to define new attributes, you can click on the Area or Line icons to display detailed dialogs, as shown in Figures 8-3 and 8-4. I do not discuss the controls in these dialogs.

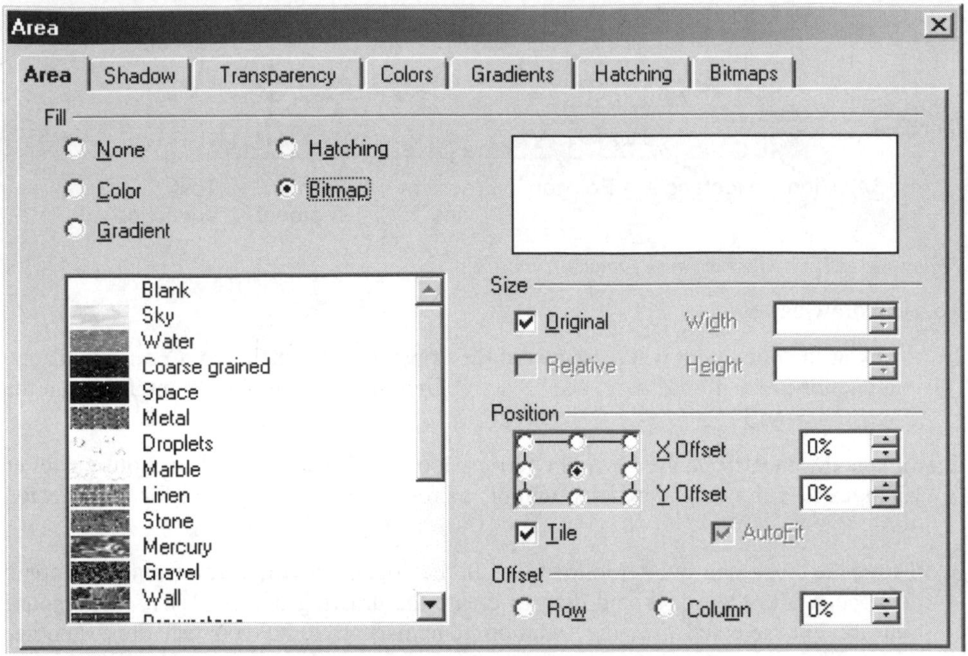

Area   ☒

| Area | Shadow | Transparency | Colors | Gradients | Hatching | Bitmaps |

Fill
- ○ None
- ○ Color
- ○ Gradient
- ○ Hatching
- ⦿ Bitmap

Blank
Sky
Water
Coarse grained
Space
Metal
Droplets
Marble
Linen
Stone
Mercury
Gravel
Wall

Size
- ☑ Original   Width   [   ]
- ☐ Relative   Height [   ]

Position

X Offset [0%]
Y Offset [0%]
- ☑ Tile   ☑ AutoFit

Offset
- ○ Row   ○ Column   [0%]

Figure 8-3. Defining area properties of a drawing object

Line   ☒

| Line | Line Styles | Arrow Styles |

Line properties   Arrow styles

Style   Style
[———— Continuous ▼]   [◄━■ Small arrow ▼]   [- none - ▼]

Color   Width
[■ Black ▼]   [0.50cm]   [0.50cm]

Width   ☐ Center   ☐ Center
[0.10cm]

Transparency   ☐ Synchronize ends
[0%]

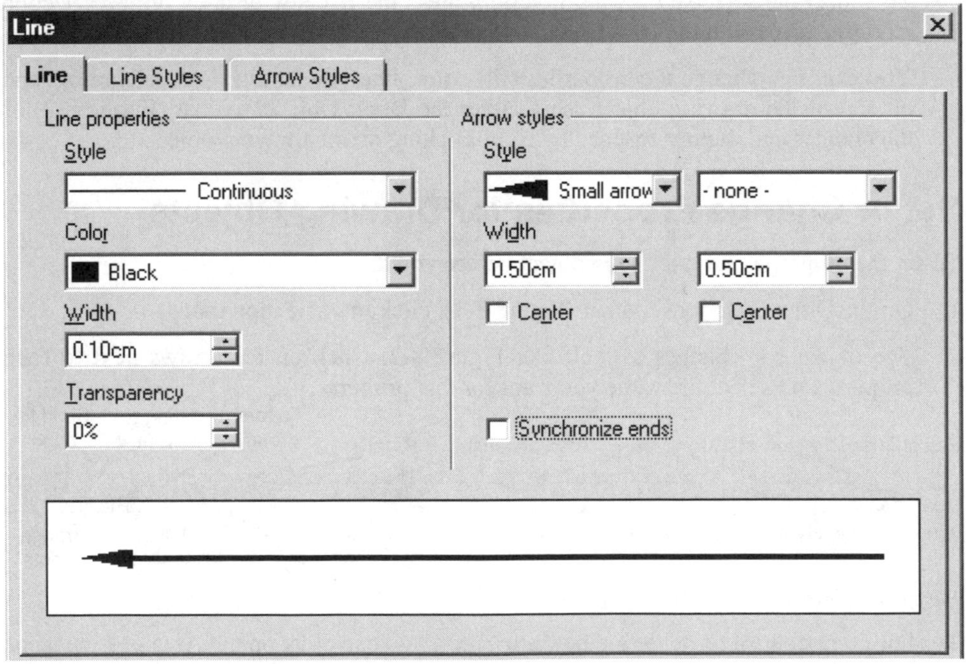

Figure 8-4. Defining line properties of a drawing object

The default you set applies to the current document and session. It is not retained when you close the document or close Writer, and it does not apply to any other document you open. The defaults apply to all the drawing objects except text objects.

To change the properties for an existing drawing object:

1. Select the object. The object bar changes to look like Figure 8-2.

2. Continue as described above.

You can also specify the position, size, rotation, slant, and corner radius properties of the drawing object:

1. Right-click on the drawing object, and then click Position and Size from the pop-up menu. The Position and Size dialog is displayed.

2. Choose properties as required.

Group Drawing Objects

1. Select one object, then hold down the Shift key and select the others you want to include in the group. The bounding box expands to include all the selected objects.

2. With the objects selected, click Format > Group > Group, or right-click and then click Group > Group on the pop-up menu.

You cannot include an embedded or linked graphic in a group with drawing objects.

Organizing Graphics Using the Gallery

The gallery is a convenient way to group reusable objects, including graphics, sounds, and video. In this document we'll consider only graphics, but the principles are the same for other objects in the gallery. Items in the gallery are grouped into collections called *themes*. The themes supplied with Writer are based on object types, but you can create themes using any criteria you choose.

In a workgroup situation you may have access to a shared gallery (where you cannot change the contents unless authorized to do so) and a user gallery, where you can add, change, or delete objects.

The location of the galleries is specified in Tools > Options > OpenOffice.org > Paths. Graphics and other objects shown in the gallery can be located anywhere on your computer's hard disk, on a network drive, or on a CD-ROM. Listings in the gallery refer to the location of the graphics. When you add graphics to the gallery, the files are not moved or copied; only the location references are added.

To open the gallery , click Tools > Gallery, or click the Gallery icon.

Figures 8-5 and 8-6 show two views of one of the themes supplied with OpenOffice.org. The list of folders shown in the Gallery on your system may vary from those shown in the illustrations, which show the default folders installed with OpenOffice.org.

You can choose between Icon view (Figure 8-5) and Details view (Figure 8-6) by clicking on icons at the top, and you can hide the Gallery by clicking on the Hide button at the bottom left.

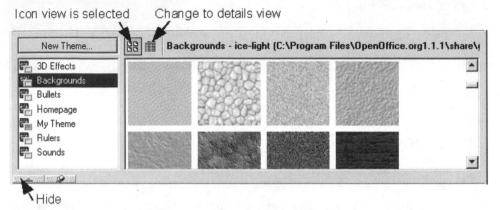

Figure 8-5. Icon view of one theme in the gallery

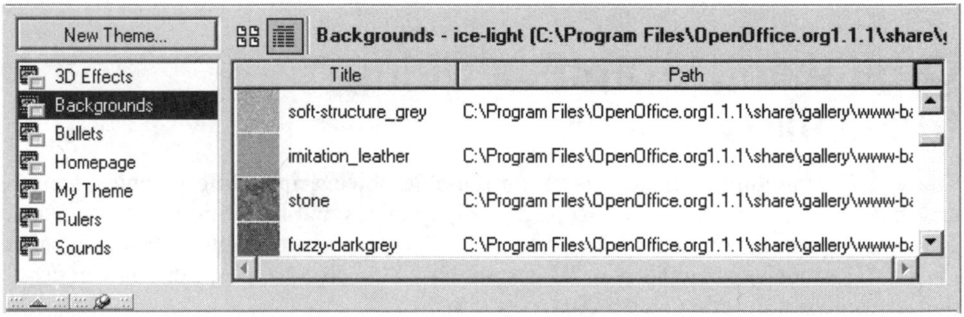

Figure 8-6. Details view of the same theme in the gallery

Add a New Theme to the Gallery

We'll add a new theme to contain the graphics for a book project.

1. Open the gallery and click the New Theme button.

2. On the General tab of the Properties of New Theme dialog (Figure 8-7), type the name for this theme.

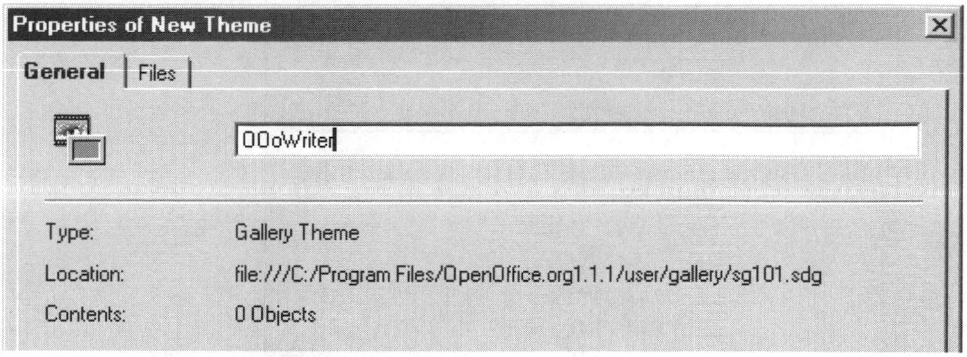

Figure 8-7. Naming the new theme in the gallery

3.   On the Files tab (Figure 8-8), click Find Files.

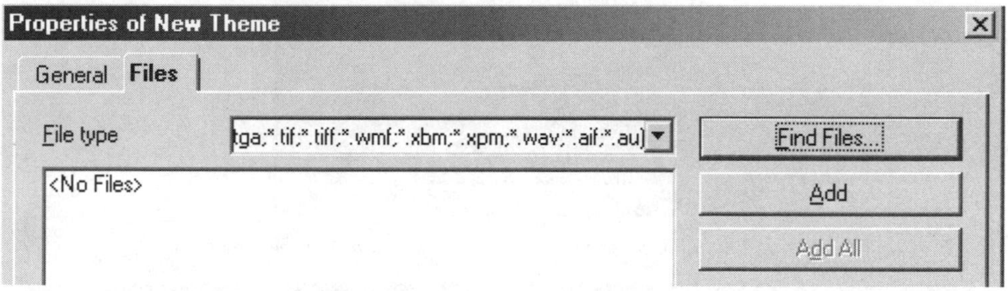

Figure 8-8. The Files tab of the Properties of New Theme dialog

4.   On the Select Path dialog (Figure 8-9), find and highlight the location of the files you want to add to the gallery. Click OK. (Use Shift-Click or Ctrl-Click to select multiple files.)

5.   Back on the Files tab of the Properties of New Theme dialog (Figure 8-10), the files have been added to the list. You can now select all the files in the list (click Add All), or select individual files to be added and click Add.

     You can also filter the list by choosing a file type and clicking Yes at the prompt to update the file list. Then you can either add all of the files of that type or select individual files from the filtered list.

6.   After you click Add or Add All, the files list is cleared. You can then repeat steps 4 through 6 to add files from another location.

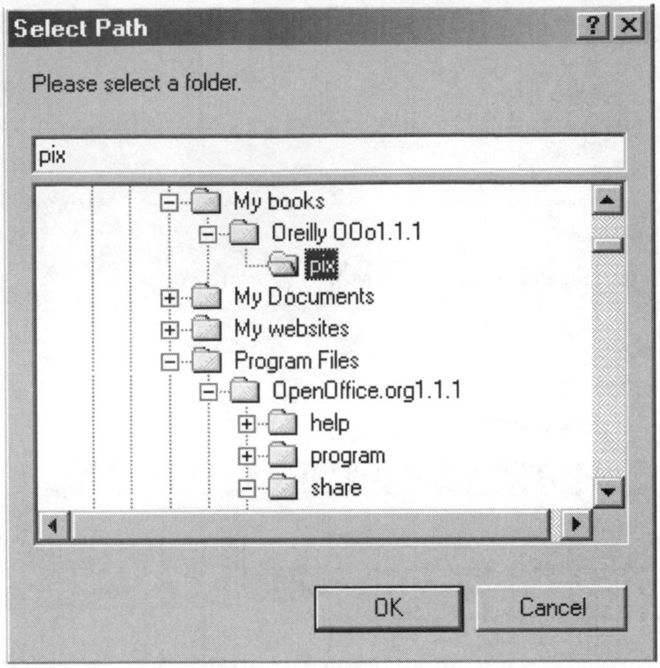

Figure 8-9. Finding the location of graphics files to be added to the new theme

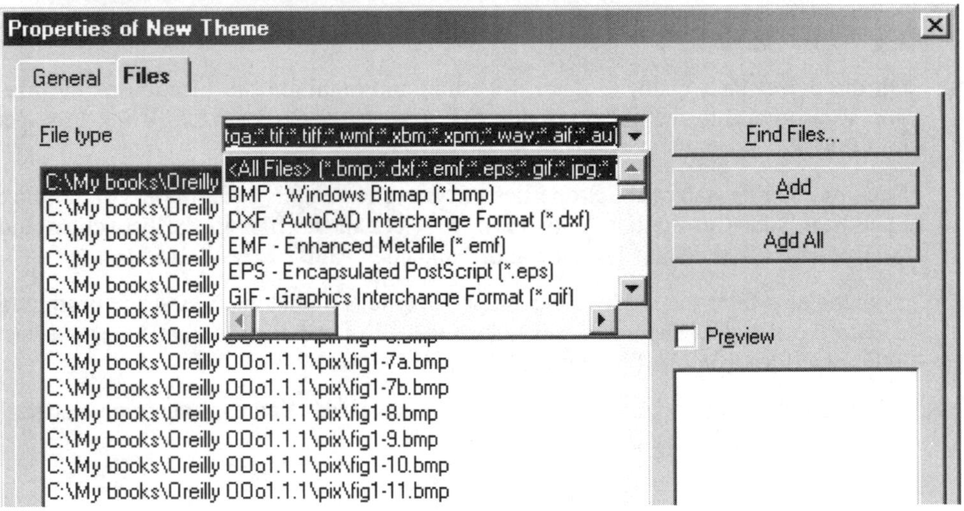

Figure 8-10. Choosing files to add to the new theme

7. When you have added all the required files, click OK on the Properties of New Theme dialog to save the new theme. Its name now appears on the list in the gallery.

Add Graphics to an Existing Theme

1. Right-click on the name of the theme in the list in the gallery, and then click Properties on the pop-up menu.

2. The Properties of [Theme Name] window opens. On the Files tab, follow the same procedure as for adding files to a new theme.

Delete Individual Graphics Files from a Theme

1. Right-click on the name of the graphics file or its thumbnail in the gallery.

2. Click Delete on the pop-up menu.

Deleting the name of a file from the list in the gallery does not delete the file from the hard disk or other location.

Copy Graphics from a Document into a Theme

You can place a graphic into the gallery by drag-and-drop.

1. In the gallery (Figure 8-5), select the theme to which you want to add the graphic.

2. In the document containing the graphic, position the mouse pointer above the graphic, without clicking.

    If the mouse pointer changes to a hand symbol, the graphic refers to a hyperlink. In this case, click the graphic while pressing the Alt key. If the mouse pointer does not change to a hand symbol, you can simply click the graphic to select it.

3. After you select the graphic, release the mouse button. Then click and hold the mouse button for a couple of seconds before dragging and dropping the graphic into the gallery.

Inserting Graphics into a Text Document

You can insert existing graphics into a text document using these methods:

*   Copy (embed) or link a graphics file.
*   Scan a graphic and embed it directly.
*   Copy or link a graphic from the gallery.
*   Copy a graphic from OpenOffice.org Draw, Impress, or Calc.

| **Tip** | OpenOffice.org saves BMP graphics in PNG format if you embed them. The file type of JPG, GIF, and TIF images is not changed. |

Copy (Embed) or Link a Graphic File

When you insert a graphic into Writer, you can either copy it into the Writer file or link it to the Writer file. Use the technique that suits your situation best.

The advantage of embedding is that the graphics won't get lost when you send a file to someone else; they are part of the file and will travel with it. You don't have to keep track of file locations and make sure you send all the files, and the recipient won't have to store all the files in the correct locations so Writer can find them. (An OOo file is a zipped format containing an XML text file and any embedded graphic files.)

The disadvantages of embedding are a larger file size and no automatic way to make sure you have the latest version of any graphics that might change. If you have linked to the files (and have chosen to automatically update links), then each time you open the Writer document, you'll be sure to have the most up-to-date graphics.

If you copy a graphic from another program and paste it directly into your Writer document, the graphic is automatically embedded. If you use one of the other insertion methods described in this chapter, you can choose whether to embed or link the graphic.

1. Place the cursor where you want the graphic to appear in the document.

2. Click Insert > Graphics > From File.

3. On the Insert Graphics dialog (Figure 8-11), select the required graphic. To link the graphic, select the Link checkbox; to embed the graphic, deselect Link.

4. Click Open. The graphic is inserted so that it is centered above the current paragraph and anchored to the paragraph. You can change the anchoring and position, as described in "Anchor Graphics" on page 175.

Tip	If the graphic is too big to fit in the space left on the page, it will move to the next page and may be anchored to the wrong paragraph. You can correct this problem afterward, but it's a nuisance. To avoid the problem, insert several blank paragraphs and attach the graphic to the first paragraph on the next page. Delete the blank paragraphs later.

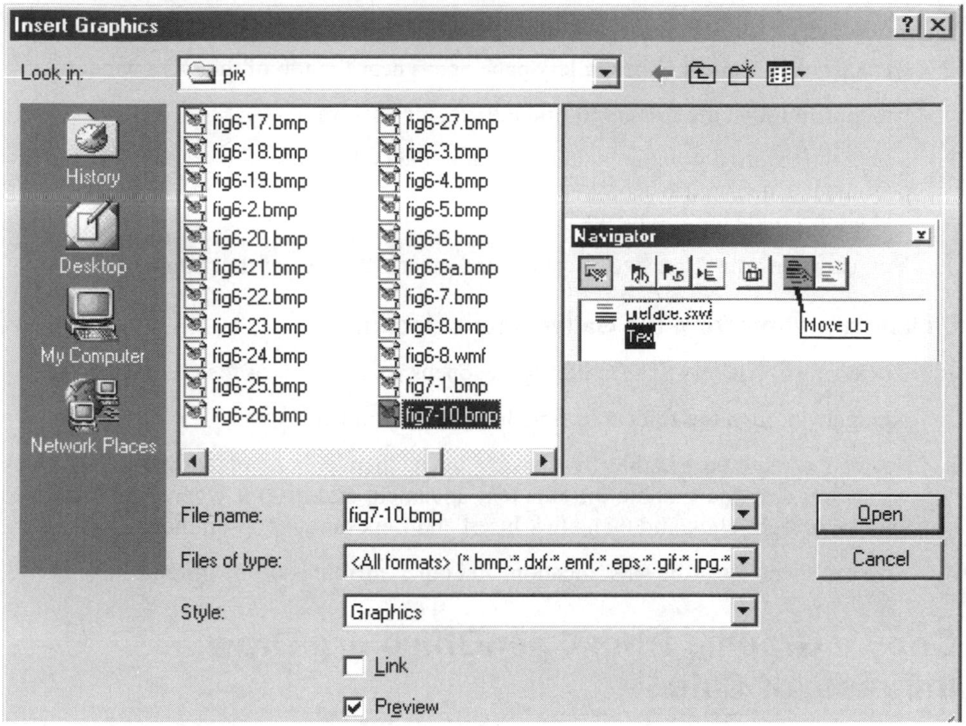

Figure 8-11. Inserting a graphic file into a text document

Scan a Graphic and Embed It Directly

You can scan a photo or graphic, save it to a file, and then embed or link that file as described in "Copy (Embed) or Link a Graphic File" on page 172 (recommended), or you can scan and embed a graphic or photo in steps, as described here:

1. Click Insert > Graphics > Scan.

2. If more than one scanner is defined on your system, choose Select Source; otherwise, choose Request.

3. What you see next depends on your scanner software. Follow your usual procedures to scan the photo or other graphic, which will be inserted directly into your text document so that it is centered above the current paragraph and anchored to the paragraph. You can change the anchoring and position, as described in "Anchor Graphics" on page 175.

Copy or Link a Graphic from the Gallery

You can copy (embed) or link a graphic from the Gallery into a document.

Copying a graphic from the Gallery into a document

1. Click Tools > Gallery. The Gallery pane opens near the top of the OOo window.

2. Navigate through the folders to find the graphic you want.

3. Select the required graphic by clicking on it, then either drag the graphic into the text document and drop it where you want it to appear, or right-click and then click Insert and Copy on the pop-up menu.

4. You can then adjust the size, location, and other attributes of the graphic.

Linking a graphic from the Gallery into a document

1. Click Tools > Gallery. The Gallery pane opens near the top of the OOo window.

2. Navigate through the folders to find the graphic you want.

3. Select the required graphic by clicking on it, then either hold down the Ctrl key while you drag the graphic into the text document and drop it where you want it to appear, or right-click and then click Insert and Link on the pop-up menu.

4. You can then adjust the size, location, and other attributes of the graphic.

Copy a Graphic from OpenOffice.org Draw, Impress, or Calc

You can copy a graphic object from one document to another using copy and paste commands, or by dragging and dropping the graphic:

1. Open the document in which you want to insert the graphic object.

2. Open the document from which you want to copy the graphic object.

3. Position the mouse cursor on the graphic object. Hold down the Alt key and click and hold the mouse button. This selects the object without activating any hyperlink that may be connected to it.

4. Drag the graphic object into the other document. If the documents are not visible side by side, first move the mouse pointer to the button of the target document in the task bar. Keep the mouse button pressed! The target document is then displayed, and you can move the mouse pointer into the document.

5. Release the mouse button as soon as the gray text cursor indicates the position where you want to insert a copy of the graphic object.

You can also drag objects out of the Navigator: in the submenu of the Drag Mode icon, specify whether to copy the object, insert it as a link, or insert it as a hyperlink.

An inserted drawing object is anchored in a text document at the current paragraph. You can change the anchor by selecting the object and clicking on the Change Anchor icon on the object bar or right-clicking on the graphic. This opens a pop-up menu where you can change the possible types of anchor.

Tips   To cancel a drag-and-drop operation at any time, press the Esc key before releasing the mouse button.

You can also copy graphics from one document to another by selecting the graphic in the source document, pressing Ctrl+C to copy it, then pressing Ctrl+V to paste it into the target document.

Placing Graphics Where You Want Them on the Page

You can anchor graphics to a page, paragraph, or character, or as a character. You can also place graphics in a frame and anchor the frame to a page, paragraph, or character. Which method you choose depends on what you are trying to achieve.

If you have automatic captioning of graphics turned on, then when you insert a graphic object, it is placed in a frame and a caption line appears below the graphic with whatever default content you have specified (for example, "Figure x").

Anchor Graphics

Here are the ways you can anchor graphics or drawing objects:

To Page
Graphic keeps the same position in relation to the page margins. It does not move as you add or delete text or other graphics. This method is useful when the graphic does not need to be visually associated with a particular piece of text. It is often used when producing newsletters or other documents that are very layout-intensive.

To Paragraph
Graphic is associated with a paragraph and moves with the paragraph. It may be placed in the margin or another location. This method is useful as an alternative to a table for placing icons beside paragraphs.

To Character
Graphic is associated with a character but is not in the text sequence. It moves with the paragraph but may be placed in the margin or another location. This method is similar to anchoring to a paragraph but cannot be used with drawing objects.

As Character
Graphic is placed in the document like any other character and therefore affects the height of the text line and the line break. The graphic moves with the paragraph as you add or delete text before the paragraph. This method is useful for keeping screen shots in sequence in a procedure, or for adding a small icon in sequence in a sentence.

To Frame
If the graphic has been placed in a frame, you can anchor the graphic in a fixed position inside the frame. The frame can then be anchored to the page, a paragraph, or a character, as required.

Arrange and Align Graphics and Wrap Text Around Graphics

Graphic *arrangement* refers to the placement of a graphic behind or in front of other graphics or text. *Alignment* refers to the vertical or horizontal placement of a graphic in relation to the page, frame, paragraph or character to which it is anchored. *Text wrapping* refers to the relation of graphics to surrounding text, which may wrap around the graphic on one or both sides, be overprinted behind or in front of the graphic, or treat the graphic as a separate paragraph or character.

Arrangement, alignment, and text wrapping choices depend on several factors, including the placement, anchoring, and wrapping of the graphic, and its relationship to other graphics. You can arrange and align graphics using commands from:

Menu options (from menu bar or right-click menu)
The Arrange submenu may include Bring to Front, Bring Forward, Send Backward, Send to Back, To Foreground, and To Background.

The Align submenu may include Left, Centered, and Right (for horizontal alignment) and Top, Center, and Bottom (for vertical alignment).

The Wrap submenu may include no wrap, page wrap, wrap through, in background, contour, and other choices.

Frame/Graphics object bar
When you select a graphic, the Graphics object toolbar (shown in Figure 8-19 on page 182) may be displayed. Click on the left-facing arrow at the right-hand end of the toolbar to display the Frame/Graphics object bar (Figure 8-12).

Here you can click icons to apply many arrangement, alignment, wrapping, anchoring, formatting, and other choices. You can toggle this object bar by clicking on the left-facing arrow at the right-hand end to display the Graphics object toolbar.

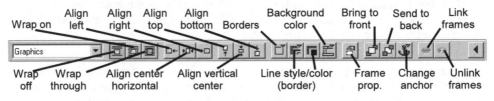

Figure 8-12. Frame object bar

Graphics dialog
Click Format > Graphics, or right-click then click Graphics on the pop-up menu, or click the Frame Properties icon on the object bar to display the dialog shown in Figure 8-13. Here you can specify the characteristics of the graphic and its placement in detail.

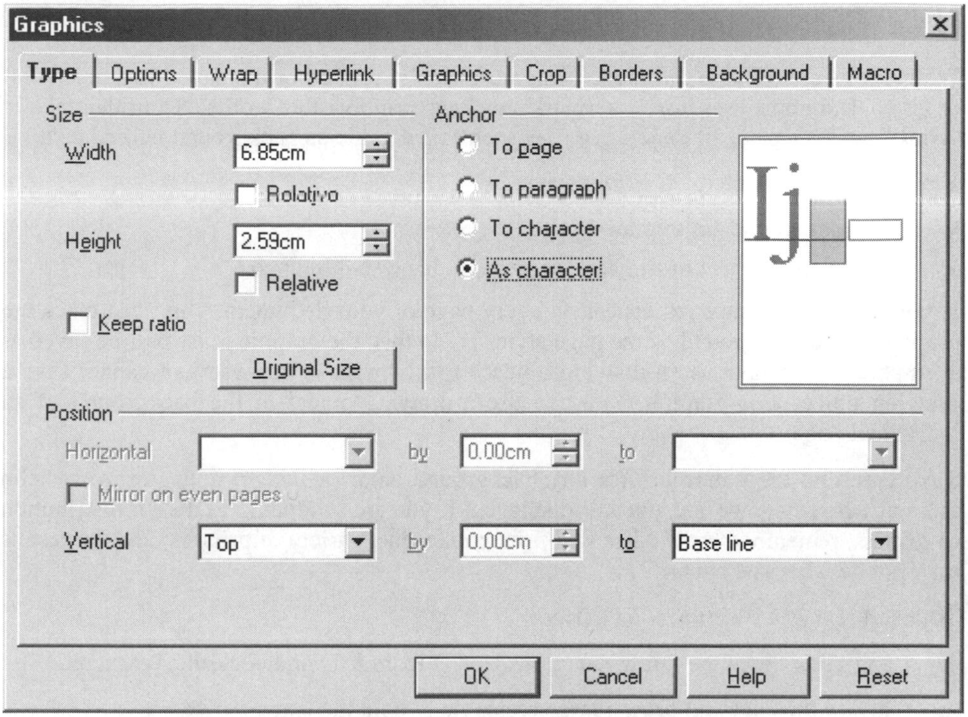

Figure 8-13. Specifying characteristics of a graphic using the Graphics dialog

Use Frames to Place Graphics on the Page

You can choose to place graphics directly on a page or into a frame. "Using Frames for Page Layout" on page 56 and "Use Frame Styles" on page 89 have more information about frames.

In two situations, your graphics will be placed in a frame automatically:

- If you have automatic captioning enabled in Tools > Options> Text Document > General.

- If you insert the graphic, then select it and click Insert > Caption.

See "Adding Captions to Graphics" on page 183 for more information.

Placing graphics in frames has both advantages and disadvantage. The main advantage is that the graphic and its caption (if any) will stay together when you move the graphic. The main disadvantages I've found are:

- Setting properties for both the frame and the graphic is extra work.

- I've had difficulty anchoring a frame as a character and getting the graphic to be placed exactly where I want it, but I've had no difficulty anchoring the graphic directly to the paragraph as a character.

Use Watermarks

Watermarks are background text or graphics, usually printed or displayed in a pale color or gray. Common uses for watermarks include printing the words "Confidential" or "Draft" across a page, or decorative uses such as a graphic as background behind text.

You can define a watermark in two ways:

- As a background graphic for a page
- As a drawing object or graphic set to "go to back" behind text

If you want a watermark to appear on every page of your document, you must place the graphic in the background of the page style. To do this, the graphic must first be saved as a graphic; you cannot use a drawing object for this purpose because you cannot save a drawing object as a graphic. You can use a drawing object in the background of an individual page.

Take care that the watermark (or any background color or image) does not overwhelm the text when the page is printed or displayed. If you are producing PDFs for distribution to readers, remember that readers will print copies on a variety of printers, and the results may not be what you intend.

To insert text as a watermark on a page:

1.   Long-click the Show Draw Functions icon (Figure 8-1) and click the Text icon.

2.   Click in the page and draw a large rectangle to hold the text.

3.   Type the text—for example, "Draft."

4.   Select the text you just typed. Click Format > Character. On the Font tab (Figure 8-14), choose the font, typeface, and size.

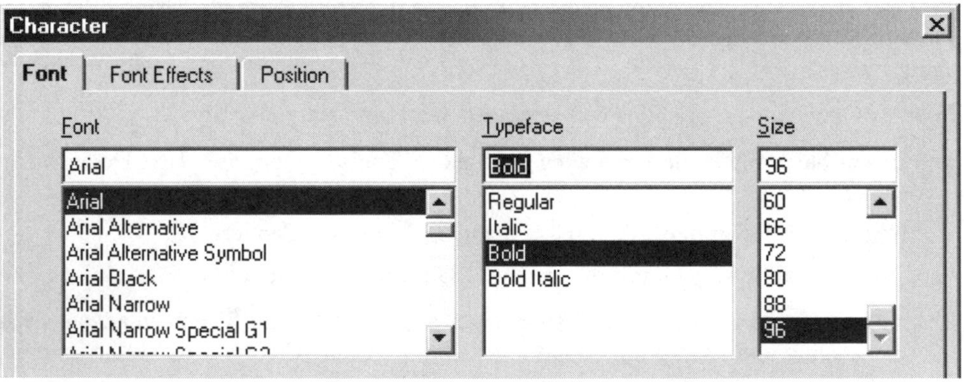

Figure 8-14. Formatting the characters in a text object

5.   On the Font Effects tab (Figure 8-15), choose a color. Gray 10% is a good pale color for a watermark. Click OK. The text now appears as formatted.

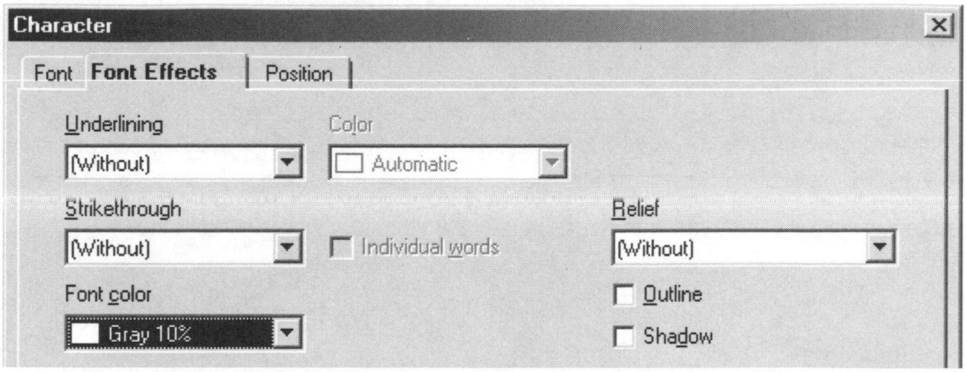

Figure 8-15. Choosing a color for a text object

6. Click outside the boundary of the text object, then click on the text object again to display the handles. Right-click, and then click Text.

   On the Text tab of the Text dialog (Figure 8-16), select the Fit width to text and Fit height to text checkboxes. Click OK.

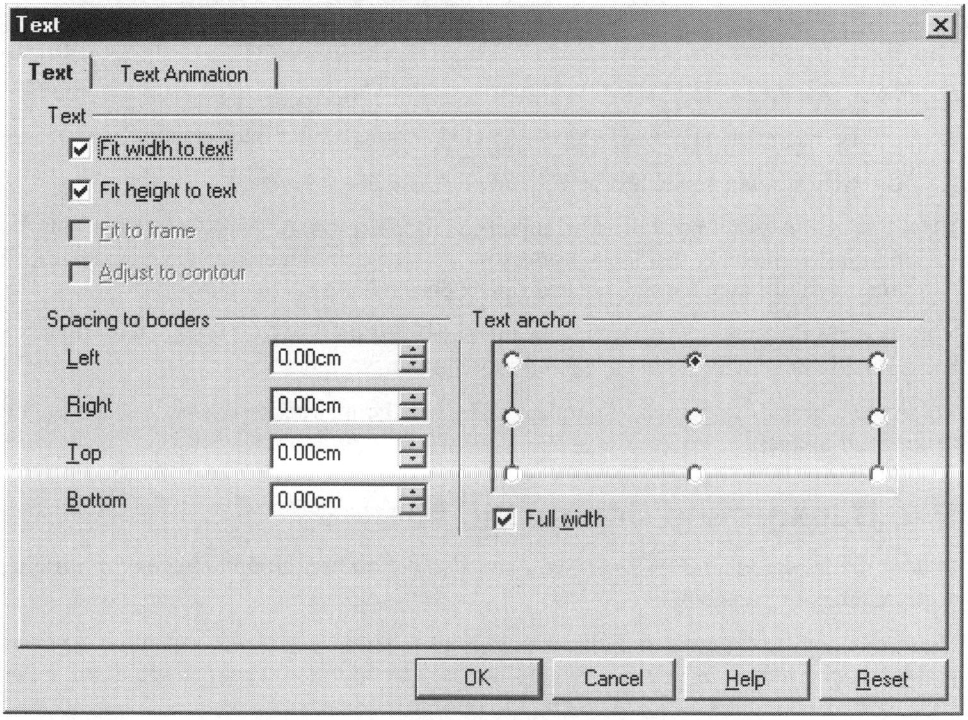

Figure 8-16. Fitting the text box to the width and height of the text object

7. Make sure the text object is selected. Right-click, and then click Position and Size.

   On the Rotation tab of the Position and Size dialog (Figure 8-17), you can choose to print the text at an angle. Click OK.

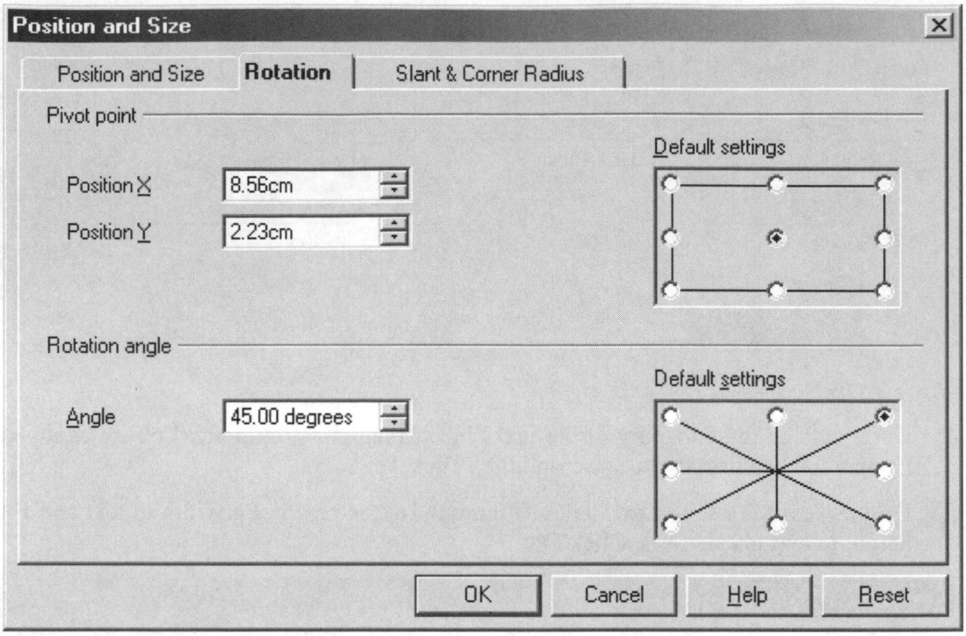

Figure 8-17. Rotating a text object

8.   Right-click again on the text object and click Arrange > To Background.

9.   Right-click again on the text object and click Anchor > To Page.

10. Click and drag to move the text object to any place on the page, including into the margins. Remember that most printers have a non-printing area at the page edges, so you may want to make sure the text object does not extend too close to the edge.

Note that if you have other graphics on the page, and they are not transparent, then the background image will be hidden behind those graphics.

To create a graphic watermark in a page style, see the instructions in "Use Background Colors and Images."

Use Background Colors and Images

In addition to watermarks on pages, you can also define background images for a frame, section, table, or paragraph.

You can manually format individual paragraphs, frames, sections, or tables to have graphic backgrounds, or you can include the background in a page, paragraph, or frame style. You cannot put a background graphic outside the page margins.

To include a background watermark in a page style:

1.   Create the graphic and save it in an appropriate format.

2.   Open the required Page Style dialog. (You can do this in several ways: select the page style in the Stylist, right-click, and then click Modify; click anywhere on the

page, right-click, and then click Page; or click anywhere on the page and then click Format > Page.)

3. On the Background tab of the Page Style dialog (Figure 8-18), select Graphic in the As drop-down list, choose the graphic using the Browse button, and then choose one of the following options:

    Position
    The graphic remains its original size and is placed in the position selected within the text margins; it may overlap the header or footer, if any.

    Area
    The graphic enlarges to fill the entire space within the text margins (including the header and footer, if any); this may distort the graphic.

    Tile
    The graphic remains its original size and is repeated (tiled) vertically and horizontally to fill the entire space within the text margins (including the header and footer).

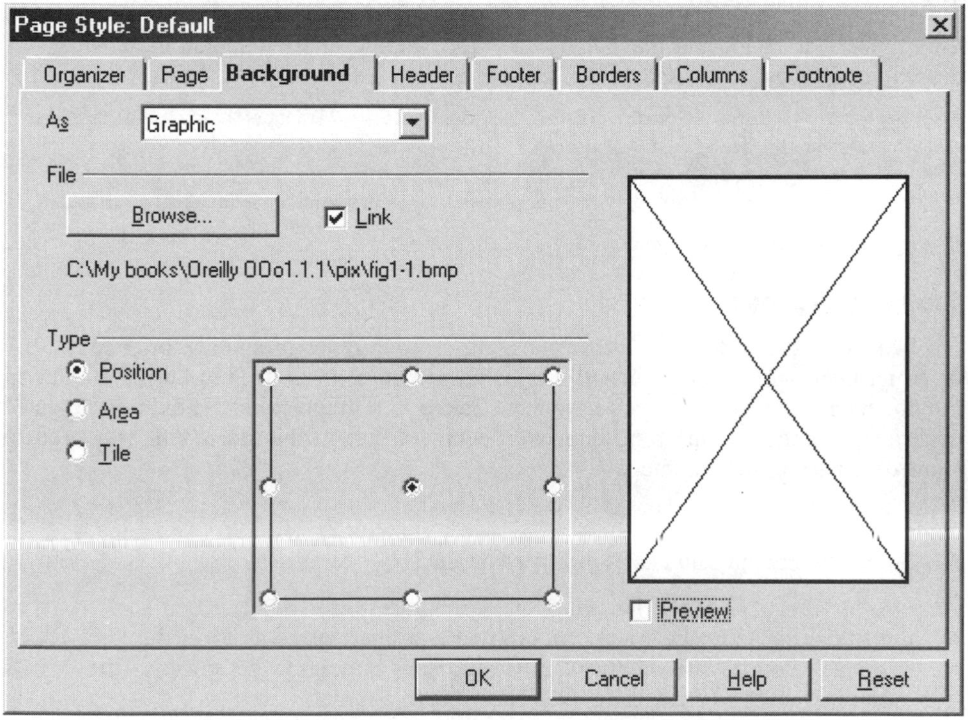

Figure 8-18. Specifying characteristics for a watermark

Note that selecting the Preview checkbox shows the graphic (so you know you've picked the right one) but not what it will look like on the page.

Tip   To remove a watermark or other background graphic, select Color on the Background tab (not shown) and No Fill. Click OK.

To insert a gallery object as a background graphic:

1. Open the gallery and select a theme.

2. Select the graphic, right-click, and then click Insert > Background > Page or Paragraph on the pop-up menu.

Editing and Formatting Graphics

Whenever possible, edit, crop, resize, and otherwise manipulate graphics in a graphics package before inserting them into a Writer document.

If necessary, you can make changes to graphics within Writer. When you select a graphic, you can toggle the object bar to show tools for editing the image itself. Click the left-facing arrow at the right-hand end of the Graphics/Frame object bar (Figure 8-12) to display the object bar shown in Figure 8-19.

Note that only a local copy is edited in the document, even if you have inserted an image as a link. Any changes you make here do not affect the original file.

This object bar includes a number of tools for filtering and manipulating an image. A description of these tools, and their effects, is beyond the scope of this book.

Figure 8-19. Graphics object toolbar

Cropping graphics

For best results, and to keep file sizes small, crop graphics in another program before inserting them into a text document. However, sometimes you need to crop a graphic in the document. For example, you may have linked to a graphic that needs to be updated occasionally and used in more than one document, but in this document you need to show only part of that graphic.

To crop a graphic within a Writer document:

1. Select the graphic and click Format > Graphics.

2. On the Crop tab of the Graphics dialog (Figure 8-20), select Keep scale (so you don't distort the image when you crop it) and then enter values in the Left, Right, Top, and Bottom boxes. You can use the spin buttons to get close to the correct cropping quickly, or you can type a value for fine-tuning.

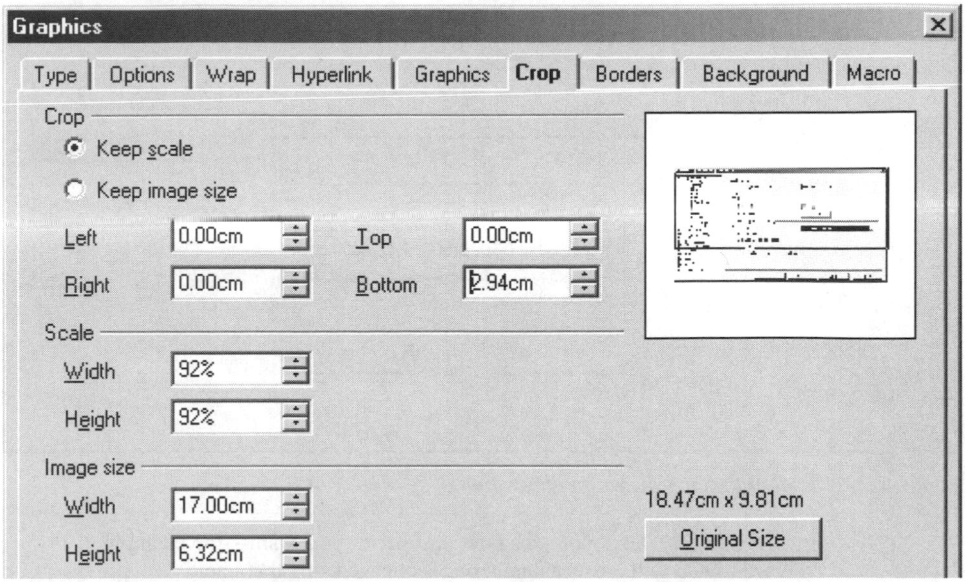

Figure 8-20. Cropping a graphic in a text document

Tip   If you convert a document to a Web page (HTML), any cropped graphics
will be saved as the full graphic, but the height and width characteristics
will be the same as the size of the cropped graphic. The resulting image
on the Web page will be distorted. Therefore, if you plan to create Web
pages from your documents, be sure to crop the images in a graphics
program, not in Writer.

Adding Captions to Graphics

You can add captions to graphics in two ways: using the Caption dialog or manually.

Add Captions Using the Caption Dialog

1. Insert the graphic, then select it and click Insert > Caption.

2. On the Caption dialog (Figure 8-21), select the caption category (Illustration in this
   example) and Arabic (1 2 3) as the numbering, and type your caption text.

3. Click OK. The graphic and its caption are placed in a frame, as in Figure 8-22.

Caption _____ [x]

Properties
              Illustration 1. This is athe caption for this illustration   [OK]

Category | Illustration   ▼ | [Cancel]

Numbering | Arabic (1 2 3)   ▼ | [Help]

Caption | . This is athe caption for this illustration | [Options]

Position | Below   ▼ |

☑ Apply border and shadow

Object name | Graphic217 |

Figure 8-21. Defining the caption for an illustration

Tip   In the Category box, you can type any name you want—for example,
             "Figure." OOo will create a numbering sequence using that name.

Add AutoFormat   [x]

Name   [OK   ]

[   ]   [Cancel]

Illustration 1. An example

*Figure 8-22. An example of a graphic and its caption contained in a frame. The outer box shows
the edge of the frame; the border is normally set to be invisible.*

If you have set captions to be inserted automatically for graphics (using Options > Text
Document > General; see Figure 1-13 on page 13), then when you insert a graphic, it will
be placed in a frame with a caption; you don't need to manually insert a caption.

Add Captions Manually

To add a caption to a graphic manually, you need to place the graphic in one paragraph
and the caption in the following paragraph. Here's how:

1. Define an appropriate paragraph style for the paragraphs containing graphics. You'll
    probably want to include the *Keep with next paragraph* attribute on the Text Flow
    tab of the Paragraph Style dialog (Figure 4-11 on page 83). (Caption is a predefined
    style, but you can modify its attributes if you wish.)

2. Insert the graphic and anchor it to its paragraph as a character.

3.. Place the cursor in the caption paragraph. Type the word Figure (assuming you want these captions to be part of the Figure sequence and a space).

4. To insert the figure number, you'll need to use a predefined numbering sequence or define your own sequence for your figure captions. Click Insert > Fields > Other and select the Variables tab (Figure 5-7 on page 100).

5. Select Number Range in the Type list. If the sequence name you want to use is shown in the Selection list, select it and click Insert. (If you have previously inserted a caption using the Figure sequence, either manually or through the Caption dialog, you will find the word Figure in the list.)

    If the sequence name you want to use is not shown in the Selection list, you can define it at the same time as you are inserting the number in the first figure caption. In the Name box (below the Type list), type the word Figure. Select Arabic (1 2 3) in the Format list. Click Insert.

6. The number 1 will appear after Figure in the caption. Type a period and a space, and continue with the text of the caption.

For the second figure caption, you don't need to create the variable. When you go to the Fields dialog, you'll see Figure in the Selection list when you select Number range. Click on Figure, then click Insert.

Tip   Using the Fields dialog can get a bit cumbersome, so you might want to make an AutoText entry containing the word Figure, the figure-number field, and the period and space after the number. See "Using AutoText to Insert Often-Used Fields Quickly" on page 99.

Define a Style for a Graphic Frame

If your graphics are in frames, you may want to define an appropriate style for a graphic frame. To position and format the frame, graphic, and caption:

1. Anchor the frame as required (I use "as character").

2. To create space between the graphic and the caption, select the graphic (not the frame) and click Format > Graphics. On the Wrap tab of the Graphics dialog (Figure 8-23), increase the value for Bottom Spacing as required.

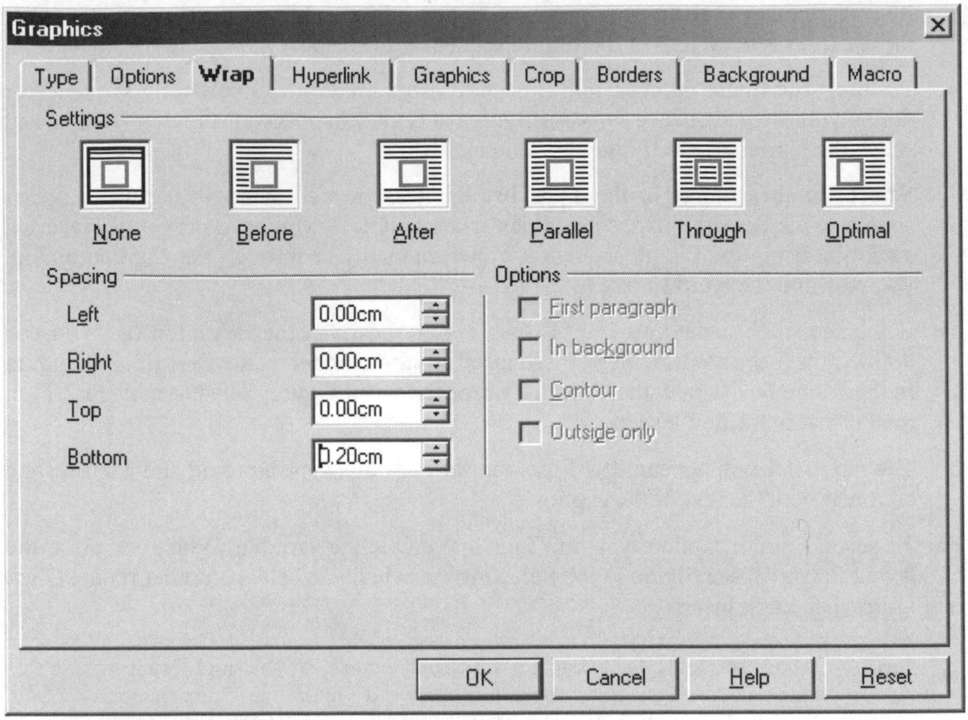

Figure 8-23. Adding space between a graphic and its caption

Line Up a Frame Precisely

1. Select the frame (not the graphic) and click Format > Frame.

2. On the Wrap tab of the Frame dialog (similar to Figure 8-23), choose values for Left, Right, Top, and Bottom spacing.

    I set all of these values to zero (0) because I prefer to have no extra spacing to the right or left of the frame, and I prefer to control the top and bottom spacing through the paragraph in which the frame is embedded.

    If I were using a different wrapping technique (before, after, or parallel), I would choose different spacing values to suit the required effect.

9

Miscellaneous Tips and Tricks

This chapter collects a few tips and tricks that didn't fit into any of the other chapters.

Converting Documents to PDF

OpenOffice.org 1.1 provides a simple way to convert files into PDF (Portable Document Format), to be read by Acrobat Reader or other PDF viewers. The process generally produces good results, but you do not have the same control over those results as you have when using Adobe Acrobat to create PDF files. The Help gives details of the built-in settings, which you cannot change.

Here are some things to keep in mind when converting files to PDF using OOo:

- Run some tests on sample files to see which export choice (Screen, Print, or Press Optimized) suits your files and your needs. The file size difference can vary from minor to very large, depending on the contents of your files, and is generally larger than the OOo (*.sxw*) file.

- PDFs created from OpenOffice.org, either by using its built-in export-as-PDF function or by printing to a PostScript file and distilling using Adobe Acrobat, do not have bookmarks or working internal links.

- You can select a range of pages or convert the entire document to PDF. To convert a range of pages, use 3–6. To export single pages, use 7;9;11. You can export a combination of page ranges and single pages by using 3–6;8;10;12.

- If you have recorded changes in the OOo file, and those changes are showing at the time you create the PDF, the changes are visible in the resulting PDF.

- Fonts are embedded in whole for Type1 or as the needed subset (for TrueType), except for the 14 PDF standard fonts, which are not embedded.

Saving Documents in DocBook XML Format

With OpenOffice.org 1.1, you can save files in DocBook XML format, the standard document type for creating product- and project-support materials for most open source projects. This format can be transformed into any format, including the Windows formats.

For more information about OOo and DocBook, visit:

http://xml.openoffice.org/xmerge/docbook/
http://www.docbook.org/

To save a document in DocBook XML, click File > Save As and select DocBook from the bottom of the list.

If you don't see DocBook as a choice on the list, it means the required filters have not been installed. (The standard installation does not include these filters.) To install the filters:

1. Go to the folder where OpenOffice.org 1.1 is installed and run Setup.

2. On the Installation program for OpenOffice.org dialog (Figure 9-1), select Modify to add new components. Click Next.

3. On the Select OpenOffice.org Modules dialog (Figure 9-2), double-click on XSLT Sample Filters. Click Modify.

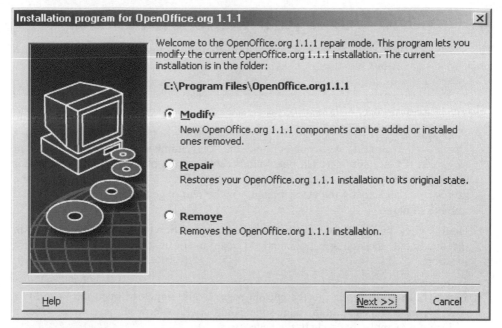

Figure 9-1. Modifying OOo to add new components

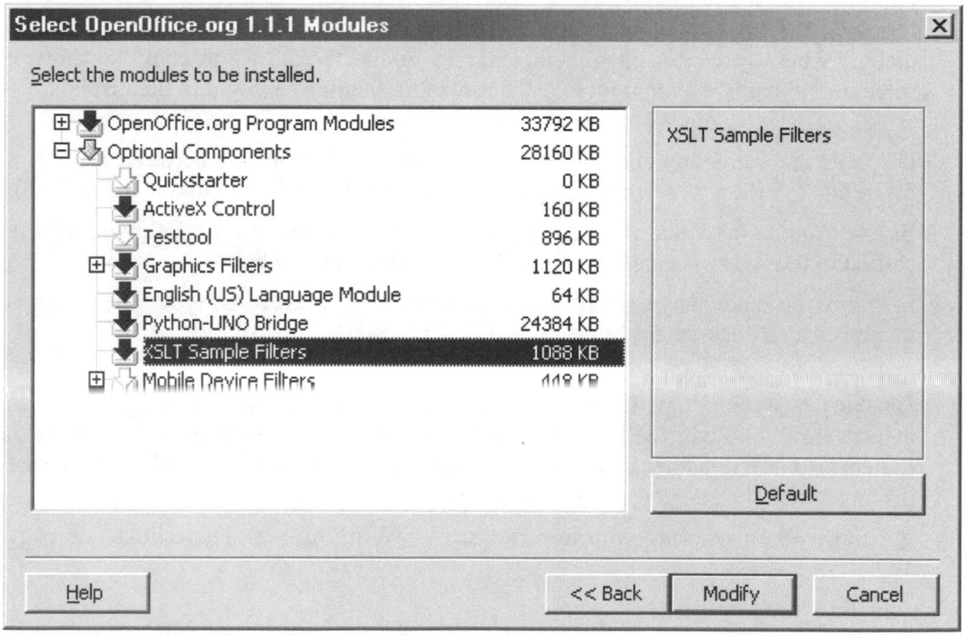

Figure 9-2. Selecting the XSLT Sample Filters for installation

Using and Configuring the Status Bar

The Status Bar (Figure 9-3) contains information about the open document and provides quick access to various functions.

| Page 171 183, Right Page | 100% | INSRT | STD | HYP | * | ↔ 0.00 / 0.01 | ⊡ 12.70 x 1.72 | 10:25 | 14/06/2004 |

Figure 9-3. The Status Bar

Page number
Displays the current page number and the total number of pages in the form *Page x/z*. If you have restarted page numbering at some point in the document (for example, after the table of contents), the form is *Page x y/z,* where *Page x* is the number that appears on the current page, *y* is the real page number, and *z* is the total number of pages.

Double-click this field to open the Navigator, right-click to show all bookmarks in the document, then click a bookmark to position the text cursor at the bookmark location.

Page style
Displays the style applied to the current page. Double-click to open the Page Style dialog, where you can edit the page style. Right-click to show all page styles. Click a style name to apply that style to the page.

Zoom
Displays the zoom factor for the current page. Double-click to open the Zoom dialog, where you can change the current zoom factor. Right-click to show a selection of available zoom factors. Click a zoom factor to apply it to the display.

Insert/overwrite mode
Displays the current typing mode. Click on this field to toggle between INSRT = insert and OVER = overwrite. (You can also use the Insert key to toggle the modes.)

In Insert mode, new text is inserted at the cursor position, and the following text is shifted to the right. The cursor is displayed as a thin vertical bar.

In Overwrite mode, any existing text is replaced by whatever you type. The cursor is displayed as a thick vertical line.

Edit/activate hyperlinks
Displays how text hyperlinks are handled. Click on this field to toggle between active (HYP) and edit (SEL). When hyperlinks are active, clicking on one jumps to the corresponding address. In edit mode, you can click on a hyperlink and edit the displayed text, just as you would normal text.

For more about working with hyperlinks, see "Working with Hyperlinks" on page 192.

Selection mode
Displays the current selection mode. Click on this field to toggle between the three choices: STD, EXT, and ADD.

Display	Mode	Effect
STD	Standard mode	Click in text where you want to position the cursor; click in a cell to make it the active cell. Any other selection is then deselected.
EXT	Extension mode	Clicking in the text extends or crops the current selection. Equivalent to holding down the Shift key while clicking with the mouse.
ADD	Additional selection mode	A new selection is added to an existing selection. The result is a multiple selection. Equivalent to holding down the Ctrl key while clicking.

Other information
Displays current information about the active document. This information varies depending on the location of the cursor.

- If the cursor is in a named section, the section name appears.

- If the cursor is in a table, the name of the table cell appears.

- If you select a frame, graphic, or drawing object, the size of the object is shown.

When the cursor is positioned within text, you can double-click this field to open the Fields dialog, where you can define a field to be inserted in your document at the cursor position.

When the cursor is positioned in a table, you can double-click in this field to open the Table Format dialog. If the cell is read-only, a note appears here.

Depending on the object selected, you can open a dialog to edit a section, a graphic object, a floating frame, an OLE object, direct numbering, or the position and size of a drawing object.

Configuring the Status Bar

You can choose which fields appear on the Status Bar. Click Tools > Configure to open the Configuration dialog (Figure 9-4). Select or deselect the fields required, then click OK.

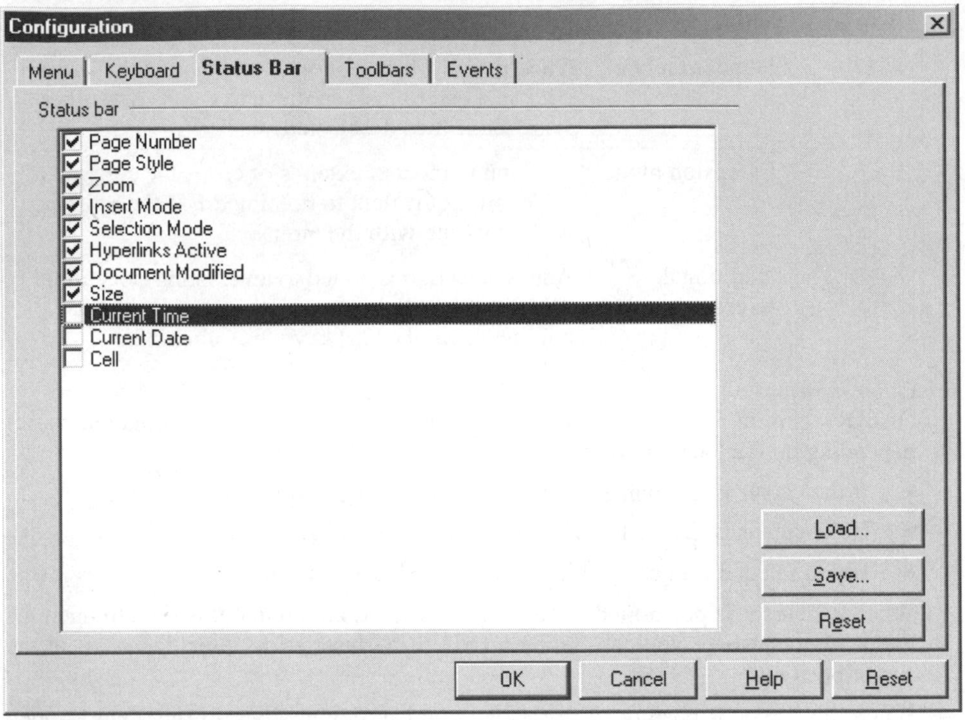

Figure 9-4. Configuring the Status Bar

Working with Hyperlinks

A *hyperlink*, also called an *Internet link*, is a cross-reference, activated by a mouse-click, that jumps a reader to another part of a Web page or a different Web page.

OpenOffice.org can recognize Web addresses (URLs) as you type them, replaces those addresses with a hyperlink, and formats the hyperlink with the font attributes (color and underline) defined for the hyperlink character style.

If you do not want OpenOffice.org to automatically recognize URLs as you are typing, you can undo or turn off this feature.

Undo Automatic URL Recognition for a Selected Hyperlink

• When you are typing and notice that text has just been automatically converted into a hyperlink, press Ctrl+Z to undo this formatting.

• If you do not notice this conversion until later, you can select the hyperlink and click Format > Default.

Turn off Automatic URL Recognition

1. Click Tools > AutoCorrect/AutoFormat. In the AutoCorrect dialog (Figure 9-5), select the Options tab.

2. Deselect both checkboxes next to URL Recognition.

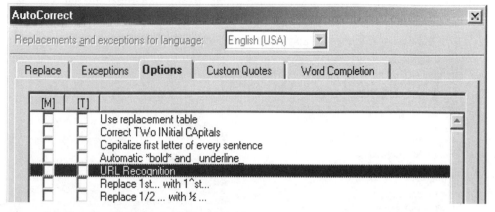

Figure 9-5. Turning off automatic URL recognition

Insert a Hyperlink

To create a hyperlink within the same document:

1. Open the Navigator (Figure 9-6), long-click on the Drag Mode icon, and select Insert as Hyperlink.

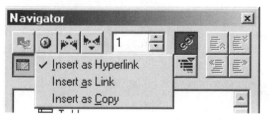

Figure 9-6. Using the Navigator to insert a hyperlink

2. In the Navigator, select the item you want to link to. Click and drag the item into your document.

Change Formatting of Hyperlinks in a Document

Hyperlinks are often underlined and in a different color from other text. If you have specified hyperlinks in the table of contents for a document (as described on page 122), the ToC entries will be displayed with the same formatting as other hyperlinks.

If you don't want your hyperlinks displayed in the default underlined format, you can change the character style for them.

1. Open the Stylist (Figure 9-7) and select the Character Styles icon.

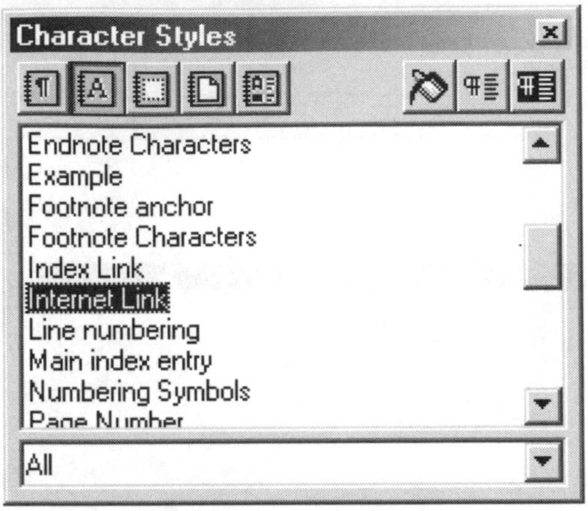

Figure 9-7. Selecting a character style

2. From the list displayed, select Internet Link, then right-click and click Modify on the pop-up menu.

3. On the Font Effects tab (Figure 9-8), choose the underlining or color you want for hyperlinks. In the example, I have made them identical to normal text, with no underlining and automatic font color (so they will be the same color as normal text). Click OK to save your changes.

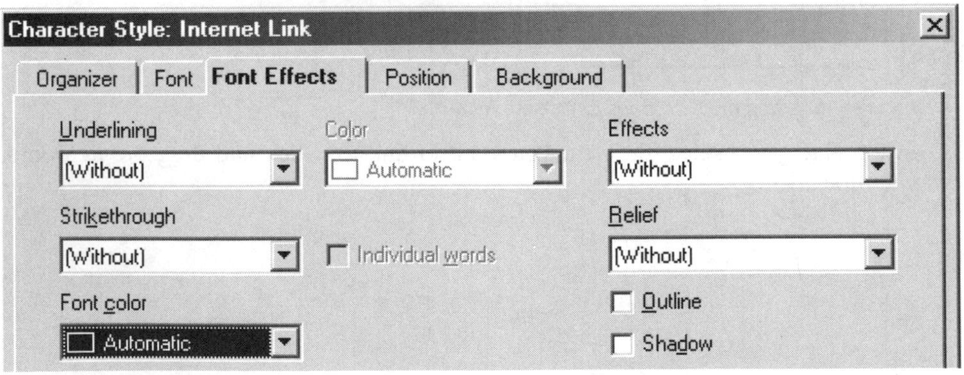

Figure 9-8. Choosing font effects for Internet links

Create a Hyperlink to Another Document

1. Click Insert > Hyperlink (or click the Hyperlink Dialog icon ![icon] if it is on the main toolbar) to display the Hyperlink dialog (Figure 9-9).

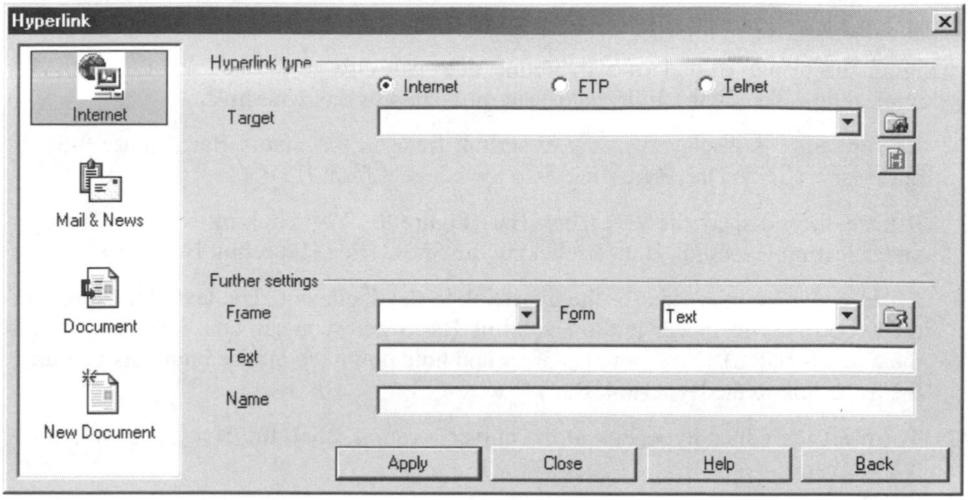

Figure 9-9. Using the Hyperlink dialog to insert a new hyperlink

2. In the Target field, type the address (URL) for the hyperlink. You can also search for the target address using one of the buttons to the right of this field.

3. In the Text field, type the text you want to appear in your document. (If you have selected some text in the document, this field will be filled in already.)

4. Click Apply to insert the hyperlink at the cursor location.

You can also insert a hyperlink using the Hyperlink Bar.

1. If necessary, display the Hyperlink Bar (Figure 9-10) by clicking View > Toolbars and selecting Hyperlink Bar. (You can also click the Show/Hide Hyperlink Bar icon if it is on the main toolbar.)

Figure 9-10. Using the Hyperlink Bar

2. In the URL name field, type the text you want displayed in your document.

3. In the URL address field, type the target address. If you are not sure of the address, and you are connected to the Internet, you can click the Find button to search for a Web address.

4. To insert the hyperlink at the cursor location, click the Hyperlink icon.

Edit the Address or Displayed Text of a Hyperlink

Hyperlinks do not behave the same as cross-reference fields. The text displayed does not update if you change the text of the source, so you may need to change the displayed text to match the source.

Changing the displayed text of a hyperlink does not change the address to which the hyperlink refers. To edit the address instead of the text of the hyperlink:

1. Be sure SEL is displayed in the hyperlink field on the Status Bar (Figure 9-3). If necessary, click on the Hyperlink field to change it from HYP.

2. If necessary, display the Hyperlink Bar (Figure 9-10 by clicking View > Toolbars and selecting Hyperlink Bar (or clicking the Show/Hide Hyperlink Bar icon).

3. Click anywhere in the text of the hyperlink in the document. The text and address of the hyperlink will appear in the Hyperlink Bar, where you can edit both the text and the address (URL). (You can also press and hold down the mouse button as you drag the hyperlink to the Hyperlink Bar.)

4. To insert the edited hyperlink at the cursor location, click the Hyperlink button on the toolbar.

Changing the Default Bullet Character

If bullets show up as strange characters or blank boxes (indicating a missing symbol), the usual cause is a missing font. This problem often arises when you send a document to someone who does not have the same fonts installed. You may also notice it in a new installation of OOo, when the program is looking for a font (usually StarSymbol) that you don't have.

To fix this problem:

1. Open the Stylist (Figure 9-7 on page 194) and select the Character Styles icon.

2. On the list displayed, select Bullets, then right-click and click Modify on the pop-up menu.

3. On the Font tab of the Character Style dialog (Figure 9-11), the current font for bullets is shown in the Font box. In this example, the font is StarSymbol. At the bottom of the dialog is a note that the font is not installed.

4. Select a common font and point size for bullets, then click OK.

Changing the bullet character here will not affect bullets already in your document, but any new bullets will use the new character.

Character Style: Bullets   ⊠

| Organizer | **Font** | Font Effects | Position | Background |

Font
```
StarSymbol
```
Abadi MT Condensed
Abadi MT Condensed Extra Bold
Abadi MT Condensed Light
Albertus Extra Bold
Albertus Medium
Algerian
Alvarana MT

Typeface
```
Regular
```
Regular
Italic
Bold
Bold Italic

Size
```
9pt
```
6pt
7pt
8pt
9pt
10pt
10.5pt
11pt

Language
```
ABC English (USA)
```

☐☐☐☐☐☐ ☐ ☐☐☐☐☐-☐☐☐☐☐☐☐☐☐

This font has not been installed. The closest available font will be used.

| OK | Cancel | Help | Reset | Standard |

Figure 9-11.Choosing a font for bullet characters

10

Moving from Microsoft Word

This chapter summarizes some information of interest to users of Microsoft Word.

The good news is that you can do almost anything in Writer that you can do in Microsoft Word, and a few things that you can't do as easily in Word. If you decide to make the change, you'll need to learn some new ways of working, but you should be happy with the results.

The bad news is that if you need to convert existing documents from Microsoft Word to Writer, you may have to do some manual cleaning up of those files, or you may need to develop templates and macros to assist in the conversion. This book does not cover macros, nor does it cover specifics of template development for this purpose.

Sharing Files with Users of Word

Will Writer read and write Microsoft Word files? Yes.

Will it do the conversion without losing any formatting? Sometimes.

If you need to share documents with users of Microsoft Word, be aware that although some files will go back and forth between the programs without any major problems, other files definitely won't. It depends on which features of Word and Writer have been used. This is what happens when files are exchanged between any two programs, including different versions of Word; conversions are never 100% complete, unless the files are very simple ones.

Generally, my advice is: If you must work with Microsoft Word files (for example, if you're editing or collaborating on documents in Word), use Word—and use the same version of Word that the other person uses, if at all possible. If you do anything else, you may have problems ranging from trivial problems to major problems.

When converting from Word to Writer, if a feature of Word isn't supported by Writer, Writer will make some substitution that may or may not be what you want. For example, Writer does not have an equivalent to Word's StyleRef field, so it turns those fields into text.

Similar problems arise when you're converting from Writer to Word. If you have used any of the powerful features of Writer described in this book, you may have serious problems with the output when it's read by Word. However, many people have no problems at all.

If you are required to provide files in Microsoft Word format (for example, when sending your resume to an employment agency), be sure to develop a template that produces clean Word files. In general, if you use text only (no cross-references, no fields, no bullets, and no tables), you'll be okay. That's fine for a letter or resume, but any document using the powerful features of Writer is unlikely to convert well.

This chapter does not attempt to summarize the problems faced by people who need to exchange files with users of Microsoft Word, or the solutions to those problems.

Comparison of Word and Writer Ways to Do Things

Experienced users of Microsoft Word may take awhile to discover how to do common tasks in Writer, because some of the menus and the terminology are a bit different; in a few cases no direct equivalent method is available.

This chapter summarizes my research and experiments with Writer 1.1.1 on Windows ME. You may find some differences if you're using another operating system or another version of OpenOffice.org.

Terminology

Microsoft Word	OpenOffice.org Writer
Office Assistant	Help Agent
ScreenTips or ToolTips	Tips
Wildcards	Regular expressions
(no equivalent)	Long-click (click and hold on an icon to display a tear-off toolbar)
Smart tags	Do not exist in OOo

Set Up the Program to Work Your Way

Most functions are found in similar places in both programs, but a few are slightly different, and the degree of control varies. This table summarizes where to find the setup choices. For more information, see Chapter 1.

To do this...	In Microsoft Word...	In OpenOffice.org Writer...
Turn off Office Assistant (Help Agent)	Help > Microsoft Word Help > Options	Tools > Options > OpenOffice.org > General
Turn off autocompletion		Tools > AutoCorrect/AutoFormat > Word Completion tab, deselect Enable Word Completion.
Set up document window (rulers, status bar, default toolbars, etc.)	View > select required items	View > select required items
Change measurement system	Tools > Options > General	Tools > Options > Text Document > General
Customize toolbars	Tools > Customize	View > Toolbars > Customize or Tools > Configure or Right-click on toolbar > Customize or Configure
Customize menus	Tools > Customize	Tools > Configure
Display font names in their font (in toolbar drop-down font list)	Tools > Customize > Options	Tools > Options > OpenOffice.org > View, select Preview in fonts lists
Always show full menus (include unavailable and little-used items)	Tools > Customize > Options	Tools > Options > OpenOffice.org > View, select Inactive menu items
Show/hide ScreenTips (ToolTips) on toolbars	Tools > Customize > Options	Help > Tips, uncheck
Always create backup copy	Tools > Options > Save	Tools > Options > Load/Save > General
Autosave every x minutes	Tools > Options > Save	Tools > Options > Load/Save > General
Show paragraph marks, tabs, etc.	Tools > Options > View	Tools > Options > Text Document > Formatting Aids
Change file locations	Tools > Options > File Locations	Tools > Options > OpenOffice.org > Paths
Change user information	Tools > Options > User Information	Tools > Options > OpenOffice.org > User Data
Set up AutoCorrect and AutoFormat options	Tools > AutoCorrect Options	Tools > AutoCorrect/AutoFormat > Options

Write, Edit, and Review Documents

Most writing, editing, and reviewing techniques in Writer are similar to those in Microsoft Word, but the details often vary. See Chapter 2 for more information on each of the topics summarized here.

To do this...	In Microsoft Word...	In OpenOffice.org Writer...
Jump quickly to other parts of a document	Edit > Go to or Outline view	Edit > Navigator, double-click on required heading, figure, table, etc.
Choose language for spelling checker	Tools > Language > Set Language	Tools > Options > Language Settings > Language. (Note: OpenOffice.org has no grammar checker.)
Ignore some text when checking spelling	Select text; Tools > Language > Set Language > Do not check or Format > Style > Modify > Format > Language	Select text; right-click > Character > Font > Language = [None]
Recheck spelling	Tools > Spelling & Grammar > Recheck Document	Always rechecks
Find and replace text, formatting, and styles	Edit > Replace > More; choices as needed	Edit > Find & Replace; details are a bit different
Use wildcards (regular expressions) in find and replace	Edit > Replace > More > select Use Wildcards checkbox	Edit > Find & Replace; select Regular Expressions checkbox. Wildcards differ from those in MSWord.
Choose, create, or edit a custom dictionary	Tools > Options > Spelling & Grammar > Custom Dictionaries	Tools > Options > Language Settings > Writing Aids
Create exception (exclude) dictionary	File > New, type words, Save As > text only, file extension .EXC	As for custom dictionary, but select Exception [-] checkbox
Track changes (choose options)	Tools > Options > Track Changes	Tools > Options > Text Document > Changes
Protect document for editing	Tools > Protect Document	Edit > Changes > Protect Records
Mark and track changes	(Word 2000) Tools > Track Changes > Highlight Changes	Edit > Changes > Record
Insert comments associated with a change	Highlight text; Insert > Comment	Edit > Changes > Comment
Insert notes (comments not associated with a change)	Highlight text; Insert > Comment	Insert > Note
View changes as pop-up text	Options > View > Screentips	Help > Tips (and) Help > Extended Tips

To do this...	In Microsoft Word...	In OpenOffice.org Writer...
Merge documents	Tools > Merge Documents	Edit > Changes > Merge Document
Accept or reject changes	View > Toolbars > Reviewing	Edit > Changes > Accept or Reject
Change document properties	File > Properties	File > Properties
Get a word count	Tools > Word Count (can get word count for selection)	File > Properties > Statistics tab (cannot get word count for selection without using a macro)
Create AutoText entry	Select text; Insert > AutoText > New	Select text; Edit > AutoText or Ctrl+F3
Insert AutoText	Type shortcut and press F3	Type shortcut and press F3 or type Name of AutoText entry and press Enter. Writer distinguishes between the "name" and the "shortcut" of an AutoText entry; Word does not.

Control Page Setup and Layout

Writer controls basic page setup somewhat differently than Word does.

In Word, page setup (paper size, orientation, margins, and so on) is a property of the document as a whole. To change the setup for a page, you need to define a separate section with the changed setup. For example, if you specify headers and footers, although you can define separate headers and footers for the first page of a section and for right and left pages, the settings apply to the entire document, unless you change them in specific sections.

In Writer, page setup is a property of the page style. You can define many page styles—for example, First Page, Left Page, Index Page, Landscape Page, and Default. If you change the page layout for one page style, only that style will be affected. When you set up a page style, you can specify which page style applies to the next page, so when text flows from one page to the next, the correct page styles will automatically apply to the following pages. For example, you could specify a First Page style to be followed by a Left Page style, to be followed by a Right Page style, to be followed by a Left Page style—a common setup in books.

For more information, see Chapter 3.

To do this...	In Microsoft Word...	In OpenOffice.org Writer...
Define margins	File > Page Setup > Margins	Format > Page > Page
Specify different headers and footers on first, odd, and even pages	File > Page Setup > Layout > Headers and Footers section	Define different page styles for First, Left (even), and Right (odd) pages, using Header and Footer tabs
Edit headers and footers	View > Headers and Footers, then type or insert fields; can also double-click in existing header or footer regions	After you have specified Header and Footer areas for a page, they are always active. Single-click to type or insert fields
Change from Roman numerals to Arabic page numbers in the footer of a page	Insert a section break, deselect "Same as Previous" in the footer of the second section, then define a new footer with page numbers restarting at 1 in Arabic numerals	Insert a manual page break and apply a different page style, specifying a starting page number of 1
Use paragraph styles for page layout	Define paragraph styles with offset from left margin, with heading styles aligned left or right	Define paragraph styles with offset from left margin, with heading styles aligned left or right
Use columns for page layout	Insert continuous sections to switch from single to multiple columns on one page	Format > Page > Columns or Insert/Format > Section > Columns or other methods
Use frames or text boxes for page layout	Frames are used in Word 97 but are mostly replaced by text boxes in Word 2000 and 2002; can be linked to flow text from one to next, as in a newsletter	Insert > Frame (can link frames to flow text from one to next, as in a newsletter); "text boxes" are fields, not positioning devices
Use tables for page layout	Table > Insert > Table (use dialog to format)	Insert > Table (use dialog to format)
Put portrait headers on landscape pages	Use rotated text box linked to header	Use rotated text in a frame
Set first page number to greater than 1	Insert > Page Numbers > Format	In first paragraph on first page, Format > Paragraph > Text Flow > Breaks, select Enable and With Page Style, choose the page style, specify the page number
View and edit facing pages	File > Print Preview; click Zoom button to enable editing	File > Page Preview shows pages on wrong sides of screen. You cannot edit in page preview mode.

Use Templates and Styles

For more information, see Chapter 4.

To do this...	In Microsoft Word...	In OpenOffice.org Writer...
Find which template is associated with a document	Tools > Templates and Add-ins	File > Document Properties > General tab
Specify default template	"Normal" template is default	File > Templates > Organize, choose any template to be the default
Create a new template	File > Save As, set type to Document Template (.DOT)	File > Templates > Save
Edit a template	File > Open, choose template	File > Templates > Edit
Copy styles between templates	Tools > Templates and Add-ins > Organizer	File > Templates > Organize. Copy styles with Ctrl + drag and drop between templates and documents
Create a new document from a template	File > New (opens a list of templates)	File > New > Templates and Documents
Apply a different template to a document	Tools > Templates and Add-ins > Attach, select template, Open	Start a new document based on the different template; copy contents of old document into new document
Apply a style to text	Select from Style List or Style dialog (Word 2000); Can also use task pane (XP).	Format > Styles (or press F11), double-click style in list; after one use, paragraph styles appear in Apply Style list on Formatting object bar
Change a style definition	Format > Style > Modify (Word 2000); can also select in task pane and click Modify (XP).	Select style in Stylist, right-click, choose Modify; or Format > Styles > Catalog, select style, click Modify
Create a new style	Format > Style > New	Format > Styles > Catalog, click New
Use outline numbering	Format > Style, select style > Format > Numbering	Tools > Outline Numbering

Use Fields

For more information, see Chapter 5.

To do this...	In Microsoft Word...	In OpenOffice.org Writer...
Insert a field	Insert > Field or Ctrl+F9 for blank field	Insert > Fields
Define a number range field	Insert > Field, use SEQ (sequence)	Insert > Fields > Other > Variables > Number range
Insert a bookmark	Select text; Insert > Bookmark	Select text; Insert > Bookmark
Insert a cross-reference to a bookmark	Insert > Cross Reference, choose Bookmark as type	Insert > Cross Reference > Bookmark
Insert a cross-reference to a heading	Insert > Cross Reference, choose Heading as type	Either bookmark the heading or use Insert > Cross Reference > Set Reference to mark the heading, then Insert > Cross Reference > Insert Reference
Insert a cross-reference to a figure or table	Insert > Cross Reference, choose type	Insert > Cross Reference > Insert Reference > Figure (or Table)
Insert a cross-reference from document A to an item in document B	Use Includetext fields	Keep a manual list of cross-reference names (case-sensitive) when you set them in document B. When you insert the cross-reference in document A, type the name of the item (in document B) in the Name box on the Fields dialog instead of selecting the name from the Selection list.
Use conditional content	Use IF or other fields, or styles (all workarounds)	Insert > Fields > Other > Variables (among other ways)

Work with Large or Complex Documents

For more information, see Chapters 6 and 7.

To do this...	In Microsoft Word...	In OpenOffice.org Writer...
Create a table of contents, list of figures, or an alphabetic index	Insert > Index and Tables	Insert > Indexes and Tables > Indexes and Tables
Insert index entries	Alt+Shift+X	Insert > Indexes and Tables > Entry or click Insert Index Marker icon
Create a bibliographic database	Use database—for example, Microsoft Access	Tools > Bibliography Database
Insert bibliographic references into text	Link to field in database	Insert > Indexes and Tables > Bibliographic Entry
Insert footnotes and endnotes	Insert > Footnote	Insert > Footnote or click Insert Footnote Directly icon
Insert other files	Insert > File, choose Insert or As Link	Insert > File
Cross-reference between documents	Use Includetext fields	Keep a manual list of cross-reference names (case-sensitive) when you set them in document B. When you insert the cross-reference in document A, type the name of the item (in document B) in the Name box on the Fields dialog instead of selecting the name from the Selection list.
Use master documents	Not recommended	File > Send > Create Master Document; use Navigator to insert subdocuments

Work with Graphics

For more information, see Chapter 8.

To do this...	In Microsoft Word...	In OpenOffice.org Writer...
Create Drawing objects	View > Toolbars > Drawing (Word 2000) Insert > Picture > New Drawing (XP).	Click Show Draw Functions icon
Combine graphics objects and drawing objects	Edit > Picture > Reset Picture Boundary (Word 2000); Use drawing canvas (XP).	Place all objects in a frame
Insert graphics files into a text document (embed or link)	Insert > Picture > From File	Insert > Graphics > From File
Anchor graphics	Format > Picture > Layout > Advanced > Picture Position	Use icons on Graphics object bar, right-click and choose from pop-up menu, or click Format > Graphics
Wrap text around graphics	Format > Picture (or Object) > Layout	Use icons on Graphics object bar, or right-click and choose from pop-up menu, or click Format > Graphics > Wrap
Crop graphics	Format > Picture > Crop or click Crop tool on Picture toolbar	Format > Graphics > Crop
Create captions for graphics	Select graphic; Insert > Reference > Caption	Select graphic; Insert > Caption
Annotate graphics	Use drawing objects; group or place in frame or on drawing canvas (XP)	Place all objects in a frame
Insert watermark	Format > Background > Printed Watermark > Picture (or Text) Watermark	Format > Page Style > Background or create drawing object, Arrange > To Background, Anchor > To Page

Index

About the Author

Jean Hollis Weber has over 25 years of experience as a scientific and technical editor and writer in the fields of biology, mathematics, engineering, and computing. She has taught short courses in writing and editing and lectured to graduate and undergraduate classes in writing and editing at several Australian universities. Jean is active in the Society for Technical Communication.

A dual U.S./Australian citizen, Jean has lived in Australia since 1974. In 1998, she escaped from the big cities to live in Airlie Beach, Queensland, a seaside resort town at the gateway to the beautiful Whitsunday Islands. Jean conducts her writing and editing business over the Internet from her home and from numerous campgrounds and motel rooms on her travels around Australia.

Jean has published six previous books, including the *Taming Microsoft Word* series. She also publishes a free e-mailed newsletter for editors and maintains three websites: Avalook at Australia (a travel website), *http://www.avalook.com.au/*; Taming OpenOffice.org, *http://www.taming-openoffice-org.com/*; and The Technical Editors Eyrie, *http://www.jeanweber.com/*.

Related Titles Available from O'Reilly

Linux

Building Embedded Linux Systems

Building Secure Servers with Linux

The Complete FreeBSD, *4th Edition*

CVS Pocket Reference, *2nd Edition*

Essential CVS

Even Grues Get Full

Extreme Programming Pocket Guide

Learning Red Hat Enterprise Linux and Fedora, *4th Edition*

Linux Device Drivers, *2nd Edition*

Linux in a Nutshell, *4th Edition*

Linux iptables Pocket Reference

Linux Network Administrator's Guide, *2nd Edition*

Linux Security Cookbook

Linux Server Hacks

Linux Unwired

Linux Web Server CD Bookshelf, *Version 2.0*

LPI Linux Certification in a Nutshell

Managing & Using MySQL, *2nd Edition*

Managing RAID on Linux

MySQL Cookbook

MySQL Pocket Reference

Practical PostgreSQL

Programming with Qt, *2nd Edition*

Root of all Evil

Running Linux, *4th Edition*

Samba Pocket Reference, *2nd Edition*

Understanding the Linux Kernel, *2nd Edition*

User Friendly

Using Samba, *2nd Edition*

Keep in touch with O'Reilly

1. Download examples from our books

To find example files for a book, go to:

www.oreilly.com/catalog

select the book, and follow the "Examples" link.

2. Register your O'Reilly books

Register your book at *register.oreilly.com*

Why register your books?
Once you've registered your O'Reilly books you can:

*   Win O'Reilly books, T-shirts or discount coupons in our monthly drawing.
*   Get special offers available only to registered O'Reilly customers.
*   Get catalogs announcing new books (US and UK only).
*   Get email notification of new editions of the O'Reilly books you own.

3. Join our email lists

Sign up to get topic-specific email announcements of new books and conferences, special offers, and O'Reilly Network technology newsletters at:

elists.oreilly.com

It's easy to customize your free elists subscription so you'll get exactly the O'Reilly news you want.

4. Get the latest news, tips, and tools

www.oreilly.com

*   "Top 100 Sites on the Web"—PC Magazine
*   CIO Magazine's Web Business 50 Awards

Our web site contains a library of comprehensive product information (including book excerpts and tables of contents), downloadable software, background articles, interviews with technology leaders, links to relevant sites, book cover art, and more.

5. Work for O'Reilly

Check out our web site for current employment opportunities:

jobs.oreilly.com

6. Contact us

O'Reilly & Associates
1005 Gravenstein Hwy North
Sebastopol, CA 95472 USA

TEL: 707-827-7000 or 800-998-9938
(6am to 5pm PST)

FAX: 707-829-0104

order@oreilly.com
For answers to problems regarding your order or our products. To place a book order online, visit:

www.oreilly.com/order_new

catalog@oreilly.com
To request a copy of our latest catalog.

booktech@oreilly.com
For book content technical questions or corrections.

corporate@oreilly.com
For educational, library, government, and corporate sales.

proposals@oreilly.com
To submit new book proposals to our editors and product managers.

international@oreilly.com
For information about our international distributors or translation queries. For a list of our distributors outside of North America check out:

international.oreilly.com/distributors.html

adoption@oreilly.com
For information about academic use of O'Reilly books, visit:

academic.oreilly.com

O'REILLY®

Our books are available at most retail and online bookstores.
To order direct: 1-800-998-9938 • order@oreilly.com • www.oreilly.com
Online editions of most O'Reilly titles are available by subscription at safari.oreilly.com